IONS

INDIAN OCEAN NAVAL SYMPOSIUM

Contemporary Transnational Challenges: International Maritime Connectivities

Editors

Ravi Vohra

PK Ghosh

D Chakraborty

KNOWLEDGE WORLD

KW PUBLISHERS PVT LTD

New Delhi

in association with

NATIONAL MARITIME FOUNDATION

New Delhi

KNOWLEDGE WORLD

A KW Publishers Book
www.kwpublishers.com

ISBN 10: 81-87966-95-5
ISBN 13: 978-81-87966-95-1

Published in India by

Kalpana Shukla
KW Publishers Pvt Ltd
4676/21, First Floor, Ansari Road, Daryaganj, New Delhi 110002
email: knowledgeworld@vsnl.net

Typeset by Black Innovation, New Delhi and Printed at Rajkamal Electric Press, New Delhi

Contents

SESSION IV

CONCLUDING SESSION

APPENDIX SPEECHES

Preface

Covering an area of 28 million sq km, with two-third of the planet's strategic resources, the Indian Ocean has for centuries been the primary medium for fostering religious, cultural and linguistic proliferation in the region. Many of its littorals share a common historical linkage of colonial subjugation, common threats and challenges and opportunities, which could well act as catalysts for bimultilateralism in the IOR. Prima facie, this multi-dimensional intercourse should by all accounts, have encouraged a strong sense of regional identity and cohesion. Regrettably, despite the oceanic thread that binds the littorals together, maritime cooperation and related issues have not received the attention and importance they deserve in the region. Hence it has often been felt by most strategists and maritime practitioners that maritime cooperation needs to be nurtured into the forefront of State agenda for the IOR littorals.

Unquestionably, there are hindrances since even the existence of the IOR as a regional entity is questioned by some thinkers. The geographical ambit of the region has resulted in endless debates about the identity of the IOR littoral and its membership in the Indian Ocean Rim Association for Regional Cooperation (IOR ARC). Apart from this basic premise, some observers view the region as a "kaleidoscope of crisis" and a hotbed of military, economic, and racial turmoil and strife.

The other primary driver of deeper cooperation has been the global trend in economic liberalisation, which has encouraged closer maritime relations since nearly half of the entire seaborne commerce of the world moves across the waters of the Indian Ocean. Nearly 20 per cent of this commerce, or $500 billion, is in the form of energy, the majority of which is shipped eastwards through the Sea Lines of Communications (SLOCs) of South-East Asia. Consequently, the IOR littorals and all other energy-dependent states have a natural interest in ensuring stability in the geopolitics of the IOR. For example, 70 per cent of Japan's need of oil is met from the energy-rich region of the Gulf. The USA too imports 20 per cent of its energy requirements from here. China has now become a major importer of Gulf energy, overtaking Japan. Thus, the entire Asia-Pacific is, and will, remain critically dependent on the energy resources of the region and on the safety of the tankers that carry this vital resource across the Indian Ocean.

With over 60,000 ships transiting the Strait of Malacca annually, effects of consequent disruption in the trade chain on the economic growth of most major economies are not difficult to visualise.

At another level, there are other challenges in the form of natural disasters. Approximately 60–70 per cent of the world's natural disasters strikes this part of the world with catastrophic consequences, given the high human density along its coastal regions. The results of the 2004 tsunami that devastated millions of coastal dwellers are still fresh in the minds of most people. The sea lanes entering and exiting through several narrow passages, e.g. the Strait of Hormuz, the Gulf of Aden, the Suez Canal, the Strait of Malacca, etc. create 'choke points' that are vulnerable to interdiction and disruption. Non-military challenges include gunrunning, drug trafficking, piracy and poaching. With the existing geopolitical atmospherics, sub regions in the IOR have emerged as hotbeds of illegal activity, e.g. piracy hotbeds (Strait of Malacca, Bay of Bengal, off the Somalian Coast, etc.), highways for drug trafficking for the drugs that emerge from the Golden crescent and the Golden Triangle, gunrunning, etc. The region is also the acknowledged hub of maritime terrorism with major hubs of the Al Qaeda, LTTE, Abu Sayyaf group, etc. all operating from the region. Thus these potent challenges need adequate multilateral coordinated response strategies that are often found lacking in the region.

In recognition of the centrality of the cooperative engagement in the IOR and as a primary means for ensuring and assuring safety, stability and security in the IOR, the Indian Navy decided to take on the role of lead facilitator in setting up a regional 'Track-I' forum of navies (and coast guard organisations) of the IOR. Taking on the role of an "unobtrusive fulcrum", the forum was termed as IONS (Indian Ocean Naval Symposium).

Thus the IONS Seminar 2008, which was co-sponsored by the National Maritime Foundation (NMF) and the Indian Navy was designed to be a specific vehicle by which the overall IONS Initiative was to be launched. Once the "regional forum" had been created, subsequent "seminars" would be subsumed into the "set" of activities of the IONS. Thus, each such subsequent seminar would undoubtedly be an important "subset" of the IONS.

The IONS seminar was held on 14–15th February 2008 in New Delhi and attended by twenty-six Chiefs of Navy (or Coast Guards in littorals where there is no Navy) along with their delegations. Internationally-renowned maritime analysts from around the globe participated in the event, with many of them presenting research papers during the conference. The Prime Minister of India, Shri Manmohan Singh, inaugurated this seminar at the awe-inspiring Plenary Hall of the Vigyan Bhavan.

The event was conducted over six sessions, which included an inaugural session. A separate Chiefs Conclave was undertaken on 15h February 2008 with the idea of having an informal session, exclusively for the attending Naval Chiefs, to discuss maritime priorities and issues associated with the setting up of the IONS forum.

This publication primarily comprises the papers presented during the Seminar. Speeches by dignitaries have also been included.

Ravi Vohra
PK Ghosh
D Chakraborty

SESSION I

PAPER 1

The Geo-Strategic Scenario in the Indian Ocean Region

Kanwal Sibal*

The geo-strategic scenario in the IOR is very complex because of the huge diversity of factors that operate in it. The IOR distinguishes itself from regions bordering other oceans by the much larger number of states around its rim, by vastly more populous countries, by considerably more points of conflict involving littoral states themselves or out-of-area powers, by more numerous military bases of foreign powers spread around, by many countries where terrorist activity with international ramifications is more intensive than anywhere else, by a greater number of choke points of strategic importance, vulnerable to State and non-State actors alike, by some of the biggest oil and gas producers in the world, by bigger sea-borne flows of vital energy resources for fuelling leading economies outside the region, by higher levels of poverty, by a whole host of high growth countries outside the industrialised world as well, by exceptional diversity in terms of civilisations, cultures and religions—Islam, Hinduism, Buddhism and Christianity, by powerful natural disasters—to recall the tsunami of December 2004.

Countries in the IOR have varying geo-strategic interests, depending on where they are located within the region and how geographically sensitive it is, how resource-rich they are and how much their resources are coveted by others, who their neighbours are, their size and strength and their relationship with them, whether they sense their security being threatened by adversaries within the region or outside it or a combination of both, and how much support they require from out-of-region powers for maximising or protecting their interests. It is conflict or competition, a desire to extend

* Former Foreign Secretary, Goverment of India.

power or minimise vulnerabilities that underlie geo-strategic calculations of individual countries. A group of countries could have shared geo-strategic interests, depending on whether they are part of an alliance system that enables them to best protect their individual interests against common challenges by working together. There are some general threats to which all or most states may feel vulnerable; others may be seen as more localised. Because the region lacks cohesion and is fractured by too many differences, it has never developed any shared thinking on security threats. No overarching collective security organisation has emerged in the region.

These characteristics of the IOR make its study that much more fascinating and, of course, challenging. Is it at all possible to have a coherent view of the region, given its wide-ranging diversities? Can such a large number of countries with different political systems and external linkages have a common understanding on security matters? Can the littoral states find sufficient common ground in the face of differing priorities, capacities and views to deal with pressing issues? How do they reflect on these issues together, in the absence of a functioning regional forum or organisation? Can a line be drawn between the issues relevant specifically to the Indian Ocean rim and problems in the forefront of international community as a whole? Is it possible to identify issues which are most germane to the geographical location of these countries around the Indian Ocean and then find a thread to connect their self-interest in addressing these issues? These are the questions that need to be answered.

To start with, a definitional issue has to be addressed. There would be logic in including in the IOR only those countries which are directly littoral and not indirectly so. The hinterland may be germane to some of the issues involved, but for that reason need not be considered a geographical part of the IOR. The approach should be dictated by geography, not politics. The countries falling into the IOR category should have coastlines that directly abut the Indian Ocean, not on one of the inland seas connecting with the Indian Ocean. This is important in the context of clarity, as we should be aware of the extent of the region with which we are concerning ourselves. If this logic were applied, then the number of countries in this region would be 29; a more inclusive approach would raise the number to 35.

From Southern Africa at one end to the Australian continent at the other, with the east coast of Africa, the Horn of Africa, the Arabian peninsula, the Gulf countries, South and South-east Asia in between, the IOR is manifestly too large and too disparate to be considered or treated as a coherent entity. The region has no distinctive overarching personality, but has quite distinctive sub-regional personalities. These sub-regional personalities express themselves more easily in regional economic organisations, because it is easier to build cooperative institutions around economic self-interest than around security-related issues. In Southern Africa, East Africa, the Gulf, South Asia and South-east Asia, for example, functioning economic groupings exist. The Association of South East Asian Nations (ASEAN) is perhaps the only sub-regional organisation in this larger region which has set up a security forum, the ASEAN Regional Forum, but not surprisingly, it has required the participation of major non-regional powers to acquire any functional credibility.

The IOR is characterised by the absence of an organisation of collective reflection and action on issues of common political, security and economic interests. On a sub-regional basis, economic cooperation arrangements, with some security-related issues, like terrorism and drug trafficking on the agenda, have been set up, such as ASEAN in South-East Asia, SAARC in South Asia, Bay of Bengal Initiative for Multi-Sectroal Technical and Economic Cooperation (BIMST-EC) spanning parts of South and South-east Asia, the Gulf Cooperation Council, economic groupings in southern and eastern Africa, etc. None of these organisations, has either maritime cooperation on its agenda or is equipped to effectively handle ocean management issues. The IOR-ARC, the only pan-Indian Ocean organisation, set up in Mauritius in March 1997, also had an exclusively economic mandate, with focus on development issues, and ignored issues of maritime cooperation. Its charter does not even mention the issue. Convergence on security issues is complicated by the fact that only India, Australia and South Africa have blue water naval capability, the US Navy has a powerful presence as well as security arrangements with individual IOR countries. The political sensitivities of non-littoral States also come into play. The recent quadrilateral exercises between the navies of the US, India, Australia and Japan, with the participation of Singapore, illustrates this point.

The geo-strategic scenario in the IOR is marked by the high concentration of vital energy resources in the western littoral of the region, which is marked by local conflicts, the rise of religious extremism, international terrorism, the danger of proliferation of weapons of mass destruction and drug trafficking. The whole expanse of the region is geostrategically important as it is through this that critical sea lines of communications (SLOCs), which are the lifeline of the littoral countries as well as China, Japan, South Korea, etc. for their trade and energy flows, pass. Two maritime choke points, one on the western end of IOR—the Strait of

Hormuz—and one on the eastern end—the Malacca Strait—complicate the geo-strategic scenario. There are, in addition, issues relating to freedom of navigation, peaceful passage, EEZs, etc. those left unresolved by the United Nations Convention on the Laws of the Sea (UNCLOS 111) which have geostrategic implications. These specific attributes of the IOR can be examined a little more in detail.

During the Cold War, the nuclear submarines of the two superpowers were engaged in powerful rivalry in the Indian Ocean. The US acquired Diego Garcia in 1968 in the southern Indian Ocean, where it located its long-range bombers, which enabled it to effectively extend its power in the IOR. France has all along kept a visible naval presence in the Indian Ocean Region to protect its overseas possessions, such as Reunion, and also to make its presence felt in areas of its traditional influence, like the Malagasy Republic, Comoro Islands, etc. It was the presence of what was seen as external powers posing a threat to the littoral states that lay behind proposals to make the Indian Ocean a zone of peace. Today the situation has altered completely with regard to the presence and role of external powers in the IOR.

The IOR contains some of the largest producers of oil and natural gas in the world and countries with the world's largest reserves of hydrocarbons. This strategic resource, vital for the economies of industrialised and developing nations alike, is concentrated in the Gulf region, which gives it great geo-strategic importance. Globally, 65 per cent of known oil reserves is in countries bordering the Persian Gulf. For powerful countries, the stake is to acquire direct or indirect control over these resources to ensure their availability, obviate the danger of their falling into the hands of adversaries, preventing any single country in the region from dominating it, to the extent of being able to challenge external control and asserting its independence beyond a point. Keeping the region divided by interfering in the politics of the region, supporting or destabilising regimes, depending on whether they cooperate with or resist the interests of powerful outside actors fits in with the objective of exercising control. A new element is the need to secure the resources of this region against threats posed to it by non-state actors.

The Western presence in this region is long-standing. The political map of the region was drawn up by Europe to serve strategic needs, with control of hydrocarbon resources in mind. During the Cold War, political competition in this region became acute, sharpened by ideological rivalry, with the former Soviet Union backing local Arab nationalism, pan-Arabism, socialist leanings, and ambitions to exert national control over the region's resources against West-backed conservative, monarchical and Islam-oriented regimes.

The Iraq–Iran conflict was provoked in part by fears of revolutionary Iran destabilising Western interests in this area. With the collapse of the Soviet Union, the ambition to tighten the grip on the region's oil and gas resources and break down resistance in the region to Western policies led to the first war against Iraq, the immediate casus belli being Iraq's invasion of Kuwait, itself an offshoot in part of oil-related differences. Despite other explanations, including that of promoting democracy in order to encourage religious moderation and combating the rising menace of terrorism, control of Iraq's huge hydrocarbon resources is considered a reason for the second war against Iraq and regime change there.

The US is the single most powerful naval factor in the IOR. It has established a new naval command (the fifth fleet) for the Persian Gulf area, where it has currently positioned a powerful carrier group to deal with the situation in Afghanistan and mounting tensions with Iran over its purported nuclear ambitions. For its general strategic needs in the area, including the continuing volatility of the situation in Iraq, it has acquired bases on land and port facilities in the Gulf region. Ships of European navies also are deployed as part of a North Attlantic Treaty Organisation (NATO) standing force supporting the US-led war in Iraq and anti-terrorism patrols along the Makran coast.

The western littoral of the Indian Ocean has spawned new challenges. Because they are interlinked, are concentrated in this geographical area and constitute a long-term threat, they have acquired the nature of a new geostrategic problem that requires to be forcefully addressed. These can be identified as religious extremism, international terrorism, drug trafficking and acquisition of WMD technologies by State and non-State actors alike. Combating this cocktail of threats will be a continuing exercise for the foreseeable future, as extremist versions of religion are being used to create a cadre of highly committed individuals and groups to fight against real or imagined historical or contemporary political grievances, to stop the cultural damage they see being done by modernity to the societies to which they belong, or to set up a new world order based on the tenets of their faith under the guidance of an institutionalised religious head. All means seem to be permitted to carry out this combat and advance their objectives, including mindless violence against innocents to instill terror in society. Access to crude WMD technologies would give such groups the capacity to inflict unimaginable damage, far beyond the casualties caused by terrorist attacks. The funds for such activities by shadowy groups operating clandestinely are provided in part by drug trafficking.

Not surprisingly, force being used to eliminate these new threats is begetting more violence. The combat is both against physical acts of terror as well as mindsets. While the former can be countered with military action and policing, bringing about a change in the mindset is an extremely complex exercise. Promotion of democracy can be a strategic goal but the timelines for this are too long and the Western version of democracy based on extreme individualism is culturally contested. The credentials of those speaking in the name of democracy are questioned because of their long support for regimes in the region considered undemocratic by the measure of their own standards. The paradox is that while the involvement of powers external to the region is necessary to effectively combat these interlinked challenges, it is the very presence of these powers and their policies in the region that are engendering these challenges in the first place.

Beneath the larger concerns about proliferation globally, there is serious concern about nuclear proliferation in the western littoral of the IOR. The other instabilities of the region can become unmanageable and could threaten international security much more ominously if suspicions about acquisition of nuclear know-how by one country lead to its neighbours acquiring it in turn, and this rivalry is further intensified by historical sectarian divides. The US, Europe, Russia, and India as well, would feel endangered by the spectre of nuclear rivalry raising its head in this already volatile region, not the least because of the number of rivals involved.

Geo-strategic considerations have brought external powers into this region. The US/Western presence both provokes and contains conflict in the region. While some countries oppose the US presence because it generates tensions, especially as the US policies are not seen as even-handed, yet for another set of countries the US presence provides protection and guarantees of peace and security. However, if the US has been successful in its efforts to establish inter-State peace in some cases, it is not in a position to maintain internal tranquillity in countries. The threat to the stability of some key Gulf States presents a paradox. At the governmental level, stability is being maintained by external support, but that very support is a case of militancy by local groups against the government.

The Strait of Hormuz is the world's most important choke point. According to statistics 2006, 16.5 to 17 million of barrels of oil per day from Saudi Arabia, Iran and the UAE pass through these straits, destined for Japan, the US, western Europe, India, and other Asian countries. This constitutes two-fifth of all sea-borne trade in oil, and three-fourth of Japanese oil imports. At its narrowest, the strait is only 33.1 kilometres wide.

Very large crude oil carriers (VLCCs) ply through the strait transporting over two million barrels of oil per voyage. In 1988, during the Iraq–Iran war sea mines were installed in the waterway. Despite the importance of this economic lifeline, the nine regional governments have not developed sufficient maritime capability to protect the strait against disruption of traffic, for whatever reason. The maritime security of the offshore oil and gas industries and ensuring safe and secure shipping are key issues, along with free and secure access to international waters, combating maritime terrorism (especially after September 11), controlling smuggling and environmental protection. Iran controls three strategically located islands—the Greater and Lesser Tunb and Abu Musa—which are also claimed by the UAE, and this unresolved issue adds to the sensitivity of the area.

The geo-strategic scenario in the eastern reaches of the IOR is different in overall character but presents similarities in that the Strait of Malacca is the second biggest choke point in the world for maritime traffic. From the economic and strategic perspective, this is one of the world's most important shipping lanes—the main shipping channel connecting the Indian Ocean to the Pacific Ocean, linking the major economies such as India, Japan, China, Republic of Korea, and Taiwan. According to statistics, 2006, 15 million bbl/d of oil shipments pass through the Straits. Over 50,000 vessels pass through the Straits every year, carrying 25 per cent of the world's traded goods, including oil, Chinese manufactures, etc. About 25 per cent of oil shipments carried by sea pass through this waterway, mainly from the Persian Gulf to the Asian markets. Near Singapore, the Straits narrow down to 2.8 kilometres, creating one of the world's significant traffic choke points. Incidents of piracy are frequent in the Straits because of a large number of minor islands, which provide safe havens. Terrorist attacks constitute a new concern in an area which has pockets of religious extremism. After Singapore unearthed in 2004 plans by an extremist organisation to attack the US naval vessels, the US proposed deployment of the US marines and Special Forces in high-speed vessels to counter possible terrorist attacks, as part of Regional Maritime Security Initiative (RMSI). As most of the Malacca Strait lies within the territorial waters of Malaysia and Indonesia, they rejected this initiative on the ground that it would infringe on their sovereignty. In June 2004, Malaysia, Indonesia and Singapore agreed to MALASINDO—an initiative to step up joint patrolling of the strait of the Strait of Malacca without participation of the US forces. But without the right of hot pursuit into territorial waters, law enforcement is weakened. In sum, regional maritime cooperation in the IOR, to ensure safe passage of maritime trade, is not well developed as the major users of the trade routes and littoral states straddling these routes have differing views and questions of sovereignty are involved.

China's phenomenal economic growth and its expanding needs for energy supplies and raw materials from various corners of the globe, as well as the movement of its export traffic, gives the IOR an increased geostrategic salience for the Chinese. The Chinese navy is as yet insufficiently equipped to protect its long lines of communication across the IOR. China has acquired footholds in Myanmar, Bangladesh, Sri Lanka, the Maldives, Pakistan and Iran to position itself to better protect its lines of communication from the Middle East to the South China Sea. This has been described as the "string of pearls strategy" of bases. Sixty per cent of China's oil supplies are shipped through the Strait of Malacca. By 2010, China's oil imports will touch 100 million tonnes. Eighty five per cent of China's trade is sea-based. China's thrust through Myanmar to the Bay of Bengal and through Pakistan to the Arabian Sea is a geo-strategic move to find outlets to the Indian Ocean for its western regions. In a situation of full normalisation of relations between India and China as a result of settlement of the boundary dispute, Tibet can be connected through Sikkim and West Bengal to the Bay of Bengal, which would be a geo-strategic development of important proportions.

India has big stakes in peace and security in the Indian Ocean. Over 70 per cent of India's oil requirements are currently being imported. This figure will go up to 80 per cent in 2010 and almost 92 per cent by 2020. India's oil supplies arrive by sea, therefore secure SLOCs are crucial. Most of the crude oil imported from the Gulf comes to India's western coast in the Gulf of Kutch, with 15 to 20 VLCCs moving between the Persian Gulf and the Gulf of Kutch at any given time. Two-third of India's oil and gas production comes from offshore fields, the most important of which are in the Arabian Sea, and most of it is transported through 49 submarine pipelines. India is doing oil and gas exploration off Chennai, in the Andaman and Nicobar Islands and in the Godavari and Cauvery basins. The security of these assets and of offshore rigs is most important. India's offshore oil assets are spread over an area of over 48,000 kilometres. Almost 95 per cent of India's trade is seaborne. About 40,000 tankers come to Indian ports annually. India shares maritime boundaries with three South Asian and three South-East Asian neighbours. Her economic interaction with the rest of Asia has grown very significantly in recent years; the trade with China alone touching 40 billion dollars this financial year. India has 7,516 km of coastline and an EEZ of two million sq km.

Given India's geographical position in the Indian Ocean, its stakes in secure SLOCs, its offshore assets, and the size of its navy, it has pursued an active policy of confidence building in the region. With the US Navy, a major player in the Indian Ocean, the Indian Navy has been carrying out exercises for over a decade, with increasing scope. Since 1992, the Indian Navy and the US Navy have been conducting the MALABAR exercises with participation of nuclear powers submarines, aircraft carriers, long-range patrol aircraft, cruisers, destroyers, etc. Procedures for inter-operability have been worked out between the two navies. As part of military cooperation between the two countries for *Operation Enduring Freedom*, at the US request, India escorted high-value US shipping through the Strait of Malacca for a few months. The tsunami that struck in 2004 demonstrated that only two navies—those of the US and of India—had the capability to provide disaster relief by sea over long distances at very short notice. Exercises have also been conducted with France, the UK, Australia, South Africa and lately with Russia. Maritime interaction with Japan is also increasing with better strategic understanding between the two countries. India has, since 1991, been conducting the biennial MILAN exercises involving the South Asian and South-East Asian navies. In 2006, nine regional navies participated in the exercise. India holds regular exercises in the IOR with South-East Asian navies. It has held exercises with China, as an important confidence-building measure. Bilateral and multilateral exercises with regional navies, involving search and rescue drills, anti-submarine warfare, advance mine counter-measures, and anti-terror tactics are held regularly. Annually, the Indian Navy makes friendly visits to important ports in the IOR. As part of general naval cooperation, the Indian Navy provides training in Indian naval establishments to trainees from IOR countries. Along with the Coast Guard, the Indian Navy conducts surveillance in the Palk Straits, the Gulf of Mannar and around its own island territories to curb the activities of the LTTE terrorists, gunrunning, poaching, and influx of refugees.

International terrorism, proliferation threats (especially from non-state actors associated with terrorism), piracy, trafficking of arms, drugs and human beings are some new and not-so-new challenges that face the international community in their sea-borne dimension. Provisions of UNCLOS 111, which deal with freedom of high seas and right of innocent passage in territorial waters, constrain the freedom of action of countries to deal with these threats. Therefore, ad hoc initiatives have been taken to deal with threats such as suicide attacks on ships, WMD material proliferation, and misuse of containers, etc. through enhanced surveillance and security of ports, coastal belts and structures on the Continental Shelf. These initiatives are driven by domestic legislation and are not based on building a large international consensus beforehand. The Container Security Initiative and the Proliferation Security Initiative are cases in point. While India has joined the Container Security Initiative (CSI) so as not to disrupt its own commercial traffic to US ports, it has not joined the Proliferation Security Initiative (PSI) because of legal issues.

The United Nations Convention on The Law of the Sea (UNCLOS) came into force in 1994, establishing a comprehensive framework for the regulation of issues of territorial waters, innocent passage, passage through straits, archipelagic waters, Contiguous Zone, Exclusive Economic Zone, the Continental Shelf, etc. The Convention deals with the peaceful uses of the world's oceans, but not with military or security matters, although such matters are the obverse side of the whole issue of peaceful use. Some of the provisions can be interpreted differently as their meaning was left ambiguous in order to be able to adopt the Convention. The US's non-adherence to the Convention has compounded the problem. The problem areas in the Convention are the delimitation of EEZ and the Continental Shelf, where a reference to equitable principles has made the resolution of maritime boundary disputes more difficult. The EEZ of island territories has become so disproportionate to the area of the islands themselves that the incentive for States to lay claim to islands has increased. The New Moore island dispute between India and Bangladesh is an example. Carrying out naval activities in the EEZs of states can be a source of potential conflict as some states want to restrict them, to which the major maritime powers are opposed, arguing that such activities are in full conformity with the UN Charter and that any limitation would presuppose a negotiated arrangement. Since September 11, the US and some other States have increased their scrutiny of military and civil aircraft and ships approaching their coasts. While for marine scientific research the Convention has established a clear regime, this is not the case with hydrographic surveys in the EEZ. The distinction between marine research and hydrographic surveys is blurred at times, to avoid taking the required permission of the coastal state. Regarding the issue of installations, structures and devices in the EEZ, there is a controversy around the question whether a State can place non-explosive devices in the EEZ of another state. Taking advantage of the lacuna in the Convention, the major maritime powers assert the right to place submarine devices on the surface and on the ocean floor because they do not interfere with the enjoyment of resource rights by coastal states. All these are the potential areas of conflict in regulating the use of oceans.

To conclude: the Indian Ocean Region is extremely diverse in its complexion politically, economically and culturally. It has more pronounced sub-regional personalities than any overarching regional identity. At the subregional level, several local conflicts exist. The region is, on the whole, militarily divided and weak. No multilateral security organisation encompassing the IOR countries has emerged. This vacuum is filled by the presence of Western powers. Their presence for some is a source of conflict and for others a source of security and stability. International terrorism, religious extremism and drug-trafficking have emerged as geo-strategic problems in the region because of the location of the hub of these international threats here. This is a long-term issue as solutions would require drastic changes in local conditions and external approaches. Geography also gives to proliferation concerns in the Gulf region an extra strategic dimension because of their nexus with other problems located here. The Gulf region is exceptionally rich in hydrocarbon resources, which are vital for big consumer countries inside and outside the region. Assured energy supplies, which includes the protection of sea-lanes through which the oil and gas are transported, is a primary concern. Two critical chokepoints on the western and eastern edges of the IOR respectively have a major geostrategic importance in this context and of trade flows in general. The problem of piracy and danger of military conflict disrupting these flows is a continuing concern. The shift in global economic growth to parts of the IOR gives to the rest of the world stakes in peace and stability in this area in the longer-term scenario. The status of EEZs, too, in the context of access to economic resources and peaceful uses of the seas, is of strategic relevance. These issues require solutions based not on exercise of power but adherence to principles and respect for sovereignty. India's central location in the IOR geographically, its dependence on the Indian Ocean sea lanes for its trade and energy flows, its island territories, its long coast line and its EEZ gives it a critical role to play in joint efforts to manage issues of freedom of navigation, peaceful uses of the sea, etc. left unsettled by UNCLOS 111. India's expanding naval capacities, already the most sizable in the region, give India the means to pursue policies which are in the common interests of all. ■

PAPER 2

Globalisation and its Impact on Maritime Trade

Rajiv Kumar*, Shrawan Nigam and Majeeta Singh*****

Introduction

Globalisation is not a new phenomenon. Countries have been trading with each other since time immemorial. However, the pace at which it has accelerated in the last few decades and the new trends it has thrown up makes it different from the rarlier phase of globalisation.

Globalisation and deepening economic integration has increased trade in merchandise. Since 90 per cent of trade is sea borne, goods loaded at ports worldwide increased to 7.4 billion tonnes in 2006 from 3.7 billion tonnes in 1980.[1] World container port traffic has expanded to 440 million TEUs in 2006, with ports of developing countries handling 65 per cent of world total. As shipping provides the most cost-effective method of bulk transport, the demand for shipping services has grown in tandem with the growth in trade. There has been expansion in tonnage in all categories of merchant fleet, be it oil tankers, dry cargo ships or container ships.

The maritime infrastructure is experiencing a revolution. Ships are becoming larger and faster to facilitate this increased trade. The trend among the new ships is more and more in favour of specialisation and tailor-made services. To deal with large ships and to move goods rapidly, there is development of a hierarchy of seaports, which include 'hub' ports and 'feeder' ports. Ports today determine the competitiveness of a country or a company, therefore port development is focused on adoption of newer technologies so as

---

* Director and CEO, Indian Council for Research on International Economic Relations (ICRIER).

** Senior Consultant, ICRIER.

*** Research Associate, ICRIER.

to be more efficient and productive. Increasing international trade has also impacted rail and road transport and the market for freight forwarding and logistics services as seaports have become the principal nodes for inter-modal movement in the international supply chain.

The aim of this paper is to lock at the impact of globalisation on trade in the world and in the Indian Ocean Region (IOR) and to discuss the key challenges that have emerged for developing countries in their effort to increase their trade and benefit from globalization. The paper is organized as follows. Section 2 describes the increasing integration of countries and the new trends that have emerged since the 1980s. Section 3 looks at regional trade in the IOR. Section 4 discusses the key issues which the developing countries must address if they want to take advantage of the opportunities created by globalisation, and Section 5 gives the conclusion.

Integration of the World Economy: Trends

The way countries have become more dependent on one another for wealth creation can be seen by the tremendous increase in cross-border trade in goods and services and in investments in the form of foreign development involment (FDI) and capital flows for portfolio investment.

Spurred by liberalisation, economic growth, new technologies in IT and telecommunications and revolution in transportation, global merchandise exports have been increasing, on an average by 8 per cent and GDP by 6 per cent since 1980. As a result, the share of trade has increased, and it represents almost 50 per cent of global GDP in 2005, 23 per cent in 1960.

Figure 2.1: Growth in World GDP and Trade

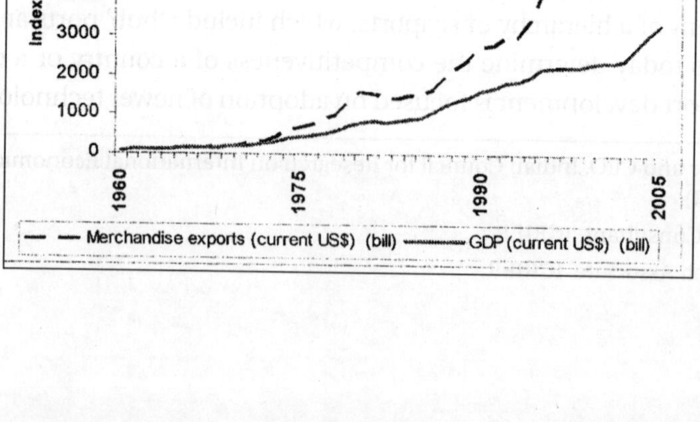

Figure 2.2: World Trade (as % of World GDP)

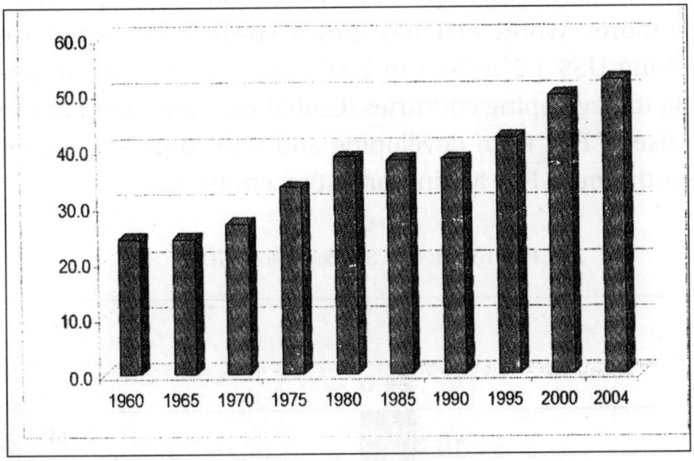

Trade in manufactures has continued to grow faster than trade in agricultural and mining products, both in terms of value and volume. Recent trends show that within manufacturing, trade is getting concentrated in goods like machinery and equipment and chemicals.

The slower growth of trade in agricultural products is said to be partly due to the restrictive trade regimes that prevail in this sector. The structure of trade in agriculture goods reveals that processed agriculture products have expended significantly more than semi-processed and unprocessed agriculture products (though not for low-income countries). The developed countries have dominated trade in this sector, with the share of developing countries improving only marginally.

From 1980 through 2005, the total global value of services export rose from US$ 450 billion to US$ 2,498 billion, representing a 4.6 times increase. The growth of services trade has outpaced the growth of world GDP. Services exports grew more strongly than merchandise exports in the 1980s and almost at the same average annual rate from 1990 to 2005. Their share in the total exports, however, has remained around 20 per cent since the mid-1980s. Over more than a decade, many services have separated from the manufacturing industry to become independent services businesses and knowledge intensive, while the share of traditional services is declining.

The expansion in international trade is linked closely to the flows of capital as FDI has played an important role in many developing countries in generating exports. World FDI has grown strongly since the 1980s with inflows reaching US$ 1.2 trillion in 2006 with about ¼ of the total ($ 325 billion) going to developing countries [Global Development Finance (GDF), 2007)]. The rise of FDI from developing and transition economies and the growth of South-South FDI are important recent trends.

Figure 2.3: FDI Stock as % of GDP

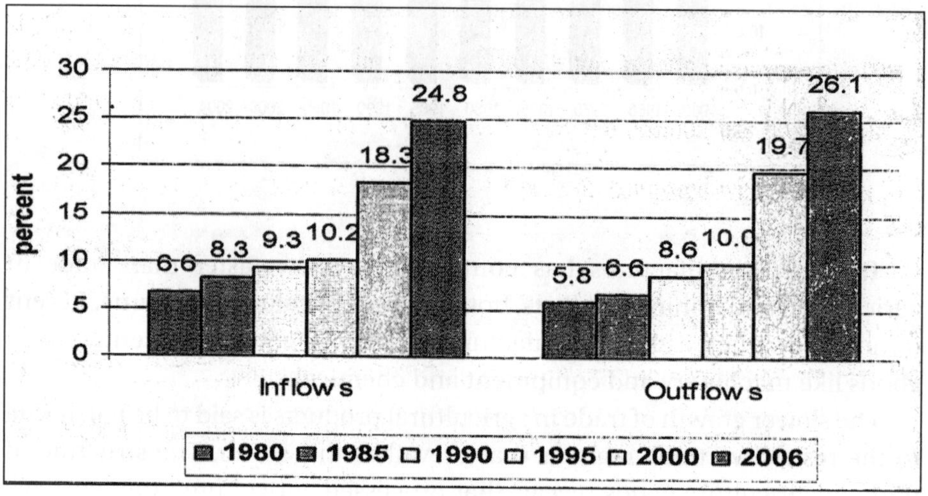

Besides FDI, the other indicator of financial integration has been a large increase in private capital flows in portfolio investments. Pension funds, mutual funds and hedge funds have been channeling equity flows in developing countries on a large scale as the stock markets in the emerging markets have been growing faster than those in the developed economies. While the TNCs of the developed countries dominate the scene, large corporations from emerging economies are internationalising rapidly (World Bank, 2007). More companies in developing countries are entering world capital markets to broaden their funding sources. Financial corporations, particularly commercial banks from India, Kazakhstan, the Russian Federation, and Turkey, have been in the forefront, tapping international debt markets to fund growing domestic loan portfolios and to meet increasing capital adequacy requirements (GDF, 2007).

Figure 2.3: Portfolio Investment Flows

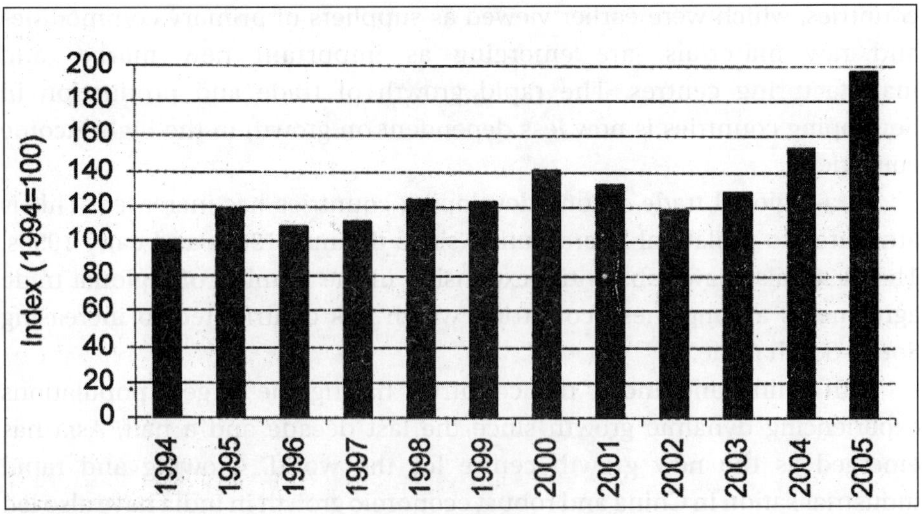

An interesting phenomenon in this phase of globalisation has been the increased participation of developing countries. During the 1990s, their exports increased at an annual average rate of 6.8 per cent, which was more or less the same as that for high-income countries. However, since 2000, developing countries exports are growingat a rate twice that of developed countries. The acceleration of imports is even more impressive. Though the imports of developing countries grew at a slower rate in the 1990s, in the last seven years the position has reversed. In 2006, import growth in developing countries registered 14.3 per cent, compared with 7.9 per cent in the high-income countries.[2]

The effect of this is seen in the increase in their marked shares. In current dollars, developing countries market share increased gradually in the 1990s from 20 to 25 per cent, but since 2000, their share has jumped to 35 per cent.[3] This is attributed to the process of trade liberalisation and market reforms that were initiated in the early 1980s and than intensified in the 1990s in these countries. Tariff barriers were lowered and economies were opened to foreign competition. Bsides this, reform programmes also included: capital account liberalization, devaluation, fiscal and financial reform and privatization. East Asia led the way in liberalizing its trade regime in the 1980s and experienced an unprecedented growth in its exports, which permanently changed the pattern of trade between developed and developing countries. Earlier, the expansion of trade in manufactures was concentrated among the industrialised countries, and East Asia in particular, have become the fastest growing component of trade. Developing countries, which were earlier viewed as suppliers of primary commodities and raw materials, are emerging as important new market and manufacturing centres. The rapid growth of trade and production in developing countries is now less dependent on growth in the high-income countries.[4]

Intra-regional trade among developing countries has increased. This is attributed to unilateral liberalisation since the mid-1980s and early 1990s. The 1990s also saw substantial expansion in the number of regional trade agreements among these countries, which has contributed to increasing South-South trade.

With China and India, the countries having the largest populations experiencing dynamic growth since the last decade and a half, Asia has emerged as the new growth centre for the world. Growing and rapid industrialisation in China and robust economic growth in India have also led to the emergence of new trade patterns, namely, Africa and Latin America are increasingly becoming important suppliers of primary commodities, while China's consumer goods are increasingly exported to Africa and Latin America. As a result, even Africa has shown high growth, along with other developing economies.

Much of the expansion in world trade over the last couple of decades reflects the development of global production linkages. Removal of trade restriction, revolution in IT and telecommunications and improvement in transportation, including containerisation have increased the ease with

Table 2.1: Share of Parts and Components in Total Trade

	Exports		Imports	
Country	**1990–96**	**2000–06**	**1990–96**	**2000–06**
China	5.7	13.9	14.5	31.4
Indonesia	4.0	12.5	17.7	16.1
S.Korea	21.8	27.5	26.3	33.2
Malaysia	38.2	42.5	35.0	50.4
Philippines	30.4	60.3	26.2	57.8
Singapore	31.0	46.5	32.7	47.6
Taipei	24.5	39.9	32.3	38.7
Thailand	18.9	26.3	22.9	30.8

Source: Jongwanich, 2007, ADB.

which goods, services, capital and technical knowledge can move around the world. Faster information flows at dramatically falling costs have broken down geographical barriers to economic activity and enabled the division of labour on a global scale. Referred to by economists as 'vertical disintegration of production', this process is increasingly reducing products to constituent components, sub-components and processes that can be manufactured anywhere in the world and then reintegrated. As a consequence the trade in parts, components and accessories is increasing rapidly.

The earlier phases of globalisation were also the result of new technologies, such as railways and electricity. However, these technologies were dispersed across the world fairly slowly, especially to the developing world. The accelerated pace of digital technologies is particularly striking. Telephone and telegram services were invented in the middle of the 19th century, and it took more than 90 years before those services reached 80 per cent of the countries. In contrast, mobile phones, computers, and cable television reached 80 per cent of the countries that currently report data in less than 25 year.[5] Thus goods embodying these technologies are being globalised faster and one witness a rapid growth of high technology exports from developing countries.

Maritime Trade

Since trade and seaborne trade are linked, goods loaded have increased from 3.4 billion tonnes in 1985 to 7.4 billion tonnes in 2006. Sixty-three per cent of world goods loaded were made up of dry cargo, including bulk, break bulk and containerised goods. A geographical breakdown of total goods loaded by continent highlights the share of Asia to be 39.1 per cent, followed by America (21.5 per cent), Europe (19.6 per cent), Africa (10.7 per cent), and Oceania (9.1 per cent). Fleet ownership of developing countries reflects the increasing participation of developing countries in trade. At the beginning of 2007, developing countries controlled 31.2 per cent of the world dwt as Compared to 19 per cent 1996.

The principal players today are tanker operators, dry-bulk operators, and liner operators. The tonnage of oil tankers in 2006 increased by 8.1 per cent and that of dry bulk carriers by 6.2 per cent; these two types of ships together now represent 72.0 per cent of total tonnage. However, to speed up port operations, containerisation is increasing and world container port throughput grew by 13.4 per cent to reach 440 million TEUs in 2006. Developing countries handled 265.4 million TEUs, or 65 per cent of the world total in 2006; this is up from 62.1 per cent for 2005.

International rail freight transport expanded in 2006, with markets in

China and India recording growth rates of 11 and 8 per cent, respectively. The global road transport market is estimated to have grown by 4.5 per cent in 2006. During the same year, the global freight forwarding and logistics market grew by 13.5 per cent. The total market size was estimated to be 93 billion Euros: the European market led with one-third, while the shares of the Asia-Pacific and North American marlets stood at 27 per cent and 29 per cent each (UNCTAD, 2007).

Growth in trade has impacted maritime trade infrastructure. There is increasing competition between seaports, and between sea and other forms of transport. Larger ships with better technologies are being built to handle large volumes of trade. To remain competitive, ports continually upgrade their facilities in terms of equipment to handle large volume break-bulk trades and resort to greater automation of terminal operations, etc. To deal with large ship, within regions, there is development of a hierarchy of main seaports where container liner vessels unload at 'hub' ports and trans-shipped cargoes are dealt with by service 'feeder' ports. Seaports are becoming inter-modal nodes in international supply chains, the efficiency of which now drives trade competitiveness.

Indian Ocean

The Indian Ocean is the world's third largest ocean. It carries half of the world's container ships, one-third of the bulk cargo traffic, two-third of world's oil shipments, and links the economies of Europe, the Indian subcontinent and Asia-Pacific with the oil-rich Gulf area and natural resources-rich Africa. The opening up, economic boom and growth of the nation as manufacturing hubs on its rim has brought this ocean in the limelight as it plays an important role in global trade. The Indian Ocean has four critically important waterways facilitating maritime trade: the Suez Canal, Bab-el-Mandeb, the Strait of Hormuz, and the Strait of Malacca. These "chokepoints" are critical to world oil trade. In 2006, about one-fifth of world's supply of oil passed through the Strait of Hormuz.

The Ocean has on its rim 40 economically and politically diverse countries of Africa, Middle East, Asia and Oceania, which are seeing acceleration of reforms with focus on outward-oriented strategies. Though most of the countries are low-income countries, there are also countries like Australia and Singapore, which are very advanced, and countries that are among the world's fast-growing economies like India, the Middle East and Far East. This is an important region as in 2005 the countries on the Indian Ocean Rim accounted for around 28 per cent of the world land mass, 40 per cent of the population, 17 per cent of the GDP in PPP terms, 13 per cent of merchandise exports, 12 per cent of merchandise imports and 16 per cent of total foreign exchange reserves.

Trade by Regional Groups

The trade passing through the Indian Ocean has grown at an annual average rate of 39 per cent between 1985 and 2006, thus making the Ocean a very busy place. However, as revealed by Table 2.2 the region pushing this growth rate was Asia. Growth of trade between Asia-Europe, Asia-Africa and Africa-Asia is way higher, at 73 per cent, 69 per cent and 79 per cent respectively.

Table 2.2: Growth in Trade Passing through India Ocean

Trade	1985	2006	1985–2006
	$ million		Average Annual Change
	40,142	3,11,802	32
Asia-Europe	20,819	3,38,716	73
Africa-Asia	2,148	37,965	79
Asia-Africa	3,435	53,111	69
Asia-Middle East	21,884	1,17,668	21
Middle-East-Asia	36,578	2,98,413	34
Total	1,25,006	11,57,674	39

Source: Estimated from DoTs.

Asia

Intra Asia trade has increased. However, if we divide Asia into South and East Asia, all the action has been in the East. In South Asia, apart from India, the other countries have not done as well.

Over the last couple of decades, East Asia has seen a change in its pattern of

Table 2.3: Asia's Trade by Region

Region/Country	Share in Asia's Trade					
	Exports			Imports		
	1990	2000	2006	1990	2000	2006
Intra Asia	41.2	48.3	51.9	43.7	54.2	55.3
USA	28.6	23.7	17.8	17.5	14.0	9.0
Africa	1.5	1.2	1.8	1.0	1.5	1.8
Middle East	2.9	2.6	3.4	8.2	8.2	10.2
Latin America	2.2	2.9	3.0	2.5	1.7	2.5
EU	18.4	16.2	15.5	15.8	11.8	10.6
Others	8.1	5.1	6.6	11.2	8.6	10.6
World	100	100	100	100	100	100

Source: Estimated from DoTs.

trade. In the 1980s, Japan had been the engine of growth for many East-Asian economies. But because of the slowdown in Japanese economy in the 1990s, it was no longer able to play as important a role in the region and the East-Asian economies had to develop new export markets and seek new foreign direct investors. Rising incomes, geographical proximity and the growing sophistication of production capacity within the region combined to create increasing trade opportunities and the share of non-Japan Asia from within the region increased. The development of cross-border production sharing made this region a manufacturing hub and the share of machinery and machinery parts and components in both total export and imports have become notably large. With the emergence of China as a major economic force and the world's manufacturing centre, this trend has further strengthened. Asian countries have become the suppliers of components to the whole world.

Africa

The African countries, like many other developing countries, embarked on a series of reforms in the early 1980s. The new trade regime moved away from inward-looking strategies towards greater integration with the world. Between 1980 and 1995, Africa's integration into global trade was increasingly based on its mining and energy industries.

Table 2.4: Africa's Direction of Trade

Trade of Partners	**Share in Africa's Total Trade (%)**		
	1995	**2000**	**2006**
EU	47.1	42.8	36.8
SA	10.9	13.8	15.4
Asia	16.0	15.8	20.8
Middle East	3.7	5.0	5.5
Latin America	2.3	3.0	4.3
Intra Africa	9.6	9.3	9.4
Others	10.5	10.4	7.8
World	100.0	100.0	100.0

Source: DoTs.

Figure 2.5: Africa's Exports to Asia

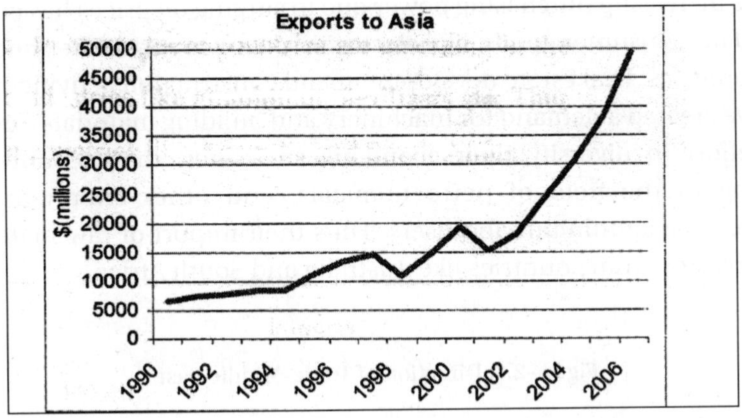

The economic crisis of the South-East Asian countries in 1996-97 had repercussions on Africa through the impact on world prices, especially those of primary commodities. The slowdown in Asia depressed the value and volume of imports from Africa. However, trade between the two regions picked up after the year 2000 and has accelerated since 2002. Africa's exports are largely driven by increasing demand for natural resources and other primary commodities from Asia's growing industrial sectors and rising purchasing power, particularly in China, India, Korea Taiwan and South-East Asian countries, like Malaysia, Singapore, Thailand and the Philippines. There has also been a growth of Africa's agricultural products which can be explained by the large population in Asia with increasing incomes. Africa's imports (mainly manufactured goods) from Asia have also grown and currently one-third of its total imports are from Asia, next only to the EU. In recent years, some African nations have become exporters of manufactured products, most notably textiles and apparels. South Africa has developed as an industrial and commercial hub in sub-Saharan Africa and an exporter of automobiles. The technical complementarities between South Africa and Asian countries have provided scope for inter-industry trade. Africa has done well in terms of growth rate since its increase in trade with Asia and rising Asian FDI there indicates further increase in trade between the two in the future.

The Middle East

Due to similarity in factor endowments and production structure, the Middle East countries have had little scope for intra-regional trade. Till the 1980s, these countries exported crude oil and imported most of the products from the USA. Now the USA accounts for only 9 per cent of their imports; the

EU contributes one-third and Asian countries about a quarter of their overall imports. Increasing purchasing power due to surging oil prices has created a demand for consumer goods, like electronics, textiles and white goods from Asian countries. Real estate development and construction activities in West Asia have created a demand for machinery and building materials from Asia. In an effort to diversify their economic structures, these countries are emerging in the field of petrochemicals, and other energy-intensive industries like aluminium, fertilisers. Thus their import of raw materials is also increasing from countries like Australia and South Africa.

Figure 2.6: Direction of Trade-Middle East

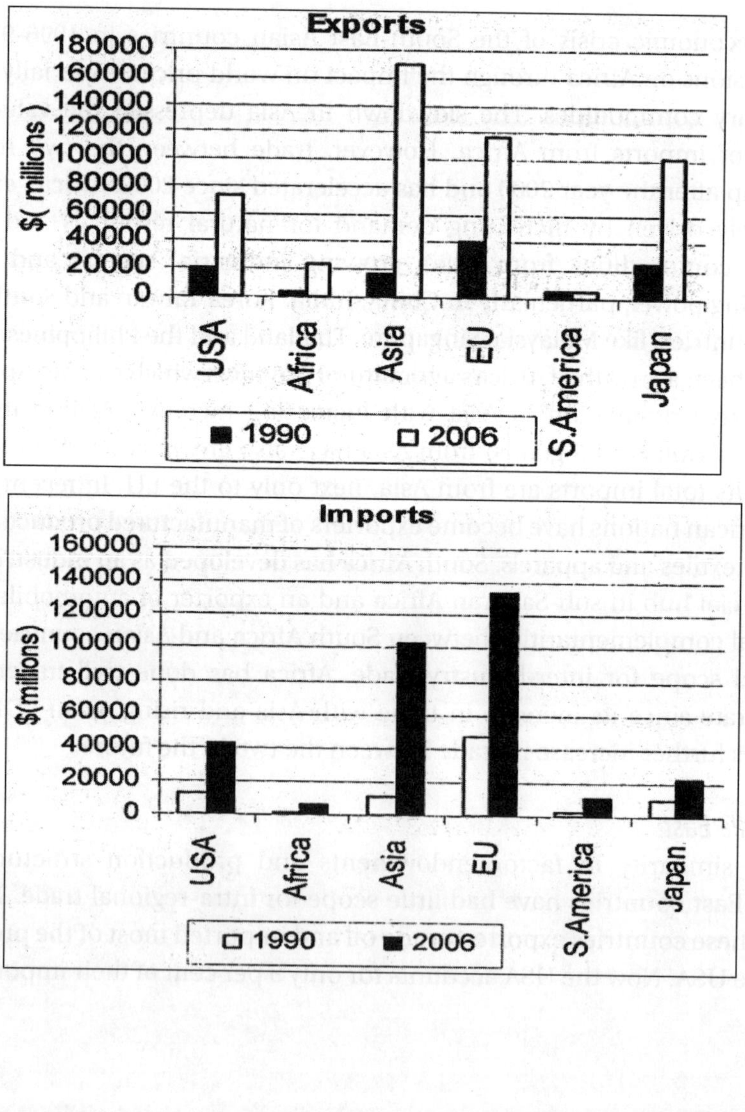

The inter-regional reliance between Asia and the Middle East is mutual: Asia is one of the three major oil markets along with the US and Europe. Asian oil consumption is expending rapidly, driven by the mega population and fast growth of China and India. The downstream sector of the oil and gas industry (refining and petrochemicals) plays an important role in India, China, Singapore, South Korea and Malaysia. While energy consumption is expected to level off in Japan, it will more than double by 2030 in developing Asia. (IEEJ) Almost two-third of the increase in India and China is expected to come from the transport sector. Geopolitical consideration, including a desire by both regions to diversify their imports and exports beyond the US and Europe, could deepen the cross-regional entente.

Apart from the increasing demand from Asia, world dependence on the middle East for hydrocarbons is also expected to increase. The Middle East countries have the largest reserves of oil and relatively low costs for expending their production capacity. World consumption of petroleum has been increasing despite rise in world oil prices. Largest increases in consumption between 2004 and 2030 are projected for North America and non-Organization for Economic Cooperation and Development (OECD) Asia (IEA). Though US oil is supplied by Canada, Venezuela and Mexico, expected investment levels in Mexico and Venezuela, are projected to be lower in coming years. The Organization of the Petroleum-Exporting Countries (OPEC) members outside Persian Gulf (excluding Angola) are projected to increase production capacity moderately because of the relatively high cost of capacity expansion. Thus dependence on West Asia for oil is expected to increase in the future.

Petroleum is the dominant commodity in commerce in the Indian Ocean as it is shipped worldwide. West Asia accounted for the largest share in world loading of crude oil (51.1 per cent) and petroleum products (43.5 per cent) the second largest crude oil exporters among the developing countries were African nations, with 24.6 per cent share of world loading. If we look at crude oil unloaded, the share of developing countries in Asia was 31.1 per cent of the world total. This shows the importance of West Asia as producers of crude oil and refinery products in Asia.

Since trade is an important determinant of maritime activity, it is therefore nor surprising that the development of maritime trade has grown in Indian Ocean region too. Asia has emerged as the leader in world container traffic. Expanding trade in China and India has played an important role. The other reason has been the good prospects for economic growth in this region in the medium to long term.

In 2006, the Asia region was the largest trader, accounting for 36.1 per cent of world goods loaded and 32.9 per cent of goods unloaded. The share of African countries was estimated at 10.7 per cent and 4.1 per cent of goods loaded and unloaded respectively.

Asia also has the largest share in dry cargo loading. The rising incomes and the growing appetite of China's industries has increased the seaborne trade in minerals, grain and soybeans and this has exerted pressure on shipping lines the world over.

The number of carriers playing through the Indian Ocean has increased with the increased participation of Asia. About a quarter of the world's bulk carriers fly an Asian flag, as do general cargo vessels. Twenty-one per cent of the world's fleet of vessels above 100 GT is registered in Asia. By far the largest registries are those of Hong Kong (China) and Singapore, each with about 32 million GT registered (UNCTAD, 2007).

Compared to Europe and America, Asia has become the most dynamic region in terms of total cargo traffic during the period 2001–2005. Today, the largest world container ports are located in Asia. Singapore and Dubai are among the world's top ten largest container ports. Due to increase in opportunities for private investment in the port sector, global terminal operators, like Cosco Pacific, DP World, Evergreen, Hanjing, Hutchision Port Holding (HPH), ICTSI, NYK/Ceres and PSA International are headquartered in Asia. Together they have a throughput of over 220 million TUEs and about half of the world's total throughput of containers (UNCTAD, 2007).

Strong economic growth and rising oil trade volumes are driving a major overhaul of the Middle East's container ports as oil wealth is being directed into intense infrastructure programmes. New regional mega hubs like Salalah and Aden are competing with established hubs of Dubai, Khor Fakkan, and Fujairah. Ports in Asia are increasingly attracting the interest of investors, and for many developing countries the main issue is no longer how finance new infrastructure projects but which partner to choose.

Challenges

Even though today all countries in the IOR trade much more and at much lower costs, their share in trade is still very small in absolute terms. They need to be concerned about some key issues if they wish to realise greater gains from international trade. They need to pay attention in particular first, to the manner in which they enter into trade agreements and second, lower their trade costs, which have become an important factor in determining a countries comparative advantage.

In recent years an increasing amount of trade is being carried out under Regional Trading Agreements (RTAs). Almost all countries are a part of some or the other trade agreement. Up to July 2007, there were around 380 RTAs in existence that have been notified to the GATT/WTO of which 205 agreements were in force. If we take into account RTAs which are in force but have not been notified, those signed but not yet in force, those currently being negotiated, and those in the proposal stage, we arrive at a figure of close to RTAs which are scheduled to be implemented by 2010.[6]

An RTA is an arrangement whereby the concerned countries can give preferential treatment in trade to each other by reducing or eliminating tariffs and other trade barriers while continuing their normal trade policies with the non-member countries that do not necessarily belong to the same geographical region. Among the RTAs that are being signed, a large majority are bilateral Free Trade Agreements (FTAs).

The economic rationale behind the formation of RTAs is that by lowering trade barriers among the members, RTAs would increase welfare through trade creation. However, this argument is contested by many economists (Bhagwati, Panagariya, etc.) who believe trade diversion is more likely to dominate when countries trade with numbers as well as with outside countries. Trade diversion happens when a countries switches imports from low cost non-number producers to a less efficient producer of a member country. They also are of the opinion that if the members of RTAs are small in relàtion to outside world, very little trade creation is likely to happen.

Initially, growth of RTAs was encouraged by the WTO as it was believed that this would complement the multilateral trade regime. However, the proliferation of RTAs with increased diversion of trade and other problems, especially for developing countries, has become a cause for concern. Concerns associated with proliferation of RTAs arise from the so-called 'noodle bowl effect' which refers to the problems arising from lack of coherence among different overlapping agreements. This leads to complexity and lack of transparency in the trading system, restricting trade because of the difficulty of implementing the rules. Problem arises mainly from the 'Rules of Origin'. For example, Bolivia has signed 28 reginol agreements with a veriety of Rules of Origin; this give custom official wide discretion and engenders corruption.[7]

Then there is the 'hub and spoke' problem, namely, when the largest RTA member or the 'hub' signs individual agreements with a number of peripheral countries or 'spokes', among whom market access is restricted. Such arrangement is advantageous to the hub as it enjoys greater access to all spokes but it can marginalise the spokes, where market access conditions are usually less advantageous than in the hub (Wonnacott, 1996). This happens when developing countries enter into an agreement with a developed country, like the USA or EU.

However, more serious is the trend of entering into free trade agreements (FTAs), which will create serious problems for the developing countries in the long run. Today, mainly developing countries are entering into FTAs because of their dissatisfaction with the progress of the negotiations at the WTO. The protectionism and lack of willingness among developed countries to provide significantly improved market access on a multilateral basis is motivating countries to look for alternative options for expanding their markets. At times these have adverse effects. For example, developing countries are entering into FTAs with the USA and EU on a bilateral basis. One of the reasons for this is the fear of being excluded from such trade blocs. This motive is particularly strong if the country competitors have already entered into such trade agreement. However, these RTAs force the developing countries to make deeper trade and investment commitments which are generally harmful to their economic interest. By pushing aggressive trade treaties, developed countries are weakening the power of developing countries in multilateral trade negotiations which not only helps the developed countries to have an upper hand in the WTO but also breaks the alliance of developing countries in the multilateral negotiations.

There are concerns that regional trading blocs might undermine the multilateral system as they may reduce enthusiasm for participation in the multilateral trade regime. This is dangerous as studies relying on simulation results, have argued that the welfare effects of multilateral liberalisation on countries are much larger than those of bacterial agreements especially for small economies. This is because in a bilateral Agreement, small economies risk being excluded as economic factors play an important role of choice of the trading Agreements partners.

Thus, given the North– South divide in the WTO and the trade barriers of the developed countries against the products which developing countries export, developing countries seek to promote trade amongst themselves. The rapidly growing economics of developing countries, especially in Asia, have reduced the need to depend on developed countries. The way forward for the developing countries should be South–South FTAs if the countries want to expand market access without compromising their national interest. Also, in the case of North–South agreements, developing countries should first consider the impact of such agreements on their policy space for longer-term development strategies.

To what extent the goods can be delivered to the destination market in a timely and cost effective manner has become extremely important. It has therefore become imperative that attention be paid to the lowering of trade cost by, inter alia, lowering transport cost, improving communication links, rationalising custom procedures, etc. In general, firms exporting goods from developing countries face higher transaction costs than those from developed countries. A large part of the transaction cost is accounted for by the transport cost.

Till recently, economic resarch paid more attention to tariff barriers while transport costs were considered to be insignificant in determining the comparative advantage of a country. Now that tariff barriers have been reduced considerably by most countries of the world, high transport costs are considered to be a significant barrier to trade. Limao and Venables[8] found that an increase in transport cost of 10 per cent would reduce the volume of trade by nearly 20 per cent. Accoreding to UNCTAD (2004), freight cost in developing countries were 70 per cent higher than in developed countries. The transport costs in Africa are almost twice that of the world average and this is considered to be one of the reasons for the region's relatively slow growth of exports.

Many developing countries export raw materials and low value-added commodities that are shipped in bulk by using not so modern logistic parctices and this increases the cost of handling the goods. Low export volumes from these countries imply smaller and less frequent consignment which leads to higher freight cost.This is because low volume of exports on the one hand does not give incentive for improvement in port infrastructure and, on the other hand, does not encourgage developing countries' shippers to enter into long-term contracts with freight carriers to offer low price transport services.

The massive volume of goods that has to be trasported and the huge sizes of container ships have lead to 'hub and spoke' based transshipment system. For shipping line, turnaround time in ports is an important factor to decide to call in any port of the world. One extra day at a port costs more than US$ 35,000 to a shipping line for a 2,200 TEU vessel.[9] Therefore, in order to reduce costs, shipping lines prefer transporting containerised goods to major ports. Countries that are able to persuade shipping companies to establish trans-shipment hubs within their borders can take advantage of substantial cost benefits since this reduced shipment distance, transit time and handling costs. Developing countries with low shipping volumes and poor port infrastructure facilities find it difficult to be at the centre of such hub and spoke networks. Without improved port efficiency and increased exports, many ports of the developing world face the danger of becoming increasingly marginalised, served only by feeder ships.

Internationally traded goods incur not only international transport costs, like cost of handling, freight and insurance, etc. but also domestic transport cost. The rise in inter-modal containerised shipments has made road and rail transport more efficient in moving goods to the ports and aiports. Facilitated transport between port and their hinterland is critical to attract increased traffic, which in turn attracts shipping lines to call at a port. It has been found that in Asia, though international transport costs have reduced between 2000 and 2005, in all countries except India and Malaysia, they suffer from bottlenecks in domestic infrastructure quality.[10] The poor condition of the roads in the developing countries adds to the vehicle operating cost per kilometre, lengthens travel time, adds to spoilage of perishable goods and damages fragile ones.

The cost of trasportation in developing countries is higher mainly because of lack of sufficient investment in infrastructure such as roads, railways, airports and ports as well as transport and logistics services and, because of inappropriate trade and transport policeis adopted by the countries. The long gestation periods, high incremental capital output ratio, low returns, etc. make infrastructure investment unattractive for private investors. As a result, infrastructure projects in developing countries have generally been finaced publicly. Fiscal stress faced by governments along with decline in funding from mulitlateral organisations menas that policy makers need to consider alternative ways of filling the infrastructure gaps.[11]

Application of new technology in field of communication besides faster and more eficient transport system has been the main factor behind this phase of globalisation. A study of traders in Ghana provides interesting findings about how the use of mobile phones has helped them to reduce transaction costs and imporve their trade.[12] Use of this simple technology has allowed them to have instant access to information about supply, demand, quality, and prices. This has ruduced search costs and information asymmetries, which have resulted in better planning. They are able to coordinate a larger number of activies, employees, and partners and save money on fuel, bus fares and on remuneration of intermediaries. Time spent on travelling amongst suppliers, customers, employees, creditors and debtors is put into productive work instead. A larger network of customers can be served by them. With the ability to provide customers with better services gives these traders a comparative advantage over those who either do not own cell phones or live in areas without coverage. Those who have been early adopters of this technology have been able to expand their businesses and profits.

The foregoing example shows the importance of technology at the micro level. It is playing the some role at the international level and impacting the volume and pattern of trade and international specialisation. Companies are locating different processes in different countries according to comparative advantage. Increasing competition is pushing firms to reduce cost by adopting just-in-time inventory managment which is highly dependent on efficient, reliable and responsive communication and transport system. If the developing countries want to be a part of these international supply chains, they will need to create an efficint transport and logistics system.

The benefits associated with technolgy are widely recongnised by policy makers in the developing countries. The degree to which the advantages may be realised, however, depends upon access to the telecommunications infrastructure, which in turn depends upon access to IT, telecommunication and the necessary supporting services, like electricity. However data reveals that by and large, developing countries are not participating in scientific innovation at the technological frontier. The intensity with which upper-middle-income countries are able to exploit both older and newer technologies is between 50 and 60 per cent of the level in high income countries. This ratio is between 30 and 40 per cent for lower-middle-income countries and is about 23 per cent for low-income countries.

Technology diffusion is quite low in developing countries. If we look at telephone mainlines, high-income countries have 54 phone lines per 100 people while East Asia has fewer than 20 phone lines per 100, South Asia 4 and sub Saharan Africa, 2 lines per 100 people. In the USA, ther are 762 computers per 10,000 people. Three quarters of low-income countries have 15 or fewer PCs per 1,000 persons and 1/4 have fewer than 5 per 1,000 people. Internet penetration in Africa is extremely low because no high-speed, low-cost backbone exists to connect eastern and central Africa to the rest of the world. As a result, Internet transactions must be made via stellite, which provides lower bandwidth at higher cost than fibre optics (Kenyan call centre operators pay $7,000 per megabyte of bandwidth compared with around $500 for operators connected by fibre optic cable in India). If we look at what is happening within the countries, the situation is no better. For example, despite several technological advanced cities in India, tele-density is as low as in sub-Sahara Africa. In June 2007, for rural India the tele-density was only 6.5 per cent. (Global Economic Prospects, 2008 World Bank)

Many developing countries are making progress in reducing the technology gap with advanced countries; however, enormous gaps in technological achievement still remain. The cost of no access to technology has increased. The countries that get disconnected from the worldwide electronic network face the danger of getting bypassed. For absorption, adaptation and integration of techonology the countries have a lot to do in providing macro-economic stablity and good governance. However, technological progress also requires an energy revolution, a literate work force and domestic R&D capacity.

Conclusion

This paper uses various indicators to show the extent of globalisation and the increasing pace at which it is progressing in Asia and the Indian Ocean Rim countries since the 1980s. It also analyses the impact of trade on maritime infastructure.

The pace of growth in international trade has gathered momentum with the rapid growth of the Asian economies,and even more so since China and India started experiencing very high rates of growth. China and India being large economies, have placed a large demand of mineral and raw material-supplying countres. As a consequence, mineral-rich countries in Africa and West Asia have also benefited and have shared in the growth of China and India. The Africa region, which in the past had lagged considerably, was also able to post respectable growth rates of about 6 per cent per annum. West Asia, which is the largest prdoucer of oil, and is expected to be the main exporter of oil in the near future, benefited both from the increased demand and also the much higher prices.

As most of the trade in goods moves by sea, its rapid growth puts immense pressure on the maritime infrastructure in the Indian Ocean Rim countries. After the decline in tariff barriers, transportation costs have become an important factor in determining the competitiveness of a country's exports. Therfore, countries need to put in place the most efficient infrastructure. Many of them are upgrading port facilities to reduce the turn-around time of ships. They are also devoting considerable resources for improving the inland transport infrastructure, such as roads and railways and the logistics managment systems. The total transport system from the exporter's factory till the port has to be streamlines to make exports globally competitive.

Funding of transport infrastructure projects is no longer a major worry, as international financiers are seeking such projects. Ther is a number of players with the necessary technical skills in port construction and managment, who are willing to collaborate with countries/ports to help develop the most modern infrastructure.

Owing to the higher cost of ship detention at ports, modern container ships and very large crude carriers (VLCC) and dry cargo carriers, perfer to call only at large ports with modern facilities. The big ships would call at the large port while the smaller ports will be catered to by feeder services from the hub (major port in the region). This places the smaller ports at a cost disadvantage, because they would need to move cargo from their port to the neighbouring hub before it is loaded on to a ship going to their final destination. This involves double handling, increases travel distance and also involves more time from cargo to be aggregated.

Thus countries that wish to benefit from the fruits of globalisation will need to increase their trade volume and also modernise their ports and transport infrastructure in the hinterland. ■

Notes

1. Review of Maritime Transport, 2007, UNCTAD.
2. Global Economic Prospects, 2008, World Bank.
3. Ibid.
4. Ibid.
5. Global Economic Prospects, 2008, World Bank.
6. World Trade Orgnisation (WTO).
7. Rajapatirana S, 2000, "The Trade Policies of Developing Countries Recent Reforms and New Challenges."
8. Limao, N and AJ Venebles, 2001 "Infrastructure, Geographical Distance, Transport Costs and Trade".
9. Harding, A Pálsson, G and G Raballand (2007). "Port and Martime Transport Challenges in West and Central Africa.
10. De P, 2007, "Trade Costs in Asia: Importance of Trade Facilitation and Improved Connectivity."
11. UNESCAP, 2006, "Enhancing Regional Cooperation in Financing Infrastructure Investment."
12. Overå, R. (2004), "Networks, Distance and Trust: Telecommunications and Changing Trading Practices in Ghana."

SESSION II

PAPER 1

Maritime-related Terrorism and Crime: A Watchlist for the Indian Ocean Region

Michael Richardson*

Geopolitical Backdrop

The Indian Ocean is a vital link in sea trade between Asia and the West. It is also a vital link in energy and other trade exchanges between Asia and the Middle East, especially the Persian Gulf—a politically volatile region rich in oil and natural gas. The Gulf is a huge source of energy for the world and one that is predicted to become even more important in the future. About 16 per cent of Gulf oil exports are shipped to Europe and 11 per cent to the US. By contrast, two-third of Gulf oil exports go to Asia. Japan imports all its oil and 89 per cent comes from the Middle East, defined as the Gulf oil exporters, plus Oman and Yemen. Asia's two emerging economic giants, China and India, are also heavily reliant on the Middle East for their oil; India for about 70 per cent of its imports and China for around 50 per cent. South Korea, Singapore, Taiwan, Thailand and the Philippines each depend on the Gulf for over 70 per cent of their oil imports. Overall, the Middle East supplies nearly 75 per cent of Asia's oil import needs, making the region by far the most important customer. This relationship is expected to strengthen even further as Asian oil production plateaus and demand rises.[1]

The Persian Gulf is also a geopolitical cockpit where the interests of many major outside powers, including the United States, Europe, Russia, China, India and Japan are deeply engaged, and often at variance. For America, the rise of Iran and its programme to enrich uranium on an industrial scale—a

* Visiting Senior Research Fellow, Institute of South-East Asian Studies, Singapore.

process that can be used to make fuel for reactors to generate electricity or fissile material for nuclear bombs—are big problems as the US and allied forces in Iraq fight the Al-Qaeda and struggle to contain growing political factionalism, as well as sectarian violence among and between the majority Shiites and minority Sunnis. For India, the revival of the Taliban in parts of southern Afghanistan close to Pakistan, despite the presence of NATO forces, and the spread of Islamic extremism and political violence in nuclear-armed Pakistan, are sources of deep apprehension.

Post-Afghanistan

The Al-Qaeda used Afghanistan as a base for operations until US-led forces entered the country shortly after the 9/11 attacks and drove its ally, the Taliban, from power in Kabul. Since then, Al-Qaeda has had to disperse. Its fighters and agents, and those trained in its camps in Afghanistan, fanned out around the world. This and the use of the Internet have helped to spread their influence.[2] Al-Qaeda's core ideology is that Islam is under attack from within by heretics, and from without by non-Muslims, and that the only way to protect the religion is to sweep away secular, nationalist government and establish exclusive theocratic rule over all areas of the world that are part of the Islamic community or were part of it at some point in history, from Spain through the Middle East, North Africa, Central and South Asia to Indonesia, Malaysia and the Philippines.[3]

Anti-American and anti-Western feeling is widespread among the world's 1.2 billion Muslims, who are concentrated in the Middle East, North Africa, Central Asia, South Asia and South-East Asia. The invasion of Afghanistan and then Iraq stoked the sentiment that Islam was under attack by non-Muslims, building on a pre-existing conviction that the US and its allies in Europe and elsewhere had long been biased in favour of Israel against the Palestinians in the Middle East's most deep-seated and emotive conflict. However, public opinion surveys suggest that only a relatively small minority of Muslims support terrorism and political violence.[4]

Iran's Rise

America's military intervention in Iraq has profoundly unsettled the Middle East. By toppling Saddam Hussein, a brutal dictator, and dismantling his secular Sunni control of the state, the US empowered and emboldened the majority Shia community centred in the oil-rich south of Iraq. But, instead of entrenching a new beacon of multi-religious democracy in the Middle East, Washington has removed a barrier to the expansion of Shiite Iranian influence in the Persian Gulf and surrounding areas. It has also turned Iraq into a magnet and operational training ground for Al-Qaeda-linked terrorists, and unleashed a sectarian conflict between Shiite and Sunni extremist factions that worsened markedly in 2006.[5]

Iran's rise as a regional power led by a militant Shiite theocracy is challenging the primacy of long-established Sunni-Arab regimes in and around the Gulf. Meanwhile, the US and its ally, Israel, are determined to try to stop Iran from following North Korea and developing nuclear weapons—something Teheran denies it will do. The US officials are seeking to tighten financial sanctions on Iran. They have accused Iranian paramilitary forces of siding with Shiite militia factions in Iraq to attack US troops. The US warships deployed in or close to the Persian Gulf are seen as a warning to Iran not to underestimate America's power and resolve despite its troubles in Iraq, Afghanistan and Pakistan.

Asymmetric Driver

Since the collapse of the Soviet Union and the end of the Cold War in the early 1990s, the US and allied military power has become both preponderant and pervasive. This has been underscored by the US-led invasions of Afghanistan and Iraq, the increased mobility of Western forces and their enhanced strike capability. It has provided an incentive, particularly for terrorists and other relatively small groups of non-state actors, to look for new ways of countering superior force, just as Communist insurgents in South-East Asia during the Cold War adopted different means and tactics for fighting numerically superior and better armed local government forces and their foreign allies. The spread of modern weapons and explosives has made it easier for militants.

Fortunately, transnational terrorists have been relatively unsuccessful so far in exploiting these developments and disrupting maritime trade. But in the concluding section of this paper, I suggest that this may change in future.

Maritime Terrorism

The paper deals first with the maritime-related plans and operations of Al-Qaeda, its affiliates and emulators in the violent jihadist network. It also deals with similar activities of the Hezbollah militia based in Lebanon. It then looks at the maritime operations of the Tamil Tigers in Sri Lanka and the overseas fund-raising and arms procurement activities that have helped to sustain the group's armed rebellion. These are all organisations with wellhoned techniques of political violence, although the international community accords each of them different weight and status in its definition of terrorism.

In the past decade, the Al-Qaeda network's plans and operations against ships and their cargo have been far less numerous than its strikes on land-based targets. The maritime-related activities of the Al-Qaeda have also been overshadowed by aircraft hijackings. The most spectacular, of course, was the 9/11 plot in which Al-Qaeda operatives seized four civilian jet airliners in the United States and crashed three of them into landmark buildings in New York and Washington on 11 September 2001, killing nearly 3,000 people from 80 nations. As a result, much is now known about the activities on land and in the air of the Al-Qaeda network. Less is known about their maritime-related activities.[6]

Yet the list of foiled, failed and successful attempts in maritime-related terrorism over the last decade is significant. Nonetheless, there remains a tendency to overlook or downplay what has happened, and thus ignore the possibility of further trouble. It is clear that terrorists can see the potential of using the maritime trading system, and its land links through the cargo container supply chain, to conceal weapons or agents for attack purposes or to provide funding or support for their operations. The terrorist network associated with Al-Qaeda understands the vital role of sea transport and has exploited it for years.

East Africa

For example, an Al-Qaeda-controlled cargo ship delivered the explosives that its operatives used to bomb two US embassies in East Africa in August 1998, killing 224 people and injuring more than 5,000.[7]

Yemen

In September 2004, two Al-Qaeda operatives were sentenced to death and four others jailed in Yemen for the suicide attack in October 2000 on the American destroyer *Cole*.[8] They used a small boat packed with explosives to ram into and seriously damage one of the US Navy's most sophisticated warships. An earlier attempt to attack another American destroyer, *The Sullivans*, in Yemen had failed when the over-laden attack boat sank. It was salvaged and used in the operation to strike the *Cole*. The blast, which left a gaping hole in the side of the destroyer, killed 17 American sailors and wounded 40. It took more than 14 months and cost around US$ 250 million to repair the ship.[9]

In October 2002, two years after the *Cole* was hit, the French-registered oil tanker, *Limburg*, carrying crude oil off the coast of Yemen, was crippled and set ablaze in another terrorist attack using an explosive-laden small boat. The Al-Qaeda claimed responsibility.[10]

Iraq

In April 2004, suicide terrorists in several small boats packed with explosives tried to attack laden tankers and pumping and storage facilities in the main oil export terminal in southern Iraq. The attack boats either blew up or were blown up before they reached their targets. But they came perilously close and it took several days to restore normal output from the terminal.[11] The assault was ordered by Abu Musab al-Zarqawi, then head of the Al-Qaeda in Iraq. He was killed in June 2006 but the movement is under new leadership and fights on, although on a more restricted scale and under increasing pressure from both local and US forces in Iraq.

Jordan

The terrorist group led by Zarqawi, who was born in Jordan, claimed responsibility for the *Katyusha* rocket attack in August 2005 that narrowly missed two US warships in the Jordanian Red Sea port of Aqaba. Three rockets were fired at the two docked vessels, the amphibious assault ship *Kearsarge* and the landing ship *Ashland*. The *Katyushas* missed the ships, but a Jordanian soldier was killed and a taxi driver wounded when the rockets exploded.[12]

Turkey

Also in August 2005, authorities in Turkey arrested Louai Sakka, a senior Al-Qaeda operative and longtime associate of Zarqawi in Iraq. Sakka was picked up and interrogated after a one-tonne bomb he was making in a rented harbour-side apartment in the resort town of Antalya, in southern Turkey, went off prematurely. He had intended to put the bomb into final shape on his 27-foot motorised yacht, the *Tufan*, which was moored in a marina close to the apartment. Sakka planned to ram the explosive-laden yacht into a cruise ship carrying Israelis—and, he believed, US soldiers on rest and recreation—as it approached Antalya to disembark passengers. Sakka said later that he was prepared to attack NATO warships in the area if he was unable to locate Israeli passenger vessels.[13]

Morocco

In March and April 2007, Moroccan officials and media reported a series of arrests of dozens of people suspected of planning attacks on a range of targets, including blowing up foreign ships in the Casablanca port and striking at facilities in three of the country's main tourist destinations. There is evidence to suggest that this was an Al-Qaeda plot.[14]

The Strait of Gibraltar

Abd al-Rahim al-Nashiri, captured in late 2002, gave investigators information that reinforced concerns about plans for terrorist attacks against shipping. He was Al-Qaeda's head of operations in and around the Arabian peninsula and its de facto naval chief. Al-Nashiri is the alleged mastermind of the attack on the *USS Cole* and the tanker *Limburg.* He has also been linked to the bombings of the two US embassies in east Africa in 1998.

In addition, Al-Nashiri was planning attacks on shipping in the Strait of Gibraltar. Early in 2002, he sent a team of several Saudis to Morocco to prepare for bomb-laden speedboat attacks on the US and British warships as they passed through the strait between the Mediterranean Sea and the Atlantic Ocean.[15] The Saudis had been trained in Afghanistan. The Moroccan intelligence service, working with Western intelligence agencies, foiled the scheme.

The Persian Gulf

Evidently drawing on information from interrogation of Al-Nashiri and other captured Al-Qaeda operatives, President George Bush said in October 2005 that America and its partners in the war on terror had disrupted at least 10 serious Al-Qaeda terrorist plots since 9/11. Two of these attempts were directed against shipping.

The White House noted that in the first, in late 2002 and 2003, the US and a partner nation disrupted a plan by Al-Qaeda operatives to attack ships in the Arabian Gulf, the name sometimes given by US officials to the Persian Gulf.[16] This may be a reference to an abortive attempt to bomb the US Navy's Fifth Fleet headquarters in Bahrain in the Persian Gulf, a plan linked to Al-Nashiri, who was captured in the United Arab Emirates (UAE) in October 2002. Or, it may be a reference to another audacious plot Al-Nashiri was working on at the time of his arrest. He was arranging funding to crash a small aircraft into the bridge of a Western navy vessel when it was docked in the UAE's Port Rashid.

The Strait of Hormuz

The White House said that in the second plot in 2002, the US and partners disrupted a plan to attack vessels transiting the Strait of Hormuz, a vital shipping channel, both for tankers carrying oil exports from the Gulf to Asia,

Europe and America, and for US and allied warships patrolling the area and supporting military operations in Iraq and Afghanistan.

Al-Nashiri's procurement arm in the UAE, through a series of front companies, had bought a general cargo vessel and several speedboats. The aim was to fit a special lifting rig on deck to lower the boats, packed with shaped explosive charges, into the water when they were close to the Strait of Hormuz, which is about 40 miles wide. The waterway consists of 2-milewide channels for separate inbound and outbound tanker traffic, with a 2-mile wide buffer zone between them. Once in position within striking distance of a passing US warship, the small craft manned by suicide crew was to be launched from the mother ship in a combined attack from different directions on the chosen target. The freighter itself was to be loaded with explosives and blown up in the shipping lanes as close as possible to the transiting US naval target. The plot was reportedly intended to coincide with the attacks on the US in September 2001. But Al-Nashiri, fearing that the operation's coordinators were under surveillance, called it off.[17]

The Philippines

Maritime terrorism has not been confined to the Middle East, Africa and the Mediterranean. In South-East Asia, Al-Qaeda's affiliates, including the Abu Sayaff Group, the ASG, and Jemaah Islamiyah, the JI, have attacked shipping or planned to do so.

Philippine officials say that the ASG—working with the Rajah Solaiman Movement, made up of converts to Islam from among the Christian majority in the Philippines—was responsible for placing the bomb that sank a passenger ferry, the *MV Superferry 14,* in Manila Bay in February 2004, killing 116.[18] In terms of loss of life, this is the worst maritime terrorist attack in recent years.[19] In August 2005, another bomb on a ferry, *MV Dona Ramona,* docked in the southern Philippines, injured at least 30 people. Security officials said the incendiary device was the work of Abu Sayaff terrorists.

Singapore

The Singapore government has said that when it started its crackdown in December 2001 on the JI—the South-East Asian terrorist network with links to both Al-Qaeda and Abu Sayyaf militants—it discovered that the group had made preliminary plans for suicide attacks on US warships visiting Singapore. The JI also intended to carry out multiple truck bomb attacks against Western and Israeli diplomatic and other targets in Singapore, including naval bases used by the American military. It had started buying the ammonium nitrate to be used in the explosives.

The plans to attack US warships with explosive-laden small boats manned by foreign suicide bombers were started in the mid-1990s and were fairly well developed, although never activated. They included a detailed targeting map for a seaborne attack using a small craft against US naval vessels travelling eastwards from Singapore's Sembawang Wharf, in the northern part of the island state opposite Malaysia, via Tekong Island. The markings on the map identified a strategic "kill" zone where the channel was narrowest and where the target ship would have had no room to take evasive action to avoid colliding with the suicide boat. The plan took advantage of local geography to hide the attack boat from radar and visual detection until the very last minute. The route and patrol schedule of Singapore's Police Coast Guard in the area had also been monitored.

In early 2001, the plans were revived when two unidentified Middle-Easterners approached Faiz bin Abu Bakar Bafana, the Malaysian JI leader, for information on US military vessels in Singapore. Faiz then instructed members of the JI in Singapore to survey Sembawang Wharf and Changi Naval Base, both of which were being used by visiting American warships. They video-recorded what they observed and a copy of the video was later given to the Middle-Easterners in Kuala Lumpur.[20]

Malaysia and Indonesia

The planning for the attack on the *USS Cole* in Yemen in October 2000 began in Malaysia. One of the key suspects—Walid Bin 'Attash, best known as Khallad—worked with Al-Qaeda maritime commander Al-Nashiri on the *Cole* attack.[21] Khallad, a Yemeni-born and raised in Saudi Arabia, was plotting another attack on a US naval vessel visiting a Malaysian port in 2000. Less than a year later, Malaysian intelligence foiled a plan to attack a second US warship. Meanwhile in Indonesia, Al-Qaeda intended to attack a US naval vessel in Surabaya, a major Indonesian naval port and the country's second largest city.[22] Planning for this attack was being handled by Omar al-Faruq, one of Al-Qaeda's leading liaison operatives in South-East Asia. It was disrupted by Al-Faruq's arrest in June 2002 in Indonesia.

Japan

Japan—along with Singapore, Australia and South Korea—is among the countries that have been singled out for attack by Al-Qaeda for supporting the US-led military coalition in Iraq. In May 2004, Japanese police arrested five foreigners—three from Bangladesh, one from India and the other from Mali—who had been in contact with Lionel Dumont, a 33-year-old French national of Algerian descent with ties to Al-Qaeda. Dumont was arrested in

Germany in December 2003 and extradited to France in May 2004.[23] He had been involved in criminal activity in France in the 1990s while belonging to a radical Islamist group known as the Roubaix gang.[24]

Dumont tried to establish an Al-Qaeda cell when he worked as a used-car exporter in Japan in 2002 and 2003. He sent substantial amounts of money to one of the arrested Bangladeshis who had an office near the US Navy base in Yokosuka on the outskirts of Tokyo. The office was being used to gather information on the base in preparation for a terrorist operation.[25] Yokosuka is the largest American naval facility outside the US and the homeport of the commander of the US Seventh Fleet and his flagship.

The United States

These are examples of terrorist attacks on naval and commercial vessels or plans to attack them and the bases from which they operated. However, Al-Qaeda has also shown interest in cargo containers on ships to ferry agents, weapons and terrorist-related material around the world. Shortly before his capture in Pakistan in March 2003, Al-Qaeda's head of global operations, Khalid Shaykh Muhammad, through two trusted lieutenants, offered to invest about 200,000 US dollars in an export firm in exchange for access to the containers used by the firm to ship garments to Port Newark in the New York-New Jersey harbour complex.[26] He wanted to use the containers to smuggle explosives into the US for various Al-Qaeda attacks.[27]

Khalid Shaykh Muhammad, one of Al-Qaeda's most capable senior operatives, is the mastermind of the 9/11 terrorist attacks on New York and Washington. His interest in ships and their cargo containers, and the fact that he was prepared to invest an unusually large amount of Al-Qaeda's money in a company that regularly moved textiles into the maritime heart of the US financial capital and sold them to leading retail outlets, must be regarded as an ominous warning sign.

Cargo Containers

The millions of containers that carry most of today's general cargo around the world are a security nightmare. These uniform steel boxes are potential Trojan Horses in the 21st century when advanced technology, including weapons and the information needed to build and operate them, is increasingly accessible to terrorists and criminals. Just as it is easy to hide smuggled goods and people inside a container, so it is easy to conceal arms or bombs. Once a container is loaded and sealed, inspection is a problem. The contents can be misrepresented and undeclared items hidden inside with relative ease. Even when sealed, containers can be surreptitiously opened and then closed again without great difficulty to remove or add contents. This is a made-to-order method of transport for terrorists—just as it is for drug and other contraband smugglers.[28]

More than 17 million containers are in circulation, criss-crossing the globe by sea and making over 230 million journeys through the world's ports each year. Some nine million containers arrive by sea in US ports alone. Physical checks of containers reaching American ports by sea increased to 5.2 per cent of total arrivals by September 2003, from 2 per cent two years' earlier. But worldwide, less than 1 per cent of shipped cargo is screened using Gamma-Ray devices and radiation detectors to peer inside and check for explosives, radioactive substances or other dangerous materials. However, homeland security officials in the US have argued that the key to preventing a terrorist attack using cargo containers is not the amount of physical inspection that takes place. It is the ability to marshal intelligence on the contents of the boxes so that only suspect ones are chosen for inspection, while the genuine trade proceeds without delay. Critics of this approach, including the world's leading container terminal operator, say that the risk analysis method being used by America is flawed and that all containers moving through the global supply chain by sea should be monitored using non-intrusive inspection equipment to scan and clear containers quickly in terminals.[29]

Italy

The fear that terrorists could exploit the container transport system was confirmed barely a month after the Al-Qaeda hijackers crashed civilian airliners into the World Trade Centre twin towers and the Pentagon. In October 2001, authorities in the southern Italian port of Gioia Tauro discovered an unusually well-equipped and neatly dressed stowaway locked inside a shipping container. It was furnished as a makeshift home with a bed, water, and supplies for a long journey. Italian police named the stowaway Rizik Amid Farid and said he was born in Egypt but carried a Canadian passport.[30]

Unlike most stowaways, Farid was smartly dressed, cleanshaven and rested as he emerged. He was found to be carrying two mobile phones, a satellite phone, a laptop computer, several cameras, batteries and, ominously, given recent events in the US, airport security passes and an airline mechanic's certificate valid for four major American airports.[31] Gioia Tauro is a leading trans-shipment hub for cargo in the Mediterranean. The container had been loaded in Port Said, Egypt. Had the occupant not been trying to widen ventilation holes when workers in Gioia Tauro were nearby, the box may well have passed unhindered to its final destination in Canada via Rotterdam. After he was discovered, Farid was investigated by Italian prosecutors who suspected that he was an Al-Qaeda operative. He was charged with illegal entry into Italy and detained. But a court released him on bail and he disappeared before further information about him and the purpose of his unorthodox means of travel could be gathered.[32]

Israel

More recently, in March 2004, two Palestinian suicide bombers gained access to the Israeli seaport of Ashdod, near Tel Aviv, by concealing themselves in a standard 40-foot long container. They hid in a secret compartment behind a false wall at the back of the container which was loaded with marble and ceramic tiles. An electronic scan and a physical inspection of the box, both inside and out, by Israeli officials failed to detect the bombers. In blowing themselves up, the militants killed 10 port workers and injured 18. This was the first attack in a closely-guarded Israeli port, which was considered one of the most secure in the world. It shows how cargo containers can be used to hide people on military or terrorist operations.[33]

In July 2002, Israeli security officials in Ashdod had seized a shipment of guns and other weapons intended for Palestinian militants. Two months earlier, a container—supposedly filled with a donation of toys sent to the Gaza Strip by an Islamic charity—had been opened by officials in Ashdod and found to be packed instead with hundreds of pounds of guns, ammunition, telescopic lenses and night-vision equipment.

In summary, if one looks at the plans and operations of the first generation of Al-Qaeda leaders like Khalid Shaykh Muhammad, Abd al-Rahim al-Nashiri and others, it is clear that by 2001 and 2002, they were conducting trial runs for opening a maritime-related front in global terrorism. They could see that:

1. the vast commercial shipping and cargo container business around the world was open to infiltration and abuse;
2. naval ships are iconic targets; and
3. busy ports, too, are tempting because they are key nodes through which so much of world trade is shipped.[34]

Reasons for the Relative Calm on the Maritime Front

Why then have terrorists not succeeded, at least so far, in causing greater damage to naval operations and to international shipping and the cargo container supply chain that carry the bulk of world trade?

First, violent jihadists have lacked modern and lethal anti-shipping weapons. Their most effective weapons so far have been small boats packed with explosives and manned by suicide bombers. But this is changing as more and better weapons fall into the hands of terrorists.

Second, many of the trans-national terrorist networks' most capable and ruthless planners have been killed or captured. They include Khalid Shaykh Muhammad, Al Nashiri, Khallad and eleven others, whom US President George Bush said on 6 September 2006 had been transferred to Guantanamo Bay detention centre in Cuba for trial before military tribunals. There have been dozens of terrorism-related prosecutions in many countries.

Third, there has also been a worldwide crackdown on the sources of terrorist finance, their communications and means of moving money around. Visa and border controls have been tightened. In addition, counter-terrorist cooperation and intelligence sharing between nations and among law-enforcement agencies have been enhanced in recent years, although there is still room for improvement.[35]

Fourth, it will take time not just to replace dead or captured planners but also to put any major maritime-related operation into effect. Remember that Khalid Shaykh Muhammad started to think about how to strike New York and Washington with hijacked planes in 1995, six years before the plot was actually carried out. According to the 9/11 Commission Report, Al-Qaeda's chief, Osama bin Laden, summoned Khalid Shaykh Muhammad to Kandahar in south-western Afghanistan in March or April 1999 to tell him that Al-Qaeda supported the "planes operation".[36] This was nearly two and a half years before the strikes took place.

Fifth, the shipping business, like the aviation industry, is now better protected by a range of measures to prevent terrorist attacks. So, too, are the US Navy and other naval forces around the world that have learned protective lessons since the attack on the *USS Cole* in October 2000.[37] The international community, spurred by the US, has also tightened controls over the movement of containerised cargo at sea and on land through the Container Security Initiative (CSI) and other measures. Nearly 90 countries, about half the member states of the United Nations, now support the Proliferation Security Initiative (PSI) to prevent illegal trade in weapons of mass destruction, related materials and technology, and their means of delivery.[38] A major focus of the PSI is on sea trade.

A sixth reason why terrorists have not succeeded, at least so far, in causing greater damage to shipping may lie in the breakdown of centralised control. In the past few years, Al-Qaeda has franchised its ideology around the world, following the loss of Afghanistan as a base and training area. Holed up—possibly in the porous border zone between Afghanistan and Pakistan—Al-Qaeda's leaders have watched as affiliates and emulators, often in home-grown and largely autonomous cells, have taken root and launched their own terrorist activity in Asia, Europe, the Middle East, North Africa, Australia, Canada and the US.

So far, this wave of second-generation Al-Qaeda-inspired terrorism has been directed against mainly land-based and air targets, including passenger airliners, crowded commuter rail systems; US embassies and consulates; landmark buildings; places frequented by tourists; expatriate housing communities; and oil production, refining and storage facilities.[39] Using remotely detonated explosions or suicide bombers to attack targets that are part of everyday urban and industrial life may be easier, cheaper and quicker to organise than striking from the sea. These attacks on 'soft' targets are planned and carried out in secret by just a few people using relatively small amounts of explosives that can be bought and put together without great difficulty. Such attacks are hard to detect and stop. Yet they are effective in causing fear and conveying a political message.[40]

Future Trends

Until now, Al-Qaeda and other Sunni extremists have shown most interest in maritime-related terrorism. They have been exclusively involved in nearly all the plans and operations outlined above. But the Shiite Hezbollah, with assistance from Iran and Syria, has also carried out maritime-related strikes against Israel, as well as bombings against Israeli and US targets abroad.

However, unlike Al-Qaeda, Hezbollah is not widely branded as a terrorist organisation. It has a well-developed political arm in Lebanon, with substantial representation in parliament and a social welfare programme than is reputed to be more effective that the Lebanese government's counterpart services. Only a small number of States, among them the US, Israel and the Netherlands, have proscribed Hezbollah as a whole. Australia and Britain treat part of Hezbollah, its paramilitary arm, as a terrorist organisation.

Hezbollah's Strikes from the Sea

Hamas, Islamic Jihad and the military wing of Fatah claimed responsibility for the container attack in the Israeli port of Ashdod in March 2004. They are all Sunni Arab militant groups. But the Lebanese Hezbollah and predominantly Shiite Iran have become increasingly involved in the Palestinian struggle against Israel in recent years, providing arms and other assistance to fighters of Hamas and other units.[41] Israeli forces have intercepted at least three major shipments of these weapons by sea in the last five years.

Abu Hassan

In the most recent, in May 2003, naval commandos boarded an Egyptian fishing boat, the *Abu Hassan*. Of the eight people aboard, at least one was a Hezbollah operative. Hidden in the vessel were fuses for *Katyusha* rockets, electronic bomb-making components, materials used to make explosive vests for suicide bombers and Hezbollah compact discs containing instructions.[42]

Karine A

The biggest arms haul was taken from a 4,000-tonne freighter, the *Karine A*, in January 2002. When boarded off the Israeli Red Sea port of Eilat, it was found to be carrying 50 tonnes of rockets, mines, anti-tank missiles, guns and C-4 plastic explosives from Iran for Palestinian terrorists. The *Karine A*'s captain was a longtime Fatah activist and adviser to the Palestinian Authority's naval police. The freighter went from the Jordanian port of Aqaba to an Iranian island in the Persian Gulf where its military cargo was loaded. Further investigation revealed that the arms were purchased through Iran's so-called "Export Committee of the Islamic Revolution" for US$ 15 million. Payment was made through Lebanon via Hezbollah agents. Senior US intelligence officers in Iraq say that the Iranian government is now spending millions of dollars to train and equip Shiite extremist groups in Iraq and that Iranian C-4 captured in Baghdad in 2006 is identical to the C-4 taken by the Israelis from the *Karine A* in 2002.[43]

Santorini

A year earlier, in May 2001, Israeli naval forces intercepted the *Santorini*, a 65-foot wooden boat laden with a large shipment of munitions that included SA-7 Strela man-portable anti-aircraft missiles. The shipment smuggled from Libya was arranged by the Popular Front for the Liberation of Palestine—General Command for delivery to Palestinian Authority representatives. Israel has thwarted many other more recent attempts to smuggle explosives, weapons and terrorists by sea into Gaza.[44]

Singapore

In June 2002, Singapore's Internal Security Department disclosed that Hezbollah had planned several years earlier to attack US naval vessels and Israeli commercial ships in Singapore or as they approached, using small boats packed with explosives.[45] The minister for home affairs said that Hezbollah had no linkages to the JI and that the Hezbollah members had been expelled. They had tried to recruit Singaporeans and establish a cell in the island-state similar to those elsewhere in Asia, Australia and in North and South America, Europe, the Middle East and Africa.[46]

Hezbollah: Iran's Arm's-Length Strike Force

These cells, front organisations and support groups have been involved in fund raising, recruitment, and intelligence gathering as well as criminal activity and money laundering. They have also been preparing for armed attacks, should Hezbollah and its main patron, Iran, decide to launch them. Hezbollah gives predominantly Shiite Iran an international capability for retaliation against US and Israeli interests on several continents.[47] Iran's Supreme Leader, Ayatollah Ali Khamenei, has warned that Iran would hit at US and allied interests worldwide if attacked. He has said that Iran would strike at them with all its capabilities. In contrast to Al-Qaeda and the now decentralized Sunni extremist network, Hezbollah is centrally directed from Lebanon and works in tandem with state patrons, Iran and Syria.

Hezbollah's Lethal Arsenal

The military wing of the Shiite Hezbollah movement in Lebanon is sometimes described as a militia. But the fighting with Israel last year revealed it to be one of the best equipped guerrilla forces in the world. Hezbollah is a militia trained like an army and equipped like a State, an Israeli soldier who had just returned from combat against the group in southern Lebanon in August 2006, told the *New York Times*. With some 3,500 fighters, an infantry brigade size force, Hezbollah's military wing proved to be very well organised, equipped and armed.

Its weapons included some that have rarely, if ever, been seen before in the hands of non-State actors:

> ...advanced anti-tank missiles and rocket-propelled grenades such as the Russian-designed RPG-29 which proved to be effective against Israeli tanks and armoured vehicles. The RPG-29, which Russia had sold to Syria, has a tandem warhead. The first explosion is designed to blow away the target's protective armour while the second penetrates it; [48]
> ...the Ababil unmanned aerial vehicle (UAV), a pilotless aircraft with a self- guidance system that is capable of carrying an 88-pound warhead for up to 150 miles. Iran builds the Ababil and supplied it to Hezbollah. Three were launched against Israel but were shot down.[49] One carried an explosive charge.

The UAVs and the armour-piercing missiles are potentially new weapons in the hands of non-State actors for use against ships.

C-802 Anti-Ship Missile

Among Hezbollah's arsenal of modern arms was a weapon not normally associated with even the fanciest guerrilla group. On 14 July last year, two days after Hezbollah triggered the conflict by capturing and killing some soldiers inside Israel, it fired two C-802 radar-guided cruise missiles. One seriously damaged an Israeli corvette about 16 kilometres off the coast. The ship was helping to enforce Israel's blockade of Lebanon. Four sailors were killed. The second C-802 narrowly missed another Israeli corvette. Instead, it hit a Cambodian-registered freighter, sinking the vessel and killing 11 Egyptian crewmen.[50]

Neither Israel nor the US knew that Hezbollah fighters had such sophisticated weapons as the C-802 in their arsenal. As a result, the Israeli vessel did not have its missile-defence system on. Even if it had, the system would probably have been unable to protect it from the sea-skimming missile traveling at just under the speed of sound.[51]

The C-802 is rated as one of the most lethal anti-ship missiles in the world. It has a range of around 120 kilometres and a warhead packed with 165 kilogrammes of high explosives. How did Hezbollah get such an advanced weapon? From Iran—by sea, air or overland through Syria, another Hezbollah ally. Iran bought at least 75 of the missiles from China in the mid-1990s. It reportedly received help from China and North Korea to extend their range and improve their accuracy. With its own product line, Teheran clearly felt it had enough of the C-802s to send some to Hezbollah in Lebanon and provide the training needed to operate them successfully.[52]

The Sea Tigers

The Liberation Tigers of Tamil Eelam (LTTE) have also shown how non-State actors can use ships in support of political violence. Indeed, some analysts believe that the Tamil Tigers and Al-Qaeda have learned from each other. They say that the Sri Lankan guerillas trained in Al-Qaeda camps in Afghanistan and that the attack on the *USS Cole* in October 2000 and the French tanker *Limburg* two years' later, both near Yemen, copied LTTE strikes against shipping. The Sri Lankan government has lost several dozen naval vessels, both in harbour and at sea, during its long war with the Tamil Tigers, who have used high-speed boats filled with explosives to ram into naval vessels. There have also been reports that members of Jemaah Islamiyah, the South-East Asian terrorist group linked to Al-Qaeda, have been trained in the seaborne guerrilla tactics developed by the LTTE.[53]

Founded in 1976, the LTTE is the most powerful group among the Tamil minority in a country with a Sinhalese majority. This ethno-nationalist rebel organisation, which is estimated to have a 10,000-strong armed force, has used both overt and illegal methods to raise funds, acquire weapons, ammunition and explosives and publicise its cause in fighting since 1983 for a separate state for Tamils in the north-east of the island. The conflict between government troops and Tamil Tiger fighters and cost the lives of 70,000 people in the past 25 years. The LTTE has frequently used suicide bombers in operations against the government and exploited commercial maritime shipping, both to make money and bring in arms, ammunition, and other war-related material for attacks in Sri Lanka. Before Norway brokered a ceasefire between the government and the Tamil Tigers that took effect in February 2002, the LTTE had developed into a prototype terrorist organisation with a potentially global reach. [54]

Suicide Attacks

Unlike Al-Qaeda, the Tamil Tigers did not strike extensively outside their home base but, like Hezbollah, has the capability to do so. The LTTE is the only group to have successfully assassinated two national leaders—Rajiv Gandhi of India in 1991 and Ranasinghe Premadasa of Sri Lanka in 1993. Both were well-orchestrated suicide operations that evaded tight official security cordons. Sri Lanka's former President Chandrika Kumaratunga narrowly survived a Tamil Tiger suicide bomb attack in 1999. Underlining its pioneer role, the LTTE had conducted 155 battlefield and civilian suicide attacks up until August 1998, compared to the 50 carried out by all other groups worldwide, including Hamas and Hezbollah in the Middle East, the Kurdish Workers' Party (PKK) in Turkey, and the Sikh Babbar Khalsa in South Asia.

The key to the LTTE's fighting strength was its international support network. It collected money from large Tamil communities in North America, Europe and Australia. There is also some evidence that the LTTE officially sanctioned drug smuggling as well as arms smuggling to support its independence struggle.[55]

Tamil Tiger Shipping

Since the mid-1980s, the Tamil Tigers had controlled an extensive and profitable network of freight forwarders and up to a dozen or so cargo ships. The latter were not registered in Sri Lanka. To help disguise their ownership, they flew Panamanian, Honduran or Liberian flags. Indeed, the heart of the LTTE's military procurement was secretive shipping network which, by 1999, included at least ten freighters, all equipped with radar and Inmarsat communication technology. Most of the time, the Tamil Tiger ships made money carrying legitimate cargo like timber, tea, rice, cement and fertiliser. But in some cases, the Tamil Tigers carried weapons and ammunition for other paying terrorist groups, among them the Harkat-ul-Mujahideen of Pakistan, which is a member of the Al-Qaeda-linked International Islamic Front. And when needed, Tamil Tiger ships and traders played a vital role in supplying explosives, weapons, ammunition and other war-related material to the LTTE in Sri Lanka.[56]

In one of the largest such shipments, in August 1994, an LTTE freighter, the *Swene*, loaded 60 tonnes of RDX and TNT bought from a factory in Ukraine. The transaction was arranged through a Tamil Tiger front company in Dhaka that had produced a forged end-user certificate showing the Bangladesh armed forces as the approved recipient. The shipment was landed on the north-east Sri Lankan coast controlled by the LTTE and transferred to jungle bases. Some of the explosives, between 300 and 400 kilogrammes, were used in the massive truck-bomb attack against the Central Bank building in Colombo in January 1996 that killed 60 people and injured as many as 1,500.[57]

The Sting

On May 23, 1997, a Greek-registered freighter, the *Stillus Limassul,* left the port Beira in Mozambique for Sri Lanka carrying over thirty-two thousand 81mm mortar bombs intended for the Sri Lankan army. The deal, worth

US$ 3 million, had been arranged between officials of the Sri Lankan Defence Ministry and the state-owned Zimbabwe Defence Industries. The munitions were shipped by train to Beira. But the Sri Lankan military never received them. This was the result of a well-organised and well-concealed "sting" operation by the LTTE that deeply embarassed the Sri Lankan government at the time.

The Tamil Tigers claimed that on July 11 they had hijacked the *Stillus Limassul* while it was on its way to Colombo. But subsequent investigations revealed that the *Stillus Limassul* was not among the vessels on Lloyds International Shipping Register. It was, in fact, owned by the LTTE itself. Further enquiries uncovered a paper trail that led to Ben Tsoi, an Israeli arms dealer who had arranged the mortar supply and apparently been bribed by the Tamil Tigers to let one of their own freighters collect the consigment. Tsoi's company, LBJ Military Supplies, reportedly persuaded some officials of the Zimbabwe Defence Industries to provide false information to the authorities in Sri Lanka that the shipment had been loaded, as scheduled, in Beira.

LBJ Military Supplies then informed the Sri Lankan government that the munitions were en route, via Walvis Bay, in Namibia, and Madagascar. This gave the LTTE time to complete the sting. By the time Colombo learned the full extent of what had happened, the mortars had been unloaded and transhipped by smaller Tamil Tiger vessels to LTTE jungle bases in Sri Lanka. Within weeks, the weapons were being used by the Tamil Tigers to cause serious setbacks to government troops.[58]

External Crackdown

The operating environment for the LTTE outside Sri Lanka has become more difficult since the late 1990s, especially since the US and other countries launched their global campaign against terrorism following the attacks against America in September 2001. The LTTE has been proscribed in the US, Canada, Britain, India and 28 other countries. Since large-scale hostilities resumed in Sri Lanka's civil war in 2006, the LTTE has faced new challenges in sustaining its international support and supply lines as foreign governments have cracked down on its fundraising and arms purchasing. Many of the arms markets and trans-shipment countries that the Tamil Tigers once used are now being more closely monitored by governments anxious to counter terrorism and protect themselves from attack.[59]

Sri Lanka's navy has been enlarged and provided with improved equipment. Naval intelligence has improved. The navy has taken the fight to the Sea Tigers. In the past two years, it claims to have destroyed eight Tiger ocean-going cargo vessels and eleven of the fishing trawlers used to offload clandestine shipments and ferry them to shore. The navy also claims to have destroyed eight Tiger floating warehouses containing arms and ammunition.[60] Three of the Tiger cargo ships were intercepted and destroyed by the navy in international waters several thousand kilometres from Sri Lanka off the coast of Sumatra, the westernmost of Indonesia's main islands in a counter-terrorist operation that spanned a number of countries, including the US. Some analysts believe that although this crackdown failed to net the LTTE's head of arms procurement based in Thailand, it nonetheless disrupted at least 75 per cent of the rebel group's supply chain.[61]

As part of the crackdown, four Indonesians, a Sri Lankan and a Singaporean were charged in US courts in 2007 with involvement in two arms-dealing conspiracies, one to illegally export arms to Indonesia and the other to funnel weapons to the LTTE in Sri Lanka. The six tried to buy sophisticated weapons that included shoulder-fired heat-seeking anti-aircraft missiles, night vision devices, sniper rifles, machine guns, grenade launchers and ammunition. According to the US Justice Department, two down payments totaling over US $700,000 were made from a Malaysian bank to an account in the US set up by FBI agents to trap the six Asians who were arrested in September 2006.[62]

Despite these setbacks, the LTTE's overseas fund-raising, arms procurement and smuggling network continues its work, reportedly raising between US $200 million to US $300 million a year from among at least 600,000 Sri Lankan Tamils living abroad, mainly in Canada, the US, Britain, Western Europe and Australia. Some of the donations are voluntary while others are coerced. The LTTE uses front companies and middlemen to buy arms from legitimate weapons manufacturers in Europe and Asia.[63]

This survey does not include "piracy", much of which is robbery or other forms of maritime crime committed not on the high seas but in waters under the jurisdiction of national governments. There were 263 such incidents reported to the International Maritime Bureau in 2007, mainly off the coast of Somalia, west Africa, Bangladesh and South-East Asia. The motives of pirates are different from those of terrorists, like those linked to Al-Qaeda, militia groups like Hezbollah and armed rebels like the Tamil Tigers. Pirates work for profit while the other non-state actors have political objectives which they are prepared to achieve through violence. Still, it is worth observing that pirate attacks on shipping are obviously dangerous and must be suppressed.

Conclusion

Weapons of Mass Destruction (WMD) Terrorism

Officials and counter-terrorism experts in Asia, Europe and the US have warned that the next step up in mass casualty terrorism may be an attack with chemical, biological, radiological or nuclear (CBRN) weapons. A ship or container is regarded as a possible delivery device for a nuclear or radiological bomb.[64] Those who worry about such an attack believe that weapons of mass destruction and terrorism have become interlocking threats that could, if more effective safeguards are not put in place, fuse in an extremely dangerous challenge to international security, stability and trade —and thus to the functioning of the globalised economy.

Achieving CBRN capability is a stated objective of Al-Qaeda, which sees weapons of mass destruction as strategic equalisers against better-armed enemies. Mustafa Setmariam Nasar, often referred to by the nom de guerre Abu Musab al-Suri, has urged clandestine terrorist cells to use weapons of mass destruction or radiological bombs if they can get them. He is the Syrian-born strategist for decentralised global jihad who was arrested in Pakistan in October 2005 and then handed over to US intelligence agents. Some analysts argue that the risk of terrorists being able to acquire or build a nuclear explosive device is overstated. Others say that the fissile material needed to build a bomb is available, or could become available, and that there are terrorists groups that have already demonstrated the technical abilities and organisational reach to make an improvised nuclear device.[65] Officials in India, the West and at the International Atomic Energy Agency (IAEA) worry that some of Pakistan's nuclear weapons or fissile material may reach extremists, although Pakistan's military leadership recently gave assurances that its stocks of both were under tight control and would not fall into the wrong hands.[66]

Most experts believe that a radiological or "dirty" bomb (which uses conventional explosives to disperse radioactive material) is well within the technical capabilities of at least some terrorist groups and that they could get all the components without much difficulty. Such a device would probably be designed as a weapon of mass disruption—to cause panic, chaos and prolonged economic dislocation in a metropolis or port-city. US-led counter-proliferation programmes, such as the CSI and the Megaports Initiative, are intended to prevent terrorists from shipping dangerous nuclear or radioactive material into American ports. But critics of existing measures say they fall far short of what is needed to detect the clandestine shipment of dirty bombs wrapped in lead shielding, bomb-grade highly enriched uranium or even a nuclear weapon into the US in cargo containers.[67]

The majority view among international officials and specialists is that some form of CBRN attack is highly likely in the next decade. The nightmare scenario, in which terrorists would move from a position of relative technological weakness to approximate symmetry of power with their perceived enemies in the US and elsewhere, is certainly no longer unthinkable. A survey was commissioned in late 2004 and early 2005 by the US Senate Foreign Relations chairman Richard Lugar. It canvassed the views of more than 80 international arms control and national security experts. They put the likelihood of a nuclear, biological, chemical or radiological attack in the next 10 years at 70 per cent. There was strong, though not unanimous, agreement that any nuclear attack is more likely to be carried out by a terrorist organisation than a government. A majority of those surveyed said a black market purchase was the most likely way for terrorists to get nuclear weapons or fissile material.[68]

Meanwhile, navies, coast guards and government intelligence and law enforcement agencies must counter the illegal or clandestine spread of conventional weapons to non-State actors, including terrorist, military and rebel organisations. Among the weapons that have been transferred through these channels are long-range anti-ship missiles, unmanned aerial vehicles and closer-range armour-piercing missiles and rocket-propelled grenades—all weapons capable of causing significant damage to ships, both big and small. The arms trade is a huge, valuable and competitive global business. Arms smuggling is rife in many parts of the world and the weapons and equipment available for use are increasingly sophisticated and difficult to counter. The Al-Qaeda network, Hezbollah and the Tamil Tigers all exploit the weapons trafficking business to get, or try to get, new and more potent weapons.

The trade in small arms and light infantry weapons is already extensive in conflict-prone parts of Asia and the demand for more advanced equipment is strong.[69] The problem is global in scope. There are around 100 countries that make weapons and ammunition. Sales of these products are estimated to be worth over US $1,000 billion in 2006—fifteen times annual spending on international aid. In October 2006, negotiations started in the United Nations General Assembly on a binding treaty to control the so-called light arms trade that kills at least 300,000 people each year, destabilises nations and ruins the lives of millions. But the negotiations are likely to be contentious and slow.[70]

For those who regard Hezbollah as an international terrorist organisation armed by Iran and Syria, its acquisition of more potent weapons is an alarming development. Hezbollah has gone one-up by showing Al-Qaeda and affiliated terrorist groups it can use these weapons in combat. As a result, navies and commercial shipping face a significantly higher level of threat, especially if there is a resurgence in fighting between Hezbollah and Israel or a major conflict with Iran over Iraq or the Iranian nuclear program. The use of the C-802 anti-ship missile by Hezbollah shows the increasingly dangerous nexus between technology and non-State actors. It is a warning about the quantum leap in the weaponry available for maritime-related attacks. ■

Notes

1. *FACTS Energy Advisory*, p. 2 of *'Outlook* for Crude Oil Demand, Supply, and Trade in the Asia-Pacific Region,' Issue #314, January 2006.
2. *Washington Post*, 'Terrorists turn to the Web as a Base of Operations,' by Steve Coll and Susan B. Glaser, 7 August 2006.
3. Al-Qaeda's second-in-command, Ayman al-Zawahiri, reiterated this irredentist world view in July 2006. Full translation of audio tape of Al-Jazeerah TV broadcast on: 'What is happening in Palestine and Lebanon proves that what the Muslims are facing is a Crusader alliance-Zionist war,' 27 July 2006.
4. *Straits Times*, Singapore, 'Fewer Muslims support Al-Qaeda,' by Derwin Pereira, 9 September 2006.
5. Vali Nasr, 'The Shia Revival: How Conflicts within Islam will Shape the Future,' pp. 241–254.
6. The phrase 'maritime-related' encompasses activities that affect merchant and private shipping, as well as the naval vessels that help protect the sealanes carrying the bulk of global trade. It also covers activities that impinge on the cargo container supply chain that is an integral part of modern commerce and now stretches into most parts of the world. Sea trade does not begin and end in ports or at the dockside. For those who have to police international trade and keep it secure, responsibility starts in the factories and warehouses on land where containers are loaded. It ends where they are unloaded. In between, the containers may have been carried by road and rail, as well as by sea, on their journeys around the world.
7. *Washington Post*, '15 Freighters believed to be linked to al-Qaeda,' by John Mintz, 31 December 2002.
8. Associated Press report in the *New York Times*, 'Two sentenced to Death for bombing of *U.S.S. Cole*,' 29 September 2004.
9. US Department of Justice press release, 'Al-Qaeda Associates charged in Attack on USS Cole, attempted attack on another US naval vessel,' 15 May 2003.
10. Lloyd's List, '*Limburg* Attackers had Inside Knowledge,' 15 May 2003.
11. *Asian Wall Street Journal*, 'US military increases Oil-facility Protection as Global Threats rise,' by Chip Cummins, 1 July 2004.
12. *New York Times*, 'Search continues for Clues and Suspects in Rocket Attack in Jordan,' by Hassan M. Fattah, 21 August 2005.

13. Jewish Institute for National Security Affairs (JINSA) online, 'Israel's Navy steps up to Security Challenges in Wake of Gaza Pullout,' pp. 7-8, 31 May 2006. http://www.jinsa.org/articles/print.html/documentid/3417
14. *Washington Post*, 'In Morocco's 'Chemist', a Glimpse of al-Qaeda,' by Craig Whitlock, 7 July 2007.
15. Office of the Director of US National Intelligence, 6 September 2006, press release on Biographies of High Value Terrorist Detainees Transferred to the US Naval Base at Guantanamo Bay, section on Abd al-Rahim al-Nashiri. http://www.odni.gov/
16. White House, Fact Sheet: 'Plots, Casings and Infiltrations Referenced in President Bush's Remarks on the War on Terror,' 6 October 2005.
17. 'Terrorism in the Early 21st Century Maritime Domain,' p.10 of paper by Rupert Herbert-Burns for the IDSS Maritime Security Conference, Singapore, 20-21 May 2004.
18. *Far Eastern Economic Review*, 'Philippines, a Dangerous New Alliance,' by James Hookway, 6 May 2004.
19. Jamestown Foundation, *Terrorism Monitor*, Volume 4, Issue 8, 20 April 2006, 'Christian Converts and Islamic terrorism in the Philippines,' by Peter Chalk. http://www.jamestown.org/terrorism/news/article.php?articleid=2369967
20. Singapore Government White Paper, 'The Jemaah Islamiyah Arrests and the Threat of Terrorism,' pp. 29–30, 7 January 2003.
21. Office of the Director of US National Intelligence, 6 September 2006 Press release on 'Biographies of High Value Terrorist Detainees Transferred to the US Naval Base at Guantanamo Bay,' section on Walid Bin 'Attash.
22. CNN.com, 'Maritime Terror Attack Alert,' by Maria Ressa, 23 October 2002.
23. *Washington Post*, 'Deadly Muslim Convert:Ttrial of French Islamic Radical sheds Light on the Role of Converts,' 2 January 2006.
24. *Time* magazine, 'Japan's Terror Threat,' by Jim Frederick, 7 June 2004.
25. Yomiuri Shimbun, 'Recent Arrests spark Fears of al-Qaeda Network in Japan,' 28 May 2004.
26. FBI criminal complaint filed before Judge Andrew J. Peck, South District of New York, 8 August 2003.
27. Office of the Director of US National Intelligence, 6 September 2006 press release on 'Biographies of High Value Terrorist Detainees Transferred to the US Naval Base at Guantanamo Bay,' sections of Majid Khan and 'Ali 'Abd al-'Aziz 'Ali, better known by his alias 'Ammar al-Baluchi.
28. OECD, Report on Security in Maritime Transport: Risk Factors and Economic Impact, July 2003.
29. US Senate Committee on Homeland Security and Governmental Affairs, Permanent Subcommittee on Investigations, pages 46 of testimony by Gary Gilbert, Senior Vice President, Hutchison Port Holdings, 30 March 2006.
30. *The Times* (UK), 'Terrorist in a Box,' by Richard Owen and Daniel McGrory, 25 October 2001.
31. *Financial Times*, 'Agencies fear Extent of al-Qaeda's Sea Network,' 21 February 2002.
32. *Economist magazine*, 'Special Report on Container Trade: When Trade and Security Clash,' 4 April 2002.
33. Jewish Institute for National Security Affairs (JINSA) online, 'Assault on Israeli Ashdod Port kills 10, Mega Attack narrowly Avoided,' 16 April 2004. http://www.jinsa.org

34. Heritage Foundation, Backgrounder no. 1930, 27 April 2006, 'Trade Security at Sea: Setting National Priorities for Safeguarding America's Economic Lifeline,' p. 5.
35. *International Herald Tribune*, 'US enters the Age of Foiled Plots,' by Scott Shane and Lowell Bergman, 9 September 2006.
36. The 9/11 Commission Report, p. 154.
37. US Department of Defence, *U.S.S. Cole* Commission Report, Executive Summary, 9 January 2001.
38. US State Department list of Proliferation Security Initiative Partipants current as of 4 June 2007. http://www.state.gov/t/isn/c19310.htm
39. Jamestown Foundation, *Terrorism Monitor*, Volume 4, Issue 9, 4 May 2006, 'Al-Qaeda and the Threat to Mass Surface Transportation, 'by Andrew Holt. http://www.jamestown.org/terrorism/news/article.php?articleid=2369984
40. The Jamestown Foundation, *Terrorism Monitor*, Volume 4, 21 September 2006, Adaptation of Fourth Generation Warfare Doctrine,' by Andrew Black. http://www.jamestown.org/terrorism/news/article.php?articleid=2370137
41. *Maariv International*, 'The Hezbollah within Us, 'by Amit Cohen, 3 June 2004.
42. JINSA online, 'IDF seizes Bombmaking Supply Ship headed for Gaza,' 26 May 2003.
43. American Forces Information Service, 'Iranian Government behind Shipping Weapons to Iraq,' by Jim Garamone, 28 September 2006.
44. JINSA online, 'Israel's Navy steps up to Security Challenge in Wake of Gaza Pullout,' 31 May 2006.
45. *New Paper*, Singapore, 'Which Terror Squad once wanted S'porean Recruits?' by Melvin Singh, 8 June 2002.
46. Ministry of Home Affairs, Singapore. Press release, 'Minister for Home Affairs comments on the Hezbollah Case,' 8 June 2002.
47. US House of Representatives Committee on International Relations, joint hearing of the Subcommittee on International Terrorism and Nonproliferation and the Subcommittee on the Middle East and Central Asia on Hezbollah's global reach, page 7 of testimony on 28 September 2006 by Frank C. Urbancic, Principal Deputy Coordinator for Counter-terrorism, US State Department.
48. *UPI*, 'Anti-tank Rockets menace Israelis,' by Joshua Brilliant, 14 August 2006.
49. *Newsweek*, 'A Worrisome Weapon,' 11 September 2006.
50. International Assessment and Strategy Centre, 'China Sows the Whirlwind: Implications of Hezbollah's Iranian-Chinese Weapons,' by Richard Fisher Jr., 26 July 2006.
51. *New York Times*, 'Arming of Hezbollah reveals US and Israeli Blind Spots,' by Mark Mazetti and Thom Shanker, 19 July 2006.
52. GlobalSecurity.org, C-802 fact sheet and history. http://globalsecurity.org/military/world/china/c-802.htm
53. Vijay Sakhuja, 'Terrorist Sea Strategy: The Kamikaze Approach,' Peace Forum Essays, April 2003, Jawaharlal Nehru University, New Delhi.
54. Peter Chalk, 'Liberation Tigers of Tami Eeelam's (LTTE) International Organisation and Operations—a Preliminary Analysis,' Canadian Security Intelligence Service, page 9 Commentary no. 77, 17 March 2000.
55. Peter Chalk, op. cit., pp. 5–6.
56. OECD Report on Security in Maritime Transport, op. cit., pp. 14–15.

57. Peter Chalk, op. cit., page 8.
58. *Sunday Times,* 'Sri Lanka, Arms Ship mystery Deepens, Possibility of LTTE Ploy: Zimbabwe official here for Probe,' 3 August 1997.
59. Australian Broadcasting Corp., 'Cambodia announces Plans to destroy its Obsolete Air Weapons Systems,' 2 March 2004. This report noted that the US had launched a global drive to secure, or eliminate, shoulder-fired or man-portable air defence rockets which it fears could be used by international terrorists to attack civilian aircraft. The report also noted that Cambodia had been accused of being a major source of illegal weapons for armed rebel groups across Asia, including the Tamil Tigers in Sri Lanka and separatists in Indonesia's Aceh province.
60. *Ceylon Daily News,* 'Navy's Pivotal Role in Battle against Terrorism,' by Rafik Jalaldeen, 10 December 2007.
61. *Straits Times,* Singapore,'Tamil Tigers' Hangout: S-E Asia,' by Robert Karniol, 22 October 2007.
62. *AFP,* 'US busts Asian Network seeking Arms for Tamil Tigers,' 5 April 2007.
63. *AP,* 'Sri Lanka's Tamil Tiger Rebels run a Global Fund-raising and Weapons-smuggling Network,' by Matthew Rosenberg, 5 November 2007.
64. US State Department, 'Preventing Weapons of Mass Destruction Terrorism in the Maritime Supply Chain,' text of remarks by Thomas Lehrman, Director, Office of WMD Terrorism, at the Maritime Security Expo, 20 September 2006.
65. See International Institute for Strategic Studies (IISS), 'Nuclear Terrorism After 9/11,' by Robin M. Frost, Adelphi Paper 378, December 2005; *IISS Survival,* vol. 48 no 2, Summer 2006, pp. 55 70 of 'Nuclear Terrorism: A Disheartening Dissent,' by Anna M. Pluta and Peter D. Zimmerman; and *Nonproliferation Review,* vol.12, no 3, November 2005, 'Does Intent Equal Capability? Al-Qaeda and Weapons of Mass Destruction,' by Sammy Slama and Lydia Hansell.
66. *Straits Times,* 'Worries over Pakistan's Nuclear Assets unabated,' by Ravi Velloor, 31 January 2008.
67. US Senate Committee on Homeland Security and Governmental Affairs, Permanent Subcommittee on Investigations, testimony by Stephen E. Flynn, Jean J. Kirkpatrick Senior Fellow for National Security Studies, Council on Foreign Relations, 28 March 2006.
68. The Lugar Survey on Proliferation Threats and Responses, June 2005. http://lugar.senate.gov
69. Associated Press, 'Six indicted in Arms brokering for Tamil Tigers and Indonesia,' by Brian White, 29 September 2006.
70. *Reuters,* 'World has Unique Chance to curb Arms Trade,' by Jeremy Lovell, 2 October 2006.

PAPER 2

Management of Large Maritime Zones for Resource-constrained Maritime States

Anbaree Abdul Sattar*

I am indeed profoundly honoured to present this paper in this important Indian Ocean Naval Symposium Seminar 2008, themed 'Maritime Opportunities and Challenges in the Indian Ocean Region' organised by the National Maritime Foundation, which, as we are all aware, is an institution of high esteem.The National Maritime Foundation has without doubt gained international fame and respect for its valuable contribution both professionally and intellectually in bringing maritime security issues to the forefront of the global maritime community. Therefore, I wish to congratulate the National Maritime Foundation and the Indian Navy, for convening this significant seminar and thank you most sincerely for allowing me to present this paper to the august audience.

At the outset, the Maldives, with its white sandy beaches, crystal clear lagoons and multicoloured reefs amid diverse marine life is recognised as one of the most exotic and idyllic holiday destinations in the world today. With nearly 90 tourist resort islands currently catering for more than a half million tourist from all over the world every year, and another 34 coming up rather soon, we all tend to forget everything else, but to make the most out of this God-given beauty. In reality, the fact is that we are speaking of a country whose 99 per cent territory is water. My focus in this paper is not about highlighting the tourism prospects of our country or small island states but to lay emphasis on the vulnerability and challenges of small island states with much larger maritime zones.

Scattered across the equator in the Indian Ocean, the Maldives

* High Commissioner of Maldives to India.

archipelago possesses an exceptionally unique geography as a small island country. Nature has fragmented the archipelago into 1,190 tiny and low-lying islands that occupy a mere one per cent of its 90,000 sq km territory. Only 194 islands are home to its 300,000 population and out of these, 134 islands have fewer than 1,000 people.[2] This extreme dispersal of the population combined with a poorly developed sea transportation system not only results in severe diseconomies of scale but also in making reaching out to them especially in case of emergencies almost impossible. Adding up to this geographical intricacy, with a coastline of approximately 868 kilometres and proportionately an enormous Exclusive Economic Zone, efficiently keeping a vigil and patrolling this vast sea surface in order to protect its interests and the marine resources are enormously challenging tasks.[2] In other words, safeguarding and managing our interests in the maritime zones continue to remain an arduous national challenge.

As many scholars put forward the view, the geopolitical importance of our region cannot be left unapprised. IOR contains one-third of the world's population, 25 per cent of its landmass, 40 per cent of the world's oil and gas reserves, while it is also the pathway of important international SLOCs. The region is home to most of the world's Muslim population as well as India, one of the world's "rising powers". On the other hand, while India and some of the few other littoral states appear to be on a path of sustained economic progress, most of the region is characterised by high levels of poverty. The IOR suffers from a high level of international and internal conflict and is a key venue for international piracy. It also is the centre of some 70 per cent of the world's natural disasters.[3] But of all these facts, the most difficult fact to accept is the reality that the region constitutes one of the key centres of gravity for international terrorism. As a result, this menace has made the regional strategic environment extremely volatile and perilous by plaguing the maritime zones of all littorals across the entire IOR with violence and instability.

Let me refer to a recent incident that had occurred in the territorial waters of the Maldives that had its links with maritime terrorism. It is an event that evidently stands proof to this judgment and has drawn region-wide attention and concern. On the 16th of May last year, an armed trawler illegally entered into the territorial waters of the Maldives. It was a vessel which originally belonged to a South Indian Company and had set sail on 7th March 2007 from Kollam in Kerala, India, and was captured during its journey by an unknown group of armed men. It appeared on Maldivian waters, just about 20 miles off a Southern Island in Gaafu Alifu Atoll on May 16th. The trouble arose when it fired at some local fishermen, inviting the attention of the Maldivian Coast Guard. After 12 hours of standoff, early the next morning, the Maldivian Coast Guard was able to sink the vessel and capture some people on board while others were killed. There are now suspicions that the vessel, which started off as an innocent deep sea fishing trawler was allegedly hijacked by a group claiming to be a faction of the LTTE (Liberation of Tamil Tigers Eelam), for gunrunning and to a later rendezvous with an ocean-going bigger LTTE arms vessel in the high seas off south of the Maldives.The Maldives Coast Guard also sought the assistance of the Indian Coast Guard and we were very fortunate to receive an Indian Coast Guard aircraft from our dearest friends here for aerial surveillance during the operation. Apparently, like in many small island-developing states, the Maldivian Coast Guard or the Defence forces do not have a military air component to undertake aerial surveillance or tasks of such nature. It is a limitation that needs to be addressed and overcome urgently, yet for a small island-developing state such as the Maldives, which is over-reliant on tourism, the resource constraints will pose a great challenge to opt for such a capability.

Although in a broader context, smaller maritime countries will have a vital stake in the security and stability of the greater IOR, yet, for the Maldives or for the other smaller island-developing states in the region, issues such as poaching, smuggling, trafficking of illegal arms and drugs are more directly related to the peace and stability of their maritime zones. Apparently, the non-official but traditional archipelagic sea lanes of the Maldives are also being extensively used by vessels on innocent passage for international maritime trade. Hence, there is a need to protect the SLOCs as menaces, such as sea piracy, human trafficking, gunrunning and narco-terrorism are becoming serious issues of common concern. I must note here with acknowledgement that the Indian Coast Guard being the National Maritime Search and Rescue Coordinating Authority for executing/coordinating SAR missions in the Indian maritime search and rescue region (SRR) had played an active role in assisting Maldives Coast Guard in undertaking SAR duties and managing other problems of our maritime zones.[4]

The maritime management, security and safety of a country are greatly reliant on its capabilities to effectively monitor, patrol, and counter illegal activities in its maritime zone. Currently, Maldivian maritime agencies have limited resources and lack the needed potential to deal with a wide range of challenges. For example, the problem of drug trafficking through sea routes has become a major problem for the nation to cope with, while other issues such as poaching, smuggling, protection of the marine environment and pollution control are also matters of serious national concern. As Cdr PK Ghosh rightly argues, drug trafficking generates fuel to maritime terrorism and thus the nexus of these two crimes is apparently deeply rooted and hence, must be dealt under same crime spectrum. With profit margins running into hundreds of per cent, drug trafficking is by far the most profitable means of generating funds to fuel ever-growing terrorist activities and insurgencies around the region.[5] Again, to note another incident, last year in April, a group of fishermen, mainly lobster catchers, had found 1,697 plastic bags of cannabis weighing almost 1.6 tonnes which were professionally packed and hidden inside a lagoon on the ocean floor near the famous Gengehi tourist resort island. It took the security and law enforcement agencies in the Maldives by surprise and caused nationwide alarm, and later suspicions were made on the involvement of the international mafia in the crime. Arms and drug trafficking in the IOR is becoming a major nuisance and the sad news is that it is estimated to be on the increase. Therefore, for a nation that predominately survives on its income from its natural beauty and tranquil environment, incidents of such nature are perceptibly matters of grave concern and serious wake-up calls. Hence, the small island-developing states in the region, such as the Maldives are forced to readjust their maritime management and security priorities and prepare realistically to counter the challenges in its maritime zones.

As in most island states in the IOR, fishing and tourism are the two main industries of the Maldives that contribute to the mainstay of the economy and hold the major shares on the foreign currency earnings. And so, the protection and preservation of these industries remain in the core of the countries, national maritime interests. Therefore, ensuring that maritime laws are not violated and unauthorised persons do not plunder the wealth of the Maldivian seas must be essentially viewed as maritime security priorities when managing our maritime zones. The Maldives Coast Guard ships have been regularly spotting and catching foreign fishing trawlers poaching in the EEZ. The fishes in the EEZ of the Maldives are considered to be exploitable assets due to their migratory nature, which attracts and has led to foreign fishing vessels to wander and poach in its waters. Consequently, there is an immediate need to enhance the reach and the surveillance capabilities of the maritime law-enforcement agencies and their assets. Another important issue that must be noted here today is the impact of oil pollution on the marine environment. The delicateness of the marine and terrestrial environment, which includes the coral reefs and marine eco system, is crucial and their protection and preservation are already urgent environmental issues. That is to say, the degree of marine environmental fragility has become a national worry for smaller maritime countries, and thus the conservation of biodiversity and the management of coastal zones are top priorities. Considering this factor, an oil-related environmental disaster in our maritime zone, such as a major oil spill or a wreck of an oil tanker will trigger hazardous repercussions beyond our imagination.

Given this broad spectrum of challenges, the small island nations in the region are faced with a management dilemma, to the extent that the maintenance of maritime order and safety of their territorial and archipelagic waters are becoming almost unattainable. The primary constraints for the maritime management and security agencies to deal with such challenges are their limited resources, lack of strategic guidance and the absence of effectual regional cooperative arrangements, and by and large the deficiency in national maritime capacity to rationally address the prevailing problems and face the challenges of an evolving maritime security environment of the IOR.

The Maldives National Defence Force (MNDF) Coast Guard, the nodal agency responsible for maintaining maritime order in the country's maritime zones, is currently faced with a major challenge of monitoring and dealing with the security issues and other illegal activities of the country's vast EEZ. As the armed maritime military service, it is assigned with the primary mission of safeguarding the territorial integrity and protecting the seas of the country, which is largely a defence role. At the same time, it has the important and broad roles of catering for homeland security, law enforcement and protecting the public and the environment. It entails tasks such as preventing illegal activities of the EEZ, undertaking search and rescue and disaster-relief operations, securing ports and the coasts, providing inter-coastal and offshore aids to navigation, pollution control and so forth. This broad mandate calls for an entire overhauling, capacity building and conceptualising of this service and, if necessary, creation of other smaller civil sister agencies. This service also needs redefined legal parameters such as a revisited 'Coast Guard Act' and formulated maritime security doctrines to guide and safeguard its operations and strategies as well as the operational activities of their servicemen. Apparently, the service is on the rise in terms of its force structure and training, yet, it needs resources to enhance its operational capability and eliteness to become a professional national service that will cater to the prevailing as well as emerging challenges of the country's maritime zone. At the same time, we need to augment the institutional capacity of national maritime agencies and increase the awareness among the public on the challenges of the maritime domain of smaller island nations. For smaller islands with constrained resources, it is crucially important to identify and prioritise the challenges in their maritime zones in order to make optimal use of their limited resources. National institutions, wherever necessary, must be integrally set up to coordinate the activities of the maritime zones and establish effective information networks that would allow maritime security intelligence gathering and information sharing internally as well as share such information within the region.[6] Meanwhile, opting for efficient cooperative arrangements will become the most viable and cost-effective option for resource constrained small island nations to enhance their maritime capacity. With the prevailing set-up, it would be an intricate affair to institute region-wide coordination and networks among the nodal national agencies to deal with emerging challenges of the EEZ and in particular, react to large-scale emergencies such as oil spills or other disasters of such nature.

Having discussed the need to develop a robust regional mechanism and to be an important partner of such a cooperative regime to deal with the maritime problems of resource constrained nations, let me also briefly highlight the possible modus operandi and attainments of such arrangements. Indian maritime law-enforcement authorities have given considerable attention to enhancing its maritime security capabilities for over many years. For example, if we look at the case of smuggling, smuggling activities were unchecked along the western sea board of India in the 1970s and 1980s, yet the Indian maritime security agencies and maritime law-enforcement authorities were able to control them considerably in recent years. India is believed to have a rapidly expanding maritime security capability and currently is the only maritime neighbour in the IOR with the potential to pragmatically address the maritime problems of its much smaller littoral neighbours. In military terms, the Indian Navy (IN) is not only the largest maritime force in the region but also has played a significant role in increasing maritime bonding with the neighbours by initiating numerous multilateral naval activities such as exercises, joint surveillance, joint SLOC patrolling, intelligence sharing, and timely reaching its neighbors in times of crisis. Therefore, smaller littoral countries will have a lot to gain by interacting with the Indian Navy, based on its experience in dealing with transnational crime and maritime terrorism. The Maldives already has a strong link with the Indian Coast Guard. Working together for over many years, the Indo Maldives Coast Guard Joint Exercise, 'Dosti' has generated greater inter-operability and joint operation effectiveness. For instance, the high degree of coordination exhibited especially between the two Coast Guards during the relief and recovery operations in tsunami was an outcome of a long-term association. Exercise 'Dosti' not only continues to be an important means to enhance the overall capabilities and operational effectiveness of the MNDF Coast Guard, it is also a vital maritime platform to professionally exchange ideas and innovation on the evolving security scenarios of our maritime zones. In the same manner, the opportunities with the Indian Navy and other maritime agencies also need to be exploited. In addition to enhancing their bilateral activities, the smaller maritime states must also hastily join the web of intense multilateral maritime activities that are steered by India in the region.

For resource-constrained smaller maritime states, it is most certain that mastering a multi-layered approach is the most favourable technique for enforcing maritime order and solve transnational maritime crimes. However, such an approach could not be practicable unless there is an efficient cooperative structure within the IOR. Hence, it is time we established a much more vigorous regional maritime arrangement and properly channelised our efforts to decisively fight maritime disorder and manage our vast maritime zones. While cooperation between regional navies and coast guards takes centre stage, attention also must be given to developing non military cooperation in this area.[7] Joint Maritime Management Centres manned by service personnel as well as professionals and other civilians need to be set up. Such centres will not only act as focal points or hubs that guide response but also as venues for intelligence and information sharing.

Finally, let me highlight that, looking at the horizon ahead, we see an ocean that has changed its currents, an ocean that is extensively infested with varied threats and challenges. To deal with them, it requires consistent cooperation among the States and the connected maritime agencies. Smaller littoral states in the region are left with no choice but to look towards regional power centres for assistance in maintaining maritime order and coping with other issues or emergencies such as natural calamities. Countries with enhanced maritime capabilities can help by not only cooperating amongst themselves, but also by taking other smaller island states on board as part of their multilateral efforts towards maintenance of maritime order. I wish to once again express my sincere thanks to the Indian National Maritime Foundation for giving this opportunity to present this paper and also let me commend the hard work of this Foundation and the

Indian Navy in organising the wonderful and productive seminar, the IONS 2008. I'm most certain that this occasion will be an important step forward in making us all more aware of the fact that we must strive to ensure the peace, calm and serenity of our vast seas, one of nature's most benevolent gifts to humankind. ■

Notes

1. Maldives Tourism Promotion Board at World Wide Web (http://www.visitmaldives.com).
2. Mansoor, Z, DG, Maldives National Defence Force Coast Guard, 'Dosti —The Bridge of Friendship and Assurance,' *Maldives in Focus, National Day Magazine*, New Delhi: Maldives High Commission.
3. India and Emerging 'Geo-politics of the Indian Ocean Region', Briefing Paper at *Conference on Indian Ocean Security*, Asia Pacific Centre for Security Studies, 2003.
4. See also 'Indian Coast Guard: 25 Glorious Years', New Delhi: Coast Guard Head Quarters, 2003, p. 158.
5. See PK Ghosh, 'Maritime Security Challenges in South Asia and the Indian Ocean Region: Response Strategies,' *Paper prepared at American Pacific Sea lanes Security Institute Conference on Maritime Security in Asia,* Centre for Strategic and International Studies, Honolulu: Hawaii, 2004.
6. See P. Paleri, 'National Defence: Maintaining the Cutting Edge,' *Role of the Coast Guard in the Maritime Security of India,* New Delhi: Knowledge World, 2004, pp. 258–280.
7. PK Ghosh, (op. cit.).

SESSION III

PAPER 1

Harnessing Technology for Maritime Cooperation

Jacob L Shuford*

As naval officers, our careers have been spent largely in a world in which threats to maritime security were well defined and emerged primarily from rival regional states or external powers. Nobody spoke of the threats from transnational networks, environmental crises, human trafficking, or failed states. Yet these are just a few of today's challenges, shared by us all, that threaten maritime security, challenging our governments, our national prosperity, and our children's future.

As our economies become more interconnected, our dependence on good order at sea increases. The sea is the global commons—it covers 75 per cent of the globe, and makes us all neighbours. Ninety per cent of the world's trade, and over two-third of the world's petroleum, is transported by sea. The vast majority of the world's population lives within a few hundred miles of the oceans, and the seas provide vital sources of food for the world's expanding population. These things you know well. You also recognise that the need for international understanding, cooperation, and partnership has never been clearer and more pronounced.

Two and a half years ago, 55 Navy and Coast-Guard Chiefs and about 30 War College Presidents met in Newport at the International Seapower Symposium (ISS) to take stock of their countries' and regions' most pressing challenges in the maritime domain. Collectively, this group of leaders recognised that "the most profound effect of today's challenges is the increased value of cooperation between friends, allies, coalition partners, and like-minded nations. Despite differences in the size or structure of our

* President, US Naval War College, Newport, RI.

navies, cooperation today is more necessary than ever before. And cooperation is growing. But we need more, much more." Because today's challenges are global in nature, we must stand together in our response. We are made neighbours by the seas—dependent upon them and bound by our responsibility to secure them—a responsibility fundamental to global stability, and economic prosperity. The ISS was categorical in asserting the view that the proactive cost of security is far more affordable than the reactive cost of war, and that navies provide unique capabilities, modes of operating, and traditions that are particularly suited to help prevent war.

This symposium proved the seminal event underpinning the new US maritime strategy announced by our Chief of Naval Operations, Admiral Gary Roughead, at Newport in October 2007. The new US maritime strategy—*A Cooperative Maritime Strategy for the 21st Century*—has at its core the concept of international cooperation, of which technology obviously plays a critical part. In the words of the maritime strategy—"trust cannot be surged". International cooperative relationships are critical in maintaining the security and stability of the maritime environment.

But this is NOT a simple task. We must *build* relationships in peacetime, and *maintain* them in times of crisis or disruption. These relationships are key to the resilient peace we discuss in our strategy. Implementing this strategy with our partners requires flexibility, adaptability, and unity of effort. Three specific elements that will contribute significantly to forming lasting partnerships are: proper preparation of our people, improving integration and interoperability, and enhancing awareness. [Note: this is not in the order listed in MARSTRAT, which has Preparing our People last!]

Prepare our People

Fostering partnerships starts with people—the fine men and women who serve in our maritime forces around the globe. Our people must develop and maintain the skills to interact with diverse international partners. We must increase the deliberativeness and comprehensiveness of our efforts to build capacity for humanitarian assistance, disaster relief, and the entire range of missions, functions and tasks that demand effective collaboration to plan and execute...and that form the basis for partnerships within the region. Our people must develop greater cultural, historical, and linguistic expertise. They must also learn to rely on their own skills and knowledge—on the software, rather than hardware, of modern military training and technology—to work flexibly and adaptably with partners with different capacities—technological, bureaucratic, and sheer numbers and platforms.

This—the human element (education, habits of behaviour)—is the foundational element for integrated effort and improved interoperability between our various navies. So, when we speak of harnessing technology for military cooperation, I think it is essential that our people have a deep understanding of one another in order to appreciate the best way to apply technology appropriately to accomplish those missions where cooperation is envisioned.

Form the Strategy: Inter-operability

"Expanded cooperation with the maritime forces of other nations requires more interoperability with multinational partners possessing varying levels of technology. The Global Maritime Partnership initiative will serve as a catalyst for increased international inter-operability in support of cooperative maritime security."

Let me talk about inter-operability first. Inter-operability has technical components to it, but it also has political, policy, and process components. Much of inter-operability is based on common understandings and common procedures rather than specific technical capabilities. The US has always known that, but we re-learned it in the 1990s when states of the former Warsaw Pact were retooling their militaries as part of their desire to join an expanded NATO. Many of them had then, and still have, significant stocks of Soviet-made (now Russian-made) equipment. However, through adoption of common procedures, practice through exercises, and technology applied to enabling communications (whether by voice or data), the military forces of many states in the former Warsaw Pact were—in relatively short order—ready for NATO membership, including the most difficult and serious of defence obligations—being ready to exercise a legal, mutual defence commitment.

Inter-operability does require compatible hardware and software, but these solutions need not be either expensive or overly-sophisticated if one understands the need to match requirements to the mission areas where cooperation is envisioned. Full cooperation in combat operations, for example, poses a much greater and more complicated array of tasks than humanitarian relief or maritime security patrols.

Consultation among partners can maximise inter-operability while minimising cost and high technology. Each partner will have a range of mission areas in which it intends to cooperate— to which our governments will commit—and a smaller set of missions to which they will not commit. Focusing our efforts on the missions most likely to be agreed upon by the widest range of participants will allow us all to enjoy simpler, cheaper, and more robust technological solutions. Inter-operability at the higher end—the cutting edge, the highly proprietary, the high risk, the high cost, the high sensitivity (both technological and political), and (with regard to application) the sensitivity of data involved as missions become oriented to conflict rather than the general security of the maritime domain— inevitably becomes more complex, politically constrained, and generally more problematic. So let's look at the high payoff areas. If we focus on priorities and the areas where we have general agreement and the most commitment, we will create an appropriate environment for cooperation and effective collaboration, an environment that may grow more sophisticated over time .... (And let me say that I have seen, during my time at the Naval War College up through the International Seapower Symposium in 2005 and now in fall 2007, how this general agreement has evolved and crystallized)... and will drive costs down and increase effectiveness.

While an implementation priority for the United States in its new maritime strategy, this type of focus and approach is critical for cooperative efforts among maritime services seeking to address shared challenges in the maritime domain. When we talk about and think about inter-operability of maritime forces in cooperative endeavours— let me make this point again—for the most part we are not talking about high-end combat. We are mostly talking about the ability to communicate and pass information. And this will need to be enabled across states operating vastly different systems with greatly divergent levels of technology and capacity (in terms of bandwidth, for example, or platforms).

These missions may be carried out with the assistance of the United States, or independent of US Navy involvement. The MALSINDO patrols in the Strait of Malacca, for example, were a combined effort by the navies of Malaysia, Singapore, and Indonesia. I think most of you are aware of the MALSINDO Initiative. Three regional navies cooperate there to carry out regional missions, (regional missions, I should add, vital to the global system and global prosperity) harnessing and adapting their independent technologies to provide the levels of interoperability for increasingly complex missions and building operational effectiveness and political confidence as a function of relationships and shared, incremental successes.

Something I incorporate routinely into the toasts I am expected to make on the occasion of the visits of some of the leaders of the great navies of the world to my home in Newport expresses best this sense of trust and confidence that is built by working together:

"The ocean makes us neighbours; working together makes us friends; and friendship makes us stronger." And I believe that.

We explored some of the technical, operational and political elements of MALSINDO's success two years ago at our Naval War College Alumni Symposium for Pacific Area alumni in Japan. Lots of lessons learned there for all of us to feast on. This sort of adaptability and capacity building is at the heart of the Global Maritime Partnership concept, and the basis of what many of you have heard called the "thousand ship navy". You appreciate that the US had nothing to do with MALSINDO. It is not our navy conducting this operation but yours. But we and others all benefit greatly from it.

Let me talk a little bit now about MDA, the piece of the new US maritime strategy focused on enhancing awareness in the maritime domain. Something which we all know is a critical requirement. I know that our host here, Admiral Mehta, has talked about the idea of a common operating picture that can be shared with neighbouring states: and there is a growing recognition of the values of a common picture of what's afloat in regional waters.

Enhance Awareness

In the new US maritime strategy, enhancing awareness is the third critical implementation priority. The language in the document is as follows:

"To be effective, there must be a significantly increased commitment to advance maritime domain awareness (MDA) and expand intelligence, surveillance and reconnaissance (ISR) capability and capacity. New partnerships with the world's maritime commercial interests and the maritime forces of participating nations will reduce the dangerous anonymity of sea borne transport of people and cargoes."

Maritime Domain Awareness is not a fully developed concept with a predetermined technology architecture—there is a lot of experimentation and concept development going on, and we are also aware of the experimentation and concept development going on in many of your own navies. The US Navy and US Coast Guard do not have a system in place for the United States nor do we have a single, fixed architecture to propose for others. I suspect the same is true for your countries as well. One reason for this is that the concept is still relatively new...and the issues to be worked out to make it truly operational are significant—both in the policy and in the technical realms. These are not issues for the United States to work out in isolation. Some issues are within the US—working on our own bureaucratic seams. But the international cooperative aspects of MDA, plus the simple fact that the world's oceans are so vast, require an international, collaborative approach.

Let me assure you, there is no need for despair. The glass is not half empty, it is half full, or more! There are many international venues and associations exploring ideas that will advance this concept.

MDA really only began to get a foothold in US national security thinking with the signing, by the President, of a national security decision direction on maritime security policy in late 2004. This directive had as its goals for the US to secure the maritime domain, meaning "All areas and things of, on, under, relating to, adjacent to, or bordering on a sea, ocean, or other navigable waterway, including all maritime-related activities, infrastructure, people, cargo, and vessels and other conveyances."

I feel compelled to note here that that particular phrase was probably made by a committee.

The Presidential directive, and the *National Strategy for Maritime Security* that resulted from it—something the Naval War College was closely involved in—tasked an inter-agency coordinating committee to build eight implementation plans, the first of which was a *National Plan to Achieve Maritime Domain Awareness,* (something the Naval War College was very much involved in) which was published in October 2005. That plan provided a policy framework, and then the hard work on technology and on questions of how one internationalises this effort began. Our thinking continues to evolve and benefit from the perspectives and experiences of many of you in this room today.

While the initial focus on these MDA efforts was on US homeland defence and homeland security, it has broadened both in terms of the fact that MDA can (and should) support the broader set of national, and indeed international, security goals. We all here today recognise that we need greater maritime domain awareness in our own territorial waters and on the high seas in areas where our national security and economic interests reside. Enhanced maritime awareness is needed to combat a wide range of ills in the maritime domain, so MDA and a shared common operating picture should be a goal among neighbouring maritime partners. And when I say neighbours, I am not just talking about your immediate, contiguous neighbours. We are all neighbours by the sea, and Admiral Mehta understands this perfectly in the context of the Indian Ocean and has responded to this reality by kindly hosting all of you for this extraordinary conference—and kindly inviting me, even though the United States is not a littoral state of this ocean. He understands, though, that we all share the commons and through that commons share interests. And you all understand that.

We have all spent our careers in the maritime environment, thinking about it, seeking to understand it, to overcome its challenges, knowing the role it plays in the security and prosperity of each of our nations. One of the challenges we all have is articulating that importance of the maritime realm to our own citizens and politicians.

Let me give you a glimpse of what we face in my own country in this regard. [CNO AFOTs Gallup Poll slide: military as most respected institution, USN as least respected of the services]. What a clear absence of maritime consciousness!

While this seems self-evident to us, it is not always self-evident to our populations or politicians. The late British Admiral John Fieldhouse talked about a concept that he called "sea blindness", where the average citizen no longer thinks about the sea. In part this was due to the advent of regular passenger air travel, which made many people no longer aware of the sea. Many countries have this "sea blindness" today, so one of our challenges is to foster a different kind of maritime domain awareness—to literally make them aware of the maritime domain and the importance it holds for their everyday lives, even if they do not see it or necessarily grasp it on a regular and intuitive basis.

The sea is no longer so commonly recognised as a highway for the transit of people, but it is vital to all of our lives as the method by which goods and services pass. The global economic system is inevitably maritime. The seas are also critical to the information revolution—the most important technological and economic sector of the globalised economy. The computers and technology that facilitate the information revolution are produced across the globe and transported by sea. Underwater cables provide the means through which information is transmitted and exchanged. Good order at sea minimises global economic disruption—and MDA is critical for good order at sea.

There will be difficulties in creating MDA networks. As I mentioned earlier, we in the United States are not entirely sure what is necessary. As we create technologies to support MDA, we will have some political constraints—there will be times when our laws and policies on sharing or releasing the technology may be frustrating. I should add, however, that in this regard there is a broadly supported effort in our navy to change our basic notion of operating with our partners at sea. We are moving from a bias towards classification of data, which is bureaucratic, to a bias towards sharing data, which is both an operational necessity and a good business practice [Fifth Fleet/NAVCENT example].

Much of the technology necessary, however, is commercial—and I should emphasise that those commercial systems are evolving from diverse countries and regions—and that's a good thing. There is no interest in the US in controlling these technologies or copyrights developed by others. The objective, again, is to create capabilities for international cooperation and good order at sea—and to make those capabilities widely available at minimum cost to encourage maximum participation.

Conclusion

I would like to conclude by thanking Admiral Mehta and VAdm Nayyar for including me in this terrific symposium. As I look out at all of the uniforms here, I have an immense feeling of pride in being part of a very special culture. It is a culture that is different from armies and air forces and land-based agencies.

I like a metaphor that has been used many times at the Naval War College when the chiefs of the world's navies gather... It is a special culture that we have of men and women who go down to the sea in ships, every night, every day. Coast Guard, Navy, we go out into this commons, and it's like the men and women of a great city walking down, flowing, day and night into the plaza, the square, the commons. They go there to do business, to work with their friends, and to enjoy their freedom.

Our business is to secure those commons...in a common, cooperative enterprise. To do so we'll have to harness technology but we will also have to harness our minds, our imaginations, and our creativity. We will have to do that collectively in a cooperative spirit, like the one that has permeated this symposium so far and I believe will continue long after we close the proceedings here in New Delhi. ■

PAPER 2

Managing International Shipping

Andrew Forbes*

Global economic growth, seaborne trade and international shipping are inextricably linked, with a predominant seaborne trade commodity being energy (oil and liquefied natural gas). As a case study, this paper will also examine energy flows from the Middle East to North Asia to highlight various issues associated with the management of international shipping.

This paper is divided into three sections: examining the importance of seaborne trade and shipping to global economic growth, issues affecting shipping and freedom of navigation, and some recent initiatives for managing international shipping in the Indian Ocean and the Strait of Malacca.

There is a variety of sources that can be used when examining international trade and shipping. This paper uses data from the United Nations Conference on Trade and Development, not because it is necessarily the best, but because it is consistent across different documents and provides historical trends; however, there is a time lag in reporting of at least 12 months.

The Importance of Seaborne Trade and Shipping

Why do nations trade? At its simplest, nations trade in order to increase their wealth; with consequential flow-on effects within their economies that include increased productivity, improved economic growth and better living

* Senior Visiting Fellow, Australian National Centre for Oceans Research and Security, University of Wollongong.

standards for their people. Strong economic growth, providing employment and goods should also provide political stability within the trading nation, which should also encourage regional security. To demonstrate the globalised nature of the world economy, global economic growth is outlined to provide context for a consideration of seaborne trade and the international shipping which moves it.

Global Economic Growth

World gross domestic product (GDP) grew from a low of 1.5 per cent in 2001 to 4 per cent in 2006 and was forecast to grow 3.4 per cent in 2007. The United States' output growth was 0.8 per cent in 2001, it peaked at 3.9 per cent in 2004, was 3.3 per cent in 2006, and is forecast to be 2.0 per cent in 2007. The European Union had a growth of 1.9 per cent in 2001, achieving a growth of 3.0 per cent in 2006, with a forecast of 2.8 per cent in 2007.

For Asia generally, the region overall had growth of 3.5 per cent in 2001, which rose to 7.6 per cent in 2006, with a forecast of 7.2 per cent in 2007. Within Asia, Japan's growth in 2001 was 0.2 per cent, rising to 2.2 per cent in 2006 and forecast to be 2.3 per cent in 2007. China's economy grew to 8.3 per cent in 2001; with a 10.7 per cent growth in 2006, and a 10.5 per cent growth was forecast for 2007. India's growth in 2001 was 5.0 per cent, rising to 9.2 per cent in 2006, and growth was forecast at 8.5 per cent in 2007. Collectively, South-East Asia grew at 2.1 per cent in 2001, 6.0 per cent in 2006, and was forecast to grow at 5.7 per cent in 2007.[1]

East Asia and South Asia were the fastest growing regions of the world economy, due to the strong economic performance of both China and India. Both regions doubled their per capita gross domestic product in 14 years (and it grew to 317.5 per cent over the period 1981–2007) and their exports by volume have increased by 160 per cent.[2]

Intra-regional trade has expanded faster than extra-regional trade and has expanded the most rapidly in East Asia since the mid-1980s, currently it represents half of the total trade of East Asian. The 'Association of South-East Asian Nations' intra-regional trade is about 25 per cent of their total trade, while it is only 5 per cent of the total trade in South Asia.[3]

Most of the growth in the world economy up to 2030 is expected to come from Asia, predominantly China and India, where the regional gross domestic product is projected to average 5.8 per cent per annum; (pa) China is projected to grow 6.5 per cent pa, and India 5.7 per cent pa.[4]

Seaborne Trade and International Shipping

Seaborne trade is a particularly important component of world trade, as there are geographical constraints impeding land transport in many countries, and often it is a cheaper form of transport for covering long distances while carrying large volumes of goods. Since the end of World War II, there has been a major growth in world trade, with 8 per cent growth by volume (double that of world output growth), 15 per cent by value and 7.4 billion tonnes of goods loaded in 2006.[5] (The difference in export value and volume rates is due to increasing commodity prices.)

Of the 7.4 billion tonnes of goods loaded in 2006, crude oil accounted for 26.9 per cent, petroleum products 9.2 per cent and dry cargo at 63.9 per cent. Of the total goods loaded, Asia had a share of 39.1 per cent, America 21.5 per cent, Europe 19.6 per cent, Africa 10.7 per cent, and Oceania 9.1 per cent.[6]

Liquid Bulk

Crude oil shipments in 2006 are estimated at 1.99 billion tonnes, with the major loading areas being: Western Asia (897.2 million tonnes), West Africa (221 million tonnes), South America (133.9 million tonnes), North Africa (133.8 million tonnes), the Caribbean and Central America (120.9 million tonnes), and Central Africa (109.8 million tonnes). These shipments were unloaded in North America (532.9 million tonnes), Europe (446.9 million tonnes), Japan (201 million tonnes), South and East Asia (439.4 million tonnes) and South East Asia (126.3 million tonnes). Petroleum product shipments continued to grow and it is estimated that 683 million tonnes were shipped in 2006.[7]

Liquefied natural gas (LNG) shipments grew at 11.8 per cent in 2006, reaching 211.1 billion cubic metres (bcm). Japan imported 81.9 bcm, and the Republic of Korea imported 34.1 bcm, with both countries accounting for 54.9 per cent of LNG shipments.[8]

Dry Bulk

Dry cargo shipments for 2006 are estimated to be 4.74 billion tonnes, with the main five dry bulk cargoes of iron ore, coal, grains, bauxite/alumina and rock phosphate accounting for 1.83 billion tonnes; and the remainder comprising minor bulks and liner cargo accounting for 2.91 billion tonnes.[9]

Seven hundred and sixteen million tonnes of iron ore were shipped in 2006, with Australia shipping 270 million tonnes (37.7 per cent) and Brazil shipping 245 million tonnes (34.2 per cent), followed by India (99 million tonnes), South Africa (28 million tonnes), Canada (22 million tonnes),

Sweden (19 million tonnes), Mauritania (12 million tonnes) and Peru (6.5 million tonnes). The importing countries were China (326.3 million tonnes), Japan (135.3 million tonnes), Western Europe (134.6 million tonnes), Republic of Korea (43.9 million tonnes), Taiwan (15.5 million tonnes), Western Asia (15.2 million tonnes), Canada and the US (9.2 million tonnes), Africa (8 million tonnes), Latin America (7.4 million tonnes), and Malaysia (4 million tonnes).[10]

Coal shipments reached 728 million tonnes in 2006, with thermal coal at 542 million tonnes (74.4 per cent) and coking coal at 186 million tonnes (25.6 per cent). Thermal coal exporters in 2006 were Indonesia (160.6 million tonnes), Australia 110.1 million tonnes), South Africa (65.4 million tonnes), Columbia (58.3 million tonnes), China (53.7 million tonnes), Russian Federation (53.7 million tonnes), and Venezuela (7.8 million tonnes). The major coking coal exporter was Australia at 124.4 million tonnes. Japan and the European Union were the main destinations for both types of coal, accounting for 54.6 per cent of all shipments.[11]

Grain shipments in 2006 are estimated at 281 million tonnes, with wheat comprising 19 million tonnes. Shipments of bauxite/alumina were 72 million tonnes and rock phosphate was 31 million tonnes. Minor dry bulks, such as steel, cement, forest and agricultural products were 949 million tonnes.[12]

The remainder of dry cargo (1.96 billion tonnes) is increasingly carried in containers (estimated at 1.13 billion tonnes) along liner trade routes. The Pacific trade is estimated at 18.5 million TEUs, with trade from Asia to the US being 13.9 million TEUs, and US to Asia trade being 4.6 million TEUs. Asia-Europe trade is 18.3 million TEUs, with trade to Europe being 12.5 million TEUs and trade to Asia being 5.8 million TEUs. Europe-North American trade is 6.2 million TEUs.[13]

The World Merchant Fleet

Table 1 outlines the size of the world merchant fleet, which continues to expand with the growth of seaborne trade. Oil tankers comprise over 35 per cent of the world fleet (with bulk carriers being a similar percentage), while LNG carriers constitute a very small, but expensive and critical component of the fleet. At the beginning of January 2007, oil tankers were 36.7 per cent of total shipping dead weight tonnage (DWT), bulk carriers were 35.3 per cent, general cargo ships were 9.7 per cent, containerships were 12.3 per cent, liquefied gas carriers were 2.6 per cent and chemical tankers were 0.8 per cent.[14]

Table 1: Size of World Fleet (thousand DWT)

	1995	2000	2005	2006	2007
Oil tankers	267,651	282,458	336,156	354,219	382,975
Bulk carriers	261,628	276,091	320,584	345,924	367,542
General cargo	104,145	101,481	92,048	96,218	100,934
Container	43,849	63,637	98,064	111,095	128,321
Liquefied gas	14,691	17,334	22,546	24,226	26,915
Chemical tankers	7,697	7,183	8,290	8,919	8,823
World Total	**734,917**	**798,995**	**895,843**	**959,964**	**1,042,328**

Sources: United Nations Conference on Trade and Development, *Review of Maritime Trade 1997,* Geneva, 1997, p.16; *Review of Maritime Trade 2001,* Geneva, 2001, p.18; *Review of Maritime Trade 2006,* Geneva, 2006, p. 21; *Review of Maritime Trade 2007,* p. 25.

The average carrying capacity of individual containerships is growing and over the last 20 years, the world fleet's total TEU carrying capacity increased almost seven-fold, with over 50 per cent of it foreign flagged.[15]

Average Age of the Fleet

The average age of the world fleet has been decreasing over time and is thought to be around 12 years for the fleet overall. The youngest fleet is containerships, with an average age of 9.1 years; nearly 35 per cent of containerships are less than 5 years old and 13 per cent are 20 years or older. Given the growth in containerisation of trade and the demand for new and larger ships, this fleet is being continually refreshed. Tankers have an average age of 10 years, probably due to the phasing out of double-hulled vessels over the past 20 years. The average age of bulk carriers is 12.9 years, while general cargo vessels are the oldest fleet, with an average age of 17.4 years.[16]

A key issue with regard to the average age profile of international shipping is safety. A general assumption is that the younger a ship is, the safer it should be due to newer designs and the incorporation of new technology. A justifiable fear if ships are not adequately maintained is that as they age, they become a greater safety risk.

Fleet Ownership and Foreign Flags

Table 2 outlines the nominal ownership of the world's merchant fleet, and a breakdown of whether it operates under national or foreign flags.

Table 2: Selected countries with largest controlled fleets (as on 1 January 2007)

		Number of vessels			Thousand DWT		
Ranking	**Country**	**National flag**	**Foreign flag**	**Total**	**National flag**	**Foreign flag**	**Total**
2	Japan	719	2,611	3,330	11,822	1,35,685	1,47,507
4	China	1,870	1,314	3,184	32,229	38,162	70,390
6	United States	847	919	1,766	22,705	25,555	48,261
7	Hong Kong	296	393	689	19,180	25,873	45,053
8	Republic of Korea	662	379	1,041	14,486	17,802	32,287
10	Singapore	499	295	794	14,887	10,836	25,723
11	Taiwan	97	477	574	4,076	20,781	24,858
15	India	404	52	456	13,288	1,529	14,817
18	Saudi Arabia	63	87	150	949	10,912	11,861
20	Iran	156	28	184	8,845	1,148	9,994
22	United Arab Emirates	51	315	366	615	6,304	6,918
23	Indonesia	679	114	793	4,382	2,301	6,684
24	Malaysia	303	54	357	6,285	372	6,657
30	Kuwait	39	29	68	3,419	1,364	4,783
32	Philippines	221	35	256	2,023	1,115	3,137
33	Vietnam	322	30	352	2,542	502	3,045
34	Thailand	260	38	298	2,498	415	2,913
35	Australia	46	39	85	1,338	1,531	2,869
	World	**16,407**	**18,415**	**34,822**	**3,29,259**	**6,49,298**	**9,78,557**

Source: United Nations Conference on Trade and Development, *Review of Maritime Trade 2007, Geneva, 2007,* Table 16, p. 32.

Overall, 66.35 per cent of the world fleet is foreign flagged, with the Panamanian flag used predominantly by Japan, Greece, China, Taiwan and Switzerland, with Japan accounting for nearly 50 per cent of Panama's DWT. The second largest flag of convenience, Liberia, is used by Germany (mostly containerships), Greece, the Russian Federation and Saudi Arabia (mostly oil tankers).

Indo-Pacific countries operating their shipping as follows: Australia's fleet is 47 per cent national flagged and 53 per cent foreign flagged; China is 46 per cent national flagged and 54 per cent foreign flagged; Hong Kong is 43 per cent national flagged and 57 per cent foreign flagged; India is 90 per cent national flagged and 10 per cent foreign flagged; Indonesia is 66 per cent national flagged and 34 per cent foreign flagged; Iran is 89 per cent national flagged and 11 per cent foreign flagged; Japan is 8 per cent national flag and 92 per cent foreign flagged; Malaysia is 95 per cent national flagged and 5 per cent foreign flagged; the Philippines is 65 per cent national flagged and 35 per cent foreign flagged; Saudi Arabia is 80 per cent national flagged and 20 per cent foreign flagged; Singapore is 58 per cent national flagged and 42 per cent foreign flagged; Taiwan is 17 per cent national flagged and 83 per cent foreign flagged'. Thailand is 86 per cent national flagged and 16 per cent foreign flagged; the United Arab Emirates is 9 per cent national flagged and 91 per cent foreign flagged; and Vietnam is 84 per cent national flagged and 16 per cent foreign flagged.[17]

The purpose of the preceding paragraph is to demonstrate the disparity across Indo-Pacific countries of ship ownership and national/foreign flags, which will have an impact on the ability of countries to undertake both flag State responsibilities and act cooperatively in port State control regimes.

Issue Affecting International Shipping

There is a number of issues that may impact upon international shipping, the free flow of goods and thus economic growth and political stability. While recent efforts have focused on the apparent threat of maritime terrorism, there also remain long-standing issues to do with ship safety and freedom of navigation.

Security Issues

Shipping is vulnerable to attack or disruption by a variety of groups with differing means and motives, including pirates and criminal gangs (potentially State-supported), terrorist groups and, least likely at the moment, nation-states. These groups may engage in attacks on ships; the hijacking of cargo, the actual ship and increasingly the ships' crew (for ransom); sinking ships, either to block narrow passages, port entrances or other focal points, or to create an environmental disaster; using the ship as a weapon, either to attack land infrastructure through a collision or explosion, or by incapacitating the crew so that the ship continues underway along a busy strait, risking collision with other ships.

Specific ship types are vulnerable to some threats more than others. Oil tankers have high economic value and could be hijacked for their cargo, or turned into an explosive weapon; the move to double hulls might have a positive mitigating effect here, limiting the ability to breach the hull. LNG carriers also have a high economic value, but are difficult to set on fire, as the conditions necessary to ignite a vapour spill are very limited; however, they are at heightened risk when they are loading/unloading in port.[18] Bulk carriers have a lower economic value but as larger ships they can be used as weapons (especially if carrying fertiliser) to crash into other ships/infrastructure, or could be sunk to block access to ports.[19]

As the naval responses to these scenarios are well known, they will not be covered in this paper.

Safety Issues

The major focus of the international shipping regulatory framework (examined in the following section) is safety and pollution. The International Safety Management (ISM) Code came into effect on 1 July 1998, and is mandatory as it has been incorporated into the International Convention for the Safety of Life at Sea 1974. The ISM Code can be traced back to increasing concerns in the late 1980s about poor management standards in the shipping industry, and it emphasises the role of sound management in safety and pollution prevention. It is aimed at forcing a culture change within the industry by establishing the following safety management objectives:

- to provide for safe practices in ship operation and a safe working environment
- to establish safeguards against all identified risks
- to continuously improve safety management skills of personnel, including preparing for emergencies.

Linked to the ISM Code is the revised International Convention on Standards of Training Certification and Watchkeeping for Seafarers 1978 (STCW), which was amended in 1995 as many flag States were ignoring its requirements. The original STCW was conceived as the minimum requirement for seafarer training and certification but its lack of clear definitions for these requirements eroded this intention. The revised STCW is based on three elements:

- it introduced new uniform standards of competence for seafarers
- it introduced new measures to ensure that governments actually fulfill their obligations under the Convention

- it introduced new responsibilities on shipping companies to ensure that seafarers employed on board ships are properly trained and are carrying properly documented certificates.

These amendments entered into force on 1 February 1997 and also required governments to advise the International Maritime Organisation (IMO) of the steps taken to implement its regulations, leading to a need for openness on the standards of training. At its most basic level, the STCW require seafarers are trained to a certain standard at a facility which is approved for that purpose and that the seafarers' knowledge is updated on a regular basis. When linked to the ISM Code, it requires seafarers joining a ship are familiar with its systems and equipment.

Although there is a variety of reasons for improved ship safety, one major concern is an accidental or deliberate oil spill. The best known example is the Exxon Valdez. On 24 March 1989, the Exxon Valdez struck a reef in Prince George Sound, Alaska and 11 million gallons of oil leaked into the water. Two months later, the resulting oil slick was 470 miles long. The initial clean-up took three years and cost US$ 2.1 billion. Exxon agreed to pay the State of Alaska and the US Government US$ 900 million over 10 years and was fined US$ 250 million. In 1994, Exxon was fined US$ 5 billion in punitive damages, but this was overturned in 2001.[20] After this accident, the US declared that only tankers with double hulls would be allowed to enter its ports, and increasingly in the world shipping fleet, single hull tankers have been phased out in favour of double hulled vessels.

Freedom of Navigation

Freedom of navigation on the oceans is an ongoing issue for trading nations, shipowners and navies. The United Nations Convention on the Law of the Sea 1982 (LOSC) guarantees freedom of navigation albeit with some restrictions. Innocent passage through the territorial sea is allowed, albeit transit is in a continuous and expeditious fashion on the surface of the ocean; and can only be impeded on a non-discriminatory and temporary basis for essential security purposes. Transit passage through international straits, and archipelagic sea lanes passage through archipelagic waters, is more generous to transiting vessels and there can be no suspensions of transit or archipelagic sea lane passage in any circumstances. Freedom of navigation also applies to the excusive economic zone and the high seas.

Although the LOSC is in force, some countries interpret its provisions differently by extending their boundaries or by attempting to apply security restrictions in certain zones. The United States navy maintains an active Freedom of Navigation programme that directly challenges these countries' restrictions.

Indonesia was the first archipelagic state to designate archipelagic sea lanes, although they should be discussed with the international community beforehand, and they must then be referred to the IMO. Indonesia worked closely with the United States and Australia (representing all user-States) in formulating three north-south archipelagic sea lanes, but since an east-west passage was not included in the proposal, these sea lanes are only a partial designation. Under its Freedom of Navigation programme, the USN transits Indonesian waters.

Case Study: Asian Energy Flows

As has been shown earlier, the Indo-Pacific is the most economically dynamic region in the world and is the driver for global economic growth and development, based predominantly on seaborne trade. Notwithstanding the level of trade within the Indian Ocean, the north Asian economies are the powerhouse of this growth and rely on energy imports from the Middle East to fuel economic growth. The Middle East supplies about 50 per cent of China's oil requirements; about 85 per cent of Japan's and about 50 per cent of South Korea's.

In 2006, China consumed 7.7 million barrels per day (mbpd) of oil, of which more than half this energy demand (3.9 mbpd) was provided by imports. Thirty-nine per cent was supplied from the Middle East, just over 12 per cent from the former Soviet Union, and 12 per cent from the Asia-Pacific region. Japan consumed 5.2 mbpd of oil, importing 5.2 mbpd to meet that demand and stockholding requirements (i.e. 100.7 per cent). Eighty-one per cent was sourced from the Middle East and a further 8 per cent from the Asia-Pacific. Singapore consumed 0.853 mbpd of oil, importing 2.2 mbpd of oil (261 per cent) for its own use as well as for refining for export to other countries. Half was obtained from the Middle East and one-third from the Asia-Pacific.[21]

In terms of natural gas, China consumed 58 billion cubic metres (bcm) in 2006, of which 1 bcm was imported from Australia.[22] India consumed 39.7 bcm of natural gas, importing approximately one-fifth (7.99 bcm) of that; with Oman, Qatar and the United Arab Emirates (UAE) supplying 89 per cent (7.12 bcm). Japan consumed 84.6 bcm, importing over 95 per cent (81.86 bcm); with Oman, Qatar and the UAE supplying 24 per cent, and Australia and South East Asia supplying 72 per cent. South Korea consumed 34.2 bcm, relying solely on imports; with Oman, Qatar and the UAE, and Australia and South East Asia supplying about half each. Last, Taiwan consumed 11.9 bcm, importing 85.7 per cent (10.2 bcm); with Australia and South East Asia supplying 93 per cent (9.5 bcm).[23]

If this tanker traffic to north Asia were impeded, the global economy would be affected, either directly, if countries were major trading partners, or indirectly, as a slowdown or downturn affected the global economy. So, what are the vulnerabilities facing this traffic from the Middle East to north Asia?

The Persian Gulf countries produce over a quarter of the world's oil while holding over half of all crude reserves. Ninety per cent of Persian Gulf oil is transported by tanker through the Strait of Hormuz into the Indian Ocean. Fifteen million barrels per day (mbpd) transit the Strait, of which 13 mbpd is bound for Asia. The Strait of Hormuz consists of two 3km wide channels for inbound and outbound tanker traffic, as well as a 3km wide buffer zone. If the Strait were to be closed, some oil could be transported via pipelines to ports on the Red Sea, entailing longer routes and increased costs.

LNG exports from the Persian Gulf come from Oman, Qatar, and the UAE; while those from Africa predominantly use the Red Sea and come from Algeria, Egypt, and Libya, with Nigerian exports primarily bound for Europe and North America.

Restrictions on freedom of navigation have come about for a number of reasons. Both offshore and land-based oil and gas installations may be attacked, ranging from the events of the 1980-88 Tanker War; shore-based attacks on oil installations in Saudi Arabia (leading to the recent decision to set up a 35,000-strong security force at a cost of US$ 4-5 billion); and attacks on Iraqi offshore oil installations, which coalition naval forces are now tasked to protect.

Iran disputes the maritime boundaries in the Persian Gulf and could harass shipping, such as its "kidnapping" of Royal Navy personnel in disputed international waters, or the recent swarming of US Navy warships, or it could attempt to close the strait. A terrorist attack against shipping, such as the attacks against the *USS Cole* and the *MV Limburg*, is distinctly possible.

Sea robbery is an increasing concern in waters outside the strait, but generally involves the theft of ships' stores and valuables rather than the cargo or ship. Endemic piracy off the Somali coast has the potential to impact tankers leaving the Red Sea. The use of mother ships, from which smaller boats operate to attack targets, extends the range of sea robbers/pirates, complicating tanker security as crews must remain vigilant for longer periods at the beginning of their transit. Critically, pirates have been found operating up to 320 nm off the coast, placing them on the high seas and enabling international action to be taken against them.[24]

Oil tankers exiting the Strait of Hormuz and oil and LNG tankers departing from African ports, are predominantly on the open ocean when transiting the Indian Ocean, except where the Strait of Hormuz traffic skirts the Malabar coast off India near Bassas de Pedro, before passing Dondra Head near Sri Lanka (tankers from the Red Sea skirt the island of Suqutra before transiting via the Eight Degree Channel to Dondra Head), and around the Andaman and Nicobar Islands near the entrance to the Strait of Malacca.

On the open ocean, the threats to shipping are at the high-end of capability, directed by a nation-state (i.e. a naval attack—due to range and endurance requirements). In regional capability terms, Iran, Pakistan and India have the capacity to interdict shipping, but a motive is not evident except for Iran, which is at odds with other countries in the region and with Western nations.

Sri Lanka suffers from maritime terrorism by the Tamil Tigers, who many analysts assess as having the most developed maritime capabilities of any non-State actor. The Sea Tigers have 2000–3000 cadres with heavily armed gunboats and speed-boats. However, it is not evident that they would attack oil tankers transiting Dondra Head, as their focus is secessionist (i.e. attacking the Sri Lankan Navy).

South-East Asia contains the major international sea-lanes for seaborne trade, while also possessing a complicated maritime geography, adjoining territorial seas and unresolved boundary delimitation issues. The trunk route between Europe and north Asia must pass through the Strait of Malacca, where it branches out through Hong Kong northwards to East Asia or the west coast of the US, or branches out southwards from Singapore to the Australian ports.[25] There is considerable intra-regional trade in LNG, through which Australia, Brunei, Indonesia, and Malaysia transport natural gas throughout the region, and there are LNG pipelines linking Singapore with Indonesia and Malaysia, and Thailand with Myanmar.[26]

A state attack on shipping in the Strait is possible but appears unlikely as there would be an immediate international response. The greater threat remains armed robbery at sea and the minor possibility of maritime terrorism. Critically, it is cross-Strait traffic that is being robbed, with the majority of attacks occurring when the ship is berthed or at anchor. It is also important to note that shipping in the Strait of Malacca has not been re-routed even when sea robbery attacks were high, calling into question how seriously shipowners consider the security threat in the strait.

Forty-one thousand ships transit the South China Sea each year, which contributes to about a quarter of global shipping. Shipping traffic becomes more congested as LNG tankers from Australia and South-East Asia begin their transit to north Asia. There are disputed territorial claims and competition over presumed oil and gas reserves.

State-directed action against tankers is more likely, given these tensions between the bordering countries. What such action would achieve is not clear but miscalculation is a possibility. Threats from non-State actors are comparable to the Strait of Malacca. Both Japan and China are keen to ensure the smooth flow of their energy supplies. In 1981, Japan declared it would protect its SLOC out to 1000nm, although the direct military application of this has never really been tested. Japan has adopted a maritime capacity-building approach in South-East Asia, using the Japanese Coastguard to assist with training and exercises. The greater concern remains China and the potential future reach of its maritime forces in protection of its trade.

The East China Sea and the Yellow Sea are critical SLOCs for north Asia but are not well known to the rest of the world. Many maritime boundaries are contested and, when combined with historical differences, the possibility of resolution appears slim. Both North Korea and China have declared extensive maritime security zones that are not in accordance with the LOSC and which complicate naval activities in this area. Economic and political competition between China and Japan, tensions between China and Taiwan, and US involvement in the region impact regional stability. The US perceives China as a peer competitor, is committed to an independent Taiwan, and has a security treaty with Japan. South Korea is in dispute with Japan over maritime boundaries and natural resource usage. Moreover, the test firing of missiles by North Korea, and that regime's nuclear programme, make this area a strategic flashpoint.

Freedom of navigation is critical to international shipping, seaborne trade, economic growth and thus political stability. This brief outline of Asian energy flows highlights a variety of issues that could impact international shipping, which may then require a response by maritime forces.

International Shipping Management Initiatives

There is a broad framework of four major stakeholders in international shipping: the IMO, the classification societies, the flag State, and the port State; although it is possible to add a fifth stakeholder: the coastal State.[27]

A regulatory regime has evolved over time to manage international shipping. Nearly 50 years ago, the International Maritime and Consultative Organisation was created as a United Nations agency responsible for maritime issues; it was renamed the IMO in 1983. The IMO produces four types of documents to manage international shipping: conventions (binding treaties), codes, resolutions (advisory,but some countries have incorporated them into their domestic legislation) and guidelines (non binding).The IMO provides regulatory oversight of international shipping in the following areas: maritime safety, marine pollution, liability and compensation, cargoes, marine technology, marine environment, navigation, life saving and search and rescue, radio communications, and training and certification.

The flag State is the state in which the ship has been registered and has primary responsibility for the conduct of the ship, that is, whether it meets requirements set by the IMO. This includes, but is not limited to: regular survey of all ships flying the flag of the flagged State, ensuring that all ships carry on board appropriate charts and navigational instruments, and that the crew is adequately trained and experienced.

The classification societies help the shipowner by assessing whether the ship meets these regulatory requirements in order to obtain insurance, and they also verify to the flagged State that the ship meets the applicable regulations.

However, over the past 40 years, there has been an increasing tendency in shipowners to move their ships to open registries or flags of convenience rather than a national flag. There are four issues that determine which flag to choose: what are the crewing levels and conditions required by the flag State; what are the tax, company tax and financial laws in the flag State; what level of enforcement does the flag State apply to compliance with maritime safety conventions; and what level of naval protection can be offered by the flag State. Often it is the first two factors that favour a flag of convenience, as operating costs can be lowered and profits increased.

Poor enforcement by some flag States of their responsibilities and the rise of flags of convenience led to gaps in the enforcement of maritime conventions, leading to increased port State control. Port States were concerned with the condition of ships calling at their ports, especially a fear of accidents, incompetent foreign crews who might endanger the ship or port, and the conditions of the foreign crews. The LOSC allows coastal and port States to make laws for the good conduct of ships in their territorial seas, and increasingly they have used articles relating to safety and pollution to develop a strong port State control regime. In 1982, the European Union (EU) became concerned at non-compliance with maritime conventions and developed and signed the Paris Memorandum of Understanding (MoU) on Port State Control, to ensure cooperation across a number of regional countries. A number of similar regional MoUs have since come into effect.

Two recent initiatives are outlined below, to show how port State control may operate, and how cooperation across a range of states can lead to improved safety of navigation in a strategic choke point.

Indian Ocean Memorandum of Understanding on Port State Control

Over the period 13–17 October 1997, 22 countries of the Indian Ocean Region met to consider a regional agreement for cooperation on port State control, and on 5 June 1998, an MoU was signed. As of 2006, there were 13 countries which are party to the Indian Ocean MoU (Australia, Eritrea, India, Iran, Kenya, the Maldives, Mauritius, Oman, Sri Lanka, Sudan, Tanzania and Yemen), with a number of countries, other MoU and international organisations as observers.

The purpose of the port State control system is to verify whether foreign flagged ships calling at a port of the State comply with relevant international maritime conventions. Each port State is expected to establish and maintain an effective port State control system, and to impose actions against ships which do not comply with international conventions. The specific conventions monitored in the Indian Ocean include:

- The International Convention on Load Lines, 1966
- The International Convention for the safety of Life at Sea, 1974 (SOLAS 74)
- The International Convention for the Prevention of Pollution from Ships 1973, as modified by the Protocol of 1978 (MARPOL 73/78)
- The International Convention on Standards of Training, Certification and Watchkeeping for Seafarers, 1978 (STCW 78)
- The Convention on the International Relations for Preventing Collisions at Sea, 1972
- The International Convention on Tonnage Measurement of Ships, 1969 identified and ship detentions for the period 2001-06.
- The Merchant Shipping (minimum Standards) Convention 1976 (ILO Convention No. 174.

Table 3 provides high-level data on ship inspection rates, deficiencies identified and ship detentions for the period 2001-06.

Table 3: Indian Ocean Port State Control Reporting

	2001	2002	2003	2004	2005	2006
Number of member countries reporting	10	8	8	9	10	7
Number of ship inspections	5,520	5,452	5,093	5,690	5,205	5,124
Ships with deficiencies	2,862	2,667	2,637	3,087	2,871	2,863
Number of deficiencies	14,644	12,732	13,233	15,142	15,006	16,045
Number of detentions	291	306	472	489	374	406

Source: Indian Ocean Memorandum of Understanding on Port State Control, Annual Reports, Goa, India, 2001-06.

Table 3 demonstrates two contradictory factors. Clearly, some States are abiding by the conditions of the MoU and their inspection, enforcement and detention of non-compliant ships appears robust. However, it is not clear whether States that are not reporting their data are undertaking their compliance monitoring role.

Initiatives in the Malacca and Singapore Straits

There has been some government concern over acts of piracy in the Strait of Malacca since the mid-1990s. Notwithstanding the incidents have primarily been of the nature of sea robber, which too have been grossly overstated. As a key choke point for Asian shipping and trade, there have been numerous efforts at managing security in the Strait.[28]

The IMO convened three meetings in South-East Asia under the 'Protection of Vital Shipping Lanes' Initiative to consider maritime security issues in the Strait. The first meeting in Jakarta in September 2005 set out the measures the three littoral states of Indonesia, Malaysia and Singapore had put in place to address concerns, providing a basis for future cooperation amongst them, user States and other stakeholders. The second meeting was held 12 months later in Kuala Lumpur where the littoral States presented their ideas about a standing mechanism for cooperation between them, user States and other stakeholders. The cooperative mechanism was agreed at the third meeting held 12 months later in Singapore.

The cooperative mechanism operates under LOSC Article 43 and consists of three components: a cooperative forum serving as a platform for dialogue between the littoral States and the international maritime community; a project coordination committee to coordinate projects involving contributions from the international maritime community; and an aid to navigation fund to receive direct financial contributions from the international maritime community.

The proposed projects for funding were:

- removal of wrecks in the traffic separation scheme in the Straits
- cooperation and capacity building on hazardous and noxious substance preparedness and response in the Straits
- demonstration project of class B automatic identification system transponders on small ships
- setting up a tide, current and wind measurement system for the Straits to enhance navigation safety and marine environment protection
- replacement and maintenance of aids to navigation in the Straits
- replacement of aids to navigation damaged by the tsunami incident.[29]

The first project was not funded due to an estimated cost of US$ 55 million to remove 11 identified wrecks; the remaining five projects will be funded.

Japan (via the Nippon Foundation), the Republic of Korea and the United Arab Emirates announced immediate contributions to the fund, while Australia, China and the United States were willing to contribute.

For many years there was extensive debate over maritime security in the Strait of Malacca, and while the littoral States rejected external naval patrols, they were willing to accept assistance in the form of training and equipment. A method for achieving this contribution was under LOSC Article 43, but user States consistently refused to consider that option. The intervention of the IMO to broker a deal between the user States and the littoral States under Article 43 is a welcome development.

Conclusion

International shipping is critical to global economic growth and seaborne trade is forecast to have continuing growth. As an example, energy demand is projected to grow 3.2 per cent pa, more than doubling over the period to 2030.[30] World consumption of petroleum and other liquid fuels is forecast to be 97 mbpd in 2015, growing to 118 mbpd in 2030; with natural gas forecast to reach 4,616 bcm in 2030.[31] For the member countries comprising the Asia-Pacific Economic Cooperation (APEC),[32] oil demand is expected to grow at 1.7 per cent to 2030, with natural gas demand growing at 2.4 per cent.[33]

To meet this forecast increase in seaborne trade international shipping will also continue to grow. While the new build of ships appears to be keeping pace with seaborne trade requirements, it is not evident that there will be enough trained personnel to crew these new ships. This is increasingly a concern for sophisticated LNG carriers, which face a shortage of experienced captains and engineers.

The IMO continues to develop a regulatory framework for international shipping, the most recent regulation being the International Ship and Port Facility Security Code, which was included as a new chapter in SOLAS Chapter XI-2 Special Measures to Enhance Maritime Security, to create an international legislative framework for regulating and assessing the security of international shipping and associated port facilities, as a reaction to concerns of an increased maritime terrorism threat.

Notwithstanding the evolving regulatory framework, if more than half of the world merchant fleet is foreign flagged, it calls into question the ability of the flag State, or in this case the flag of convenience, to monitor compliance. This can only lead to an increasing reliance on port State control, which appears to be more effective when operating through a regional MoU. However, this is partially offset if parties to an MoU do not meet their compliance monitoring and enforcement commitments, which might occur if their own fleet is predominantly foreign flagged.

As shown in the case study examining energy flows to north Asia, there are a variety of constraints that could disrupt tanker traffic. Importantly, many of these are outside the scope of the international regulatory framework and would require the intervention of maritime forces (navies, cost guards and marine police) to manage them.

The overall conclusion of this paper is that there is a growing need for maritime capacity building in the areas of ship safety and security, both for flag and port States. There may also be a need for improved cooperation between a State's maritime forces to enforce ship safety and security, and if serious disruption occurs, then cooperation between the maritime forces of a number of States may be necessary. ■

Notes

1. United Nations Conference on Trade and Development (UNCTAD), *Trade and Development Report 2007*, New York and Geneva, 2007, Table 1.1, p. 2.
2. UNCTAD, *Trade and Development Report 2007*, pp. ii, 3.
3. UNCTAD, *Trade and Development Report 2007*, pp. xiii, xiv, 98.
4. Energy Information Administration (EIA), *International Energy Outlook 2007*, Washington, May 2007, p. 11.
5. UNCTAD, *Review of Maritime Transport, 2007*, New York and Geneva, 2007, p. 2; *Trade and Development Report 2007*, p. 4.
6. Ibid, pp. 4-5.
7. Ibid, p. 12.

8. Ibid, p. 13.
9. Ibid, p. 14.
10. Ibid, p. 17.
11. Ibid, pp. 17-18.
12. Ibid, pp. 18-19.
13. Ibid, pp. 19-20.
14. Ibid, p. 25.
15. Ibid, p. 24.
16. Ibid, p. 24.
17. Ibid, Table 16, p. 32.
18. A specific safety concern associated with LNG carriers is the possibility of a catastrophic explosion or fire that could devastate a port and its surrounds; this prospect resulted in the US Department of Homeland Security, including them in a list of potential terrorist targets. There are three possible scenarios. A pool fire may occur if LNG spills near an ignition source — if the combustible gas-air concentration is right, the evaporating gas will burn. As the LNG pool expands, so does the fire, which is very intense and far hotter than an oil or gasoline fire. Importantly, such a fire cannot be extinguished and will only end when all the LNG has been consumed. If LNG spills but does not immediately ignite, the evaporating gas will form a vapour cloud that may drift from the spill site. If the cloud then achieves the right gas-air concentration, it becomes volatile and again prone to ignition, with disastrous consequences. An-LNG spill on water could theoretically heat up in what is called a flameless explosion; but this event is less likely to occur than a pool fire or a flammable vapour cloud. Notwithstanding these 'possibilities', LNG carriers appear relatively safe as the conditions necessary to create a fire are difficult to achieve, thus the major vulnerability of LNG is actually ashore.
19. Philippe Crist, *Security in Maritime Transport: Risk Factors and Economic Impact,* Maritime Transport Committee, Organisation for Economic Co-operation and Development, Paris, July 2003.
20. 'The Exxon Valdez Oil Spill Disaster', ExploreNorth, www.explorenorth.com/library/weekly/aa032499.htm
21. British Petroleum, *Statistical Review of World Energy,* London, June 2007, pp. 11, 20.
22. In 2004, China and Australia signed an LNG supply contract for 3.5 million tonnes pa for 25 years at a price of $25 billion; a further contract was signed in September 2007 for another 1 million tonnes pa for 20 years at a price of $45 billion. 'Chinese ties enter new era after $45bn gas deal', *The Australian,* 7 Sep 2007.
23. British Petroleum, *Statistical Review of World Energy 2007,* p. 30.
24. Hans Tino Hansen, 'Piracy off the Coast of Somalia and the Hijacking of Danica White', *Protocol,* June 2007, p. 3.
25. D. Sukhakanya, 'The Security of the Sea Lanes in Southeast Asia', in Lau Teik Soon and Lee Lai To (eds), *The Security of the Sea Lanes in the Asia-Pacific Region,* Heinemann, Singapore, 1988, p.23.
26. British Petroleum, *Statistical Review of World Energy 2007,* p. 30.
27. The coastal State will play an increasing role with the introduction of Long Range Identification and Tracking, which will provide them with information about ships transiting their eaters but not necessarily planning to enter a port.

28. While international shipping is being attacked in the Strait of Malacca, the methodology adopted by the International Maritime Bureau's (IMB) Piracy Reporting Centre causes confusion over both the scale and types of attacks being perpetrated and does not assist with the development of appropriate policy responses to the assessed problem. The IMB is funded by shipowners, who might have a vested interest in overstating the threat facing international shipping, in order to pass on protective security costs to the littoral states (Indonesia, Malaysia, Singapore) rather than absorb them. It has been shipping policy to shrink crew numbers to lower costs, but now the ships have no crew to 'protect' the ship if it is boarded. It also appears the shipowners do not wish to fund ship 'defences'—electric fences and the like— preferring the littoral states to patrol the waters to stop the 'pirates'. There is no evidence that shipowners have begun to reroute shipping from the Malacca Strait, so it is not clear how seriously they actually regard the 'threat'. Notwithstanding the possibility of overstating the threat to shipping, the number of attacks is probably lower than what is actually occurring as ships often do not report an incident. Shipmasters might not report an attack to the authorities as they cannot afford the delay (which might be a couple of days) to be interviewed by law enforcement officials. There are growing concerns that ship hijackings are not being reported with shipowners instead paying the ransom—this only encourages more attacks. Confusingly the number of reported attacks is overstated because attempted attacks are combined with actual attacks. The IMB does not use the internationally accepted definition of piracy, theirs is much broader—so someone getting on board while the ship is berthed and stealing a wallet or ship's stores is classified as a pirate attack. The use of the IMB data is misleading and has led to calls for increased naval patrols in the Malacca Strait. However, many attacks occur while the ship is berthed or at anchor — which means that it is up to port authorities or for the ship to protect itself. If the ship is steaming through the Strait then responsibility is with the ship to repel boarders in the first instance and then for maritime forces (navies and coastguards) to respond.
29. Maritime Port Authority of Singapore, *New Historic Milestone in International Cooperation for Straits of Malacca and Singapore,* 4 September 2007, www.mpa.gov.sg/infocentre/newsreleases/2007/nr070904.htm.
30. EIA, *International Energy Outlook 2007*, p. 6.
31. EIA, *International Energy Outlook 2007*, pp. 29, 39. The natural gas forecast in 2030 is 163 trillion cubic feet (ie 163 x 1012), which has been converted at the rate of 1 cubic foot = 0.028316846592 cubic metres.
32. Member economies are: Australia, Brunei, Canada, Chile, China, Hong Kong, Indonesia, Japan, Malaysia, Mexico, Papua New Guinea, Peru, the Philippines, New Zealand, Russia, Singapore, South Korea, Taiwan, Thailand, the United States, and Vietnam.
33. Asia Pacific Energy Research Centre, *A Quest for Energy Security in the 21st Century: Resources and Constraints*, Tokyo, 2007, pp. 3, 13.

SESSION IV

PAPER 1

The 1982 UN Law of the Sea Convention: The Need for Change

Jon M Van Dyke*

The 1982 United Nations Law of the Sea Convention is a monumental achievement, providing a true constitution for the oceans that addresses and resolves many disputes concerning the uses of the oceans and their resources. But much has changed in the world since it was completed, and new challenges have emerged. And many of the provisions in the Convention are ambiguous compromises that leave practical problems of implementation unresolved. The balance between navigational freedom through straits and the need for strait states to protect their coastal environments is an example of continuing tension that is unresolved in the Convention. The extent to which countries can engage in military activities in the exclusive economic zones of other countries is another problem area. The rules governing straddling and highly migratory fish stocks need further development. Allocation of fish from the high seas needs attention. National enforcement and international dispute resolution procedures need strengthening. Procedures for limiting the movement of weapons of mass destruction need to be clarified. The world community is still struggling to find ways to deal with piracy and other threats to navigation and coastal security. The applicability of the Convention in times of armed conflict remains a gray area. Should these issues be addressed in a new comprehensive treaty, or should they be dealt with through piecemeal issue-specific documents? The world community is still feeling its way through these issues. This paper will outline the issues that need attention and will offer recommendations on how to approach them.

* Professor, William S Richardson, School of Law, University of Hawaii.

The 1982 United Nations Law of the Sea Convention

The Law of the Sea Convention[1] is a comprehensive document that provides rules to govern most ocean activities and procedures for resolving competing and overlapping uses. It was drafted after more than a decade of preparatory meetings and formal negotiations that involved countries from all parts of the globe. The Convention is a monumental achievement, which entered into force November 16, 1994, after the 60th nation submitted its ratification. As of February 2008, it had been ratified by 155 of the 192 members of the United Nations,[2] but has not yet reached universal adherence, with key nations such as Turkey, Iran, and Thailand, as well as the United States, still withholding ratification.

The 1982 Convention was produced by the Third United Nations Conference on the Law of the Sea, which began with much fanfare and high expectations in Caracas in 1974, and then continued with meetings every six months thereafter, alternating between New York and Geneva. The need for a comprehensive treaty became clear after countries began making wildly conflicting claims to their coastal waters and the resources in them. The first formal claim to an extended maritime zone had been made by the United States in the 1945 Truman Proclamation, which claimed sovereign rights and jurisdiction over the nonliving resources on the US continental shelf.[3] This claim was designed primarily to allow the United States to drill for oil and natural gas in the gently-sloping continental shelf extending off the US coast in the Gulf of Mexico. In making this claim, the United States sought to protect its navigational freedoms by distinguishing between the ability to claim resources on the one hand, and the ability to regulate navigation on the other, but other countries ignored this distinction and responded to the US action by making a bewildering array of claims to the resources near their coasts.

Four treaties were drafted in Geneva in 1958,[4] but countries ratified some of them and not others, producing a patchwork of legal principles, and, most notably, the Territorial Sea Convention failed to define the breadth of the territorial sea. An attempt to reach consensus on that matter in 1960 also failed. During the mid-1960s, attention began to focus on the polymetallic nodules found on the sea floor.[5] The debates over this potential resource brought countries back to the table, leading to the eight-years of formal negotiations. When the Conference began, the central disputes concerned the width of the territorial sea, coastal state control of adjacent offshore resources, and the navigational rights of commercial and military vessels to pass through straits and island archipelagoes. The United States initially resisted the concept of extended fisheries zones, because it was concerned that such zones would limit navigational freedoms. The United States was particularly concerned about its continuing ability to navigate its warships, including submerged submarines, through key international straits such as the Strait of Gibraltar (into the Mediterranean Sea), the Strait of Hormuz (into the Persian/Arabian Gulf), the Strait of Bab el Mandeb (into the Red Sea), the Strait of Malacca (connecting the Indian Ocean with the Pacific), the Dover Strait (through the English Channel), the Bering Strait (in the Arctic), and the Strait of Lombok (through the Indonesian archipelago). The United States worried that if countries were allowed to extend their territorial seas from three to 12 nautical miles, no high-seas corridors would remain in these narrow straits, and control over passage might fall under the control of the countries bordering these key waterways. The United States maintained that free movement through these straits was essential to its national security, and protested claims of expanding territorial seas.[6]

The compromise that emerged consisted of: (a) allowing coastal states to extend their territorial seas to 12 nautical miles, (b) recognizing the right to transit passage through international straits, and (c) allowing countries to establish an "exclusive economic zone" (EEZ) out to a distance of 200 nautical miles from its coast. The right of "transit passage through international straits" is nonsuspendable and applies to all vessels and also to airplanes. Submarines are allowed to remain submerged when they exercise this right of transit passage. In the newly-created EEZ, the adjacent or coastal state has sovereign rights over the living and nonliving resources and can exercise certain forms of jurisdiction to protect the marine environment, regulate scientific research, and govern artificial structures. Coastal states must also exercise "due regard to the rights and duties of other States" under Article 56(2) and must permit navigational passage, but debates continue regarding the types of restrictions that can be imposed upon the movement of ships. The EEZ was designed to balance carefully the interests of both the coastal and the maritime states. Maritime countries contend that they have the same navigational freedoms in the EEZs of other countries as they have on the high seas, but a number of coastal countries, including some of the maritime powers, have imposed restrictions on navigation in their EEZs in order to protect coastal resources and coastal populations. Disputes continue regarding the nature of military activities one country can engage in while its vessels are in the EEZ of another country, and disputes also exist regarding whether hydrographic surveying by one country is permitted in the EEZ of another country.[7] Countries cannot engage in marine scientific research in the EEZs of other countries without permission, but coastal countries are encouraged to grant permission when it is requested.[8] The Convention also addresses a wide variety of other issues, and, inevitably, left some issues unresolved. Should ships be free to move freely in all parts of the oceans? Even if they are warships carrying nuclear weapons? Even if they are carrying ultrahazardous radioactive cargoes that impose risks on coastal populations? What law applies when vessels collide? Or when a crime takes place on a vessel sailing on the high seas or other waters off the coast of a foreign state? Should fishing vessels be free to harvest fish wherever they can be found, or should the people living near the sea have priority over, or even ownership of, the fish that live near their coasts? Should a different approach be taken regarding fish that "straddle" adjacent fishing nations or a fishing nation and the high seas? Who should own the petroleum and mineral resources found under the sea? Can scientific research been done freely in all parts of the ocean, or in certain parts only with permission of an adjacent country? How should ocean boundaries be drawn?[9] Some of these issues have been resolved, but others remain ambiguous, and the question has been raised whether a new treaty is now needed to address these issues.

The Innovative Provisions of the Convention

What does the Convention contain, and why has it been controversial in the United States and elsewhere? Some articles repeat language from earlier treaties, and many of the articles are based on longstanding norms of customary international law. Other sections were new and innovative in 1982, and their status as customary international law remains uncertain.

Archipelagic States

Articles 46–49 of the Convention describe the concept of "archipelagic waters". These provisions specify that countries made up exclusively of islands, and have a water-to-land ratio of between 1:1 and 9:1, can become "archipelagic states" and exercise unique jurisdiction over the waters within their islands. These provisions apply to countries such as the Bahamas, Fiji, Indonesia, Papua New Guinea, the Philippines, the Solomon Islands, and Vanuatu. Other countries can exercise the right of innocent passage through archipelagic waters and can exercise "archipelagic sea lanes passage" in "archipelagic sea lanes," which is a right of nonsuspendable passage applicable to all vessels and planes, like the right of transit passage through international straits.

The Exclusive Economic Zone

The recognition of exclusive economic zones (EEZs) in the Law of the Sea Convention transferred most of the productive fishing areas from the high seas where fishing freedoms have traditionally been recognized to the exclusive jurisdiction of the adjacent coastal or island community. This transfer was based on the views, recognized in the Anglo-Norwegian Fisheries Case,[10] that coastal communities tend to have an economic dependence on their nearby fisheries and that they are more likely to manage these resources carefully to protect them for future generations.

Management under this new regime has not always been enlightened or orderly, however, and new disputes have arisen, particularly when fish stocks overlap or "straddle" between an EEZ and its adjacent high seas zone. In areas such as the productive fisheries off the east coast of Canada, European fishing vessels have harvested just outside the 200 nautical-mile EEZ in a way that has impacted the stocks within the EEZ. This activity has led to disputes and also led in 1995 to the creation of an innovative new treaty designed to reduce such conflicts, the Straddling and Migratory Fish Stocks Agreement.[11]

Fisheries Management

The provisions of the 1982 U.N. Convention on the Law of the Sea are general in nature but nonetheless clearly articulate an overarching duty to cooperate in all situations involving shared fisheries. Article 56 gives the coastal state sovereignty over the living resources in the 200 nautical-mile EEZ, but Articles 61, 62, 69 and 70 require the coastal state: (a) to cooperate with international organizations to ensure that species are not endangered by over-exploitation, (b) to manage species in a manner that protects "associated or dependent species" from over-exploitation, (c) to exchange data with international organizations and other nations that fish in its EEZ, and (d) to allow other states (particularly developing, land-locked, and geographically disadvantaged states) to harvest the surplus stocks in its EEZ. Article 63 addresses stocks (or stocks of associated species) that "straddle" adjacent EEZs, or an EEZ and an adjacent high seas area, and requires the states concerned to agree either directly or through an organization on the measures necessary to ensure the conservation of such stocks. Article 64 requires coastal states and distant-water fishing states that harvest highly migratory stocks such as tuna to cooperate either directly or through an organization to ensure the conservation and optimum utilization of such stocks. Article 65 contains strong language requiring nations to "work through the appropriate international organization" to conserve, manage, and study whales and dolphins. Article 66 gives the states of origin primary responsibility for anadromous stocks (i.e. salmon), but requires the states of origin to cooperate with other states whose nationals have traditionally harvested such stocks and states whose waters these fish migrate through.

On the high seas, Articles 118 and 119 require states to cooperate with other states whose nationals exploit identical or associated species. Article 118 recognizes mandatory duties by stating that nations "shall enter into negotiations with a view to taking the measures necessary for the conservation of the living resources concerned," and advocates creating regional fisheries organizations, as appropriate. Article 120 states that the provisions of Article 65 on marine mammals also apply on the high seas.

These provisions thus reinforce the duty to cooperate that has always existed in customary international law. Because they were not specific enough to resolve conflicts that have arisen as species have been over-exploited, the 1995 Straddling and Migratory Fish Stocks Agreement was negotiated.[12] This treaty requires countries to cooperate with each other directly and through regional fishery organizations, to utilize the precautionary approach with regard to fishery regulation, to collect and share data, and to assess carefully the health of each fish stocks. It expands enforcement powers and authorizes countries to utilize the dispute-resolution procedures established in the Law of the Sea Convention for fishery disputes involving the straddling and migratory fish stocks.

Standards Governing the Marine Environment

The environmental provisions in Part XII of the Convention use broad, general language but confirm the importance of protecting the marine environment for its own sake. The simple, direct, and elegant language of Article 192 articulates the importance of human stewardship of the ocean: "States have the obligation to protect and preserve the marine environment." Each word in this sentence has importance and power. The operative word "obligation" makes it clear that countries have positive duties and responsibilities and must take action. The verbs "protect" and "preserve" reinforce each other, to emphasize that countries must respect the natural processes of the ocean and must act in a manner that understands these processes and ensures that they continue for future generations. The "marine environment" is a purposively comprehensive concept covering all aspects of the ocean world—the water itself, its resources, the air above, and the seabed below—and it covers all jurisdictional zones (internal waters, territorial seas, contiguous zones, exclusive economic zone, continental shelves, archipelagic waters, and high seas. Article 192 thus recognizes the responsibility that all countries have to govern the oceans in a manner that respects the marine creatures that inhabit them. The marine environment must be preserved for the benefit of those who will come later to exploit its resources, to study its mysteries, and to enjoy the many pleasures that the oceans offer us.

Deep Seabed Mining and the International Seabed Authority

Part XI of the Law of the Sea Convention regulates seabed mining on the sea floor in the area beyond the exclusive economic zones of coastal countries. As explained above, the primary resource thought to be of some potential value are the soft-ball sized polymetallic nodules on the sea floor, particularly in the Pacific and Indian oceans, which contain nickel, manganese, cobalt, copper and trace amounts of other metals.

The Convention declared this resource to be "the common heritage" of humankind and established an International Seabed Authority, based in Jamaica, to regulate it.[13] The structure of this Authority was one of the major reasons the Reagan Administration refused to sign the Convention in 1982 and refused to participate in the Preparatory Commission to establish the details of the international regime to govern exploitation of the polymetallic nodules. The dispute over these resources was based in part on a disagreement regarding whether the concept of the "freedom of the seas," which protects navigational freedoms and fishing activities on the high seas, also includes the ability to harvest mineral resources.[14] Because the nodules are on the floor of the abyssal plains in the deep seabed, they have never been exploited historically, and the question was not addressed in earlier agreements.

The Clinton Administration worked with the international community to modify the provisions of Part XI of the Law of the Sea Convention to address the concerns that had been identified during the Reagan Administration. The modifications made to the regime governing the nonliving resources of the deep seabed are dramatic and reveal a new approach to international decisionmaking and resource sharing. The detailed provisions of Part XI of the 1982 Law of the Sea Convention have been simplified through an agreement signed on July 29, 1994, generally referred to as the "Part XI Agreement."[15] Some of the provisions of Part XI are put on hold for the time being, and others are scaled down or altered to meet new perceptions of the economic potential of the seabed minerals and the greater acceptance of free market principles by the world community.[16] The Agreement is effectively an amendment to the Law of the Sea Convention, although its creation was not in compliance with the Convention's provisions on amendments, reservations, or modifying agreements. It should also be emphasized that the fundamental principle that the resources of the seabed are the common heritage of humankind, first established in 1970, remains unchanged, and that the obligation to share these resources, particularly with the least developed nations, remains firm.

The Dispute Resolution Procedures

The dispute-resolution provisions in Part XV of the Law of the Sea Convention are innovative and are carefully crafted to maintain the Convention's delicate balances between competing interests. Article 287 instructs each ratifying nation to pick from among four possible means of settling disputes over the interpretation of the Convention: (i) the International Tribunal for the Law of the Sea (ITLOS) (a 21 -judge court located in Hamburg, Germany, established according to Annex VI); (ii) the International Court of Justice (in The Hague, Netherlands); (iii) an arbitral tribunal established pursuant to Annex VII; or (iv) a special arbitral tribunal established pursuant to Annex VIII to deal with specialized scientific issues. If the disputing countries have picked different procedures and cannot agree on a procedure, their dispute will be resolved through an Annex VII arbitration.

According to Article 297, controversies subject to mandatory dispute-resolution procedures include those involving coastal state environmental regulations that limit navigation (Article 297(1)(a) & (b)), allegations that a coastal state is violating internationally-established environmental regulations (Article 297(1)(c)), and allegations that a coastal state has improperly seized a vessel flying the flag of another country (Article 292). Coastal states are not required to submit to these dispute-resolution procedures their decisions regarding marine scientific research on their continental shelf and exclusive economic zone (Article 297(2)) and their decisions regarding management of their EEZ fisheries and the allocation of their surplus catch (Article 297(3)). Ratifying countries have the option of withdrawing from mandatory dispute resolution disagreements over maritime boundaries (Article 298(1)(a)), disputes concerning military activities (Article 298(1)(b)), and disputes that are pending before the U.N. Security Council (Article 298(1)(c)). Disputes relating to deep seabed mining are subject to a special regime, and the Seabed Disputes Chamber of ITLOS will deal with most of these controversies.

Emerging and Unresolved Issues

Is the Regime of Transit Passage through International Straits now Binding Customary International Law?

The United States has not yet ratified the Law of the Sea Convention, but has argued vigorously that the regime of transit passage through international straits is now part of binding customary international law. On August 17, 1987, the United States said:

The United States particularly rejects the assertions that the right of transit through straits used for international navigation, as articulated in the LOS Convention, are contractual rights and not codification of existing customs or established usage. The regimes of transit passage, as reflected in the Convention, are clearly based on customary practice of long standing and reflect the balance of rights and interests among all States, regardless of whether they have signed or ratified the Convention.[17]

Other countries have, however, viewed transit passage as emanating directly from the Law of the Sea Convention, and thus not applicable to countries that are not contracting parties,[18] and some commentators have suggested that the transit passage regime in the Law of the Sea Convention may not yet have been confirmed as customary international law because of "the attitude taken by a significant number of States which appear reluctant, either explicitly or implicitly, to accept the transit passage regime as a whole or some of its implications."[19] Some Greek scholars have argued, for instance, that Turkey would not be entitled to invoke the right of transit passage through the Aegean Sea (if Greece were to claim 12-mile territorial seas around its Aegean islands), because Turkey is not a contracting party to the Law of the Sea Convention.[20] Professor Scovazzi has explained that the Convention does not adequately protect the "vital concern" of states bordering straits regarding the protection of their marine environment.[21] In particular, the Convention provides only limited authority to the bordering states to enforce their environmental regulations, it does not create an adequate liability regime, nor does it require the prior notification of transit of ultrahazardous cargoes that would allow coastal states to protect their coastal populations and resources.[22] These inadequacies have led a number of straits-bordering states to promulgate regulations that appear to go beyond what is permitted by the Convention.[23] Professor Scovazzi concludes, therefore, that " [i]t is therefore possible to argue that the LOS Convention transit passage regime is still far from fully corresponding to present customary international law."[24]

Security Concerns

Article 39(1)(b) requires vessels and planes that are exercising their right of transit passage to "refrain from any threat or use of force against the sovereignty, territorial integrity of political independence of States bordering the strait, or in any other manner in violation of the principles of international law embodied in the Charter of the United Nations." Warships can, however, according to Professor Bernard Oxman, travel through straits in "squadron formation", and they may "communicate by radio, use radar or sonar, and, where circumstances permit, travel in defensive formation and use defensive maneuvers".[25] Professor Oxman, of the University of Miami, who was a member of the US delegation to the Law of the Sea negotiations, has also contended that the launching and recovery of aircraft from an aircraft carrier is a permitted activity during transit passage, so long as it does not constitute a threat or use of force against a straits state.[26]

If a vessel does engage in an activity other than those permitted under the transit passage regime, Article 38(3) states that it remains subject to the "other applicable principles" of the Convention. But it is unclear exactly what actions the coastal state can take in the light of such a threat. What should happen if an airplane that is purporting to exercise transit passage over a strait strays over land and then drops anti-government leaflets to the residents below? Professor Oxman has acknowledged that straits states can take action under Article 233 against nongovernmental ships "causing or threatening major damage to the marine environment of the straits". He suggests that no action can be taken against military ships or planes no matter how nefarious their behavior might be.[27] Satya Nandan has suggested that the only appropriate action is to require the ship or plane to continue expeditiously through the strait:

It is implicit therefore, that any activity threatening a coastal State would bring the ship or aircraft under the general regime of innocent passage and enable that State to require the vessel to leave the area expeditiously (Art. 30) presumably, in the direction it was travelling, since transit passage cannot be suspended for any reason (Art. 44) (including threats to security.[28]

The recent security concerns of countries adjacent to the Strait of Malacca and those using the Straits have been focused on piracy, and concerns about terrorist bombings are also serious ones. In early July 2006, for instance, pirates boarded and robbed in the Strait of Malacca two ships chartered by the United Nations carrying construction materials for tsunami-torn Aceh and attempted to board a Japanese cargo ship that was able to defend itself with floodlights and fire hoses.[29] The major military powers and main users of the Straits have frequently expressed an interest in helping to patrol the Straits, but Malaysia and Indonesia have strenuously resisted this idea, saying that the only assistance they would be willing to accept would be information, intelligence, and technical equipment. Singapore and Indonesia have established a joint radar surveillance system in the Singapore Strait, called Project Supric, to allow their navies to observe activities in the Strait.[30] These countries want to undertake the active security operations themselves, but activities such as providing armed escorting vessels to commercial vessels are expensive, and the question inevitably arises whether it would be lawful to introduce a compensation scheme so that the users of the straits would pay for the necessary security measures.

Can Ships be Charged for Passing through Straits?

Historically, ships have been required to pay for passage through straits, in the Baltic Straits in particular and also in the Strait of Malacca when they were under Portuguese control, payments are now required for certain services related to passage through the Turkish Straits, and payments are always required for passage through canals. Article 37(1) of the Law of the Sea Convention says that "the right of transit passage...shall not be impeded," but Article 42 allows countries bordering on straits to promulgate a variety of laws regulating passage and Article 43 says that "[u]ser States and States bordering a strait should by agreement cooperate" to establish navigational aids and "for the prevention, reduction and control of pollution from ships". No such formal agreements have, however, yet been established under Article 43.

Article 26 is entitled "Charges Which May Be Levied Upon Foreign Ships," and its paragraph 2 indicates that a coastal state can charge ships passing through its territorial sea "for specific services rendered to the ship." Does this provision apply to a ship in the territorial sea of a country bordering on a strait while the ship is exercising its right to transit passage through the strait? No provision in Part III on "Straits Used for International Navigation" says explicitly that it does not apply, and application of Article 26(2) does not directly conflict with the purposes of Part III.

If a ship is passing through a strait narrower than 24 nautical miles wide, it must of necessity be in the territorial sea of one of the strait states, but is a ship in the territorial sea of a strait state as a juridical matter when it is exercising its right of transit passage through the strait? One author has suggested that "[t]he transit passage regime implies, as regards navigation, that the strait is no longer to be considered as part of the territorial sea of a strait State and that coastal State powers in the strait are different from those it can generally exercise in the territorial sea."[31] The strait states would generally disagree with this characterization, and would argue that "sovereignty and jurisdiction over the waters, air space, seabed, and subsoil of the straits are still subject to other rules of international law."[32] Satya Nandan has sided with the straits states on this issue and has said that "[t]here is nothing in the Convention which prohibits charges for similar services [similar to the (specific services rendered to the ship allowed under Article 26(2)] in straits which are part of the territorial sea."[33]

The subject of compensation came up during the negotiations, with the strait States arguing in 1971 that they should be compensated for expenditures designed to promote navigational safety[34] and the United States opposing any requirement of compensation.[35] Professor Oxman has contended that the absence of specific language in Part III comparable to that of Article 26(2) was not unintentional, that Article 43 was included to address the issue of fees in the context of straits, and hence that straits states cannot charge fees for services absent an Article 43 agreement.[36] Article 43 is cast in "conditional, non-mandatory terms,"[37] according to Satya Nandan and Judge David Anderson, and efforts to make its language obligatory were not accepted by the negotiating conference.[38] As Satya Nandan has explained, the problem of compensating strait States for their services was "addressed in a perfunctory manner in article 43 of the Convention, which exhorts user States to cooperate through agreements to assist strait States, [but] the fact is that apart from the exceptional case of Japan's cooperation in respect of the Malacca and Singapore Straits, such cooperation has not materialized."[39]

Satya Nandan has noted that the issue of compensation to strait States "has been festering for some time" and has explained that:

Straits States are legitimately concerned with the financial burdens they have to bear for establishing and managing traffic separation schemes, for installing and maintaining navigational aids, and by the pollution they must endure, without receiving any corresponding benefits, since many ships transit straits en route to ports in other States.[40]

Nandan has noted that this "matter remains unresolved" and that "a meaningful global solution would be difficult to achieve," and has suggested that the special circumstances of each strait need to be examined separately and has recognized that " [a]ccount also has to be taken of the sensitivity of the straits States to any diminution in the exercise of sovereignty over the strait."[41]

If Article 26(2) does apply to straits, what "specific services" could strait States charge for? Among those that might fall into the "specific services" category would be pilotage, towing, and escorting services, because they would be applied to specific vessels to ensure they success of their voyages. If the ship requests such services from the coastal state, then the charging of a fee would certainly seem appropriate. But can the strait state require the passing ship to accept such services if it does not want them?

One strait where a compulsory pilotage scheme seems to be emerging is the Torres Strait, between Australia and Papua New Guinea. In May 1996, the IMO approved a reporting regime for the Torres Strait region between Australia and Papua New Guinea and the inner route of Australia's Great Barrier Reef.[42] In 2003, Australia and Papua New Guinea jointly applied to have the Torres Strait area declared to be a particularly sensitive sea area (PSSA),[43] which was subsequently approved. The IMO's Maritime Safety Committee (MSC) and its Marine Environment Protection Committee (MEPC) have both endorsed Australia's initiative to extend the mandatory pilotage provisions governing passage through the Great Barrier Reef (which has previously been designated as a PSSA) to the Torres Strait area.[44] Although the United States has noted that this IMO action is only "recommendatory,"[45] it will become mandatory, at least under Australian law, when Australia acts to extend its compulsory pilotage program to the Torres Strait region. If the user States accept the duty to utilize an Australian pilot during passage through the Torres Strait pursuant to the IMO resolutions, then their agreement would conform to the responsibility under Article 43 to reach agreements for navigational safety and "for the prevention, reduction and control of pollution from ships".

The Strait of Malacca might be a logical candidate to be designated as a "particularly sensitive sea area" because of the human and economic dependency on this Strait. Its economic importance as a transport channel is unquestioned,[46] and the closure of the Strait because of an accident or act of terrorism would be disastrous to the region and the world, and other economic activities to the region include offshore fishing, tourism, and mangrove harvesting. The vulnerability of the Strait from an accident, act of terrorism, or act of piracy is also clear. If the Strait were to be designated as a PSSA, the countries bordering on the Strait would have strong arguments that they could require escorts and charge users for activities related to patrolling and protecting the Strait. Under Article 211(6)(a) they could petition the IMO to approve "laws and regulations for the prevention, reduction and control of pollution from vessels".

In September 1997, the United Kingdom submitted an information paper to the Legal Committee of the IMO entitled Developing Principles for Charging Users the Cost of Maritime Infrastructure, which suggested that the organization should develop a set of fair and equitable principles governing the charges that strait States could charge users for navigational aids and other services to passing vessels.[47] The paper argued that such aids were important to the shipping industry and that it was unfair to impose the expenses solely on the coastal states.[48] The paper suggested that charges should be exacted on a nondiscriminatory basis and that they "would be linked to the recovery of costs, including capital investment and improvements, but there would be no element of profit since that would amount to tax on traffic."[49] The Committee did not act on this proposal because of the complexity of the legal issues.

One further reason why this problem is so vexing is that "[t]he issue cannot be left just for straits States and flag States to resolve, for many flag States, as it is well known, are mere flags of convenience with little or no capacity to assist. The term 'user States' in Article 43 must therefore include States other than flag States, whose nationals benefit from safe passage."[50] The category of "user States" must therefore also include "exporting states, receiving States, and States of ship-owners, insurers of ships and cargoes and major oil corporations whose global trade is facilitated."[51]

Military Activities in the EEZ[52]

Can countries engage in military exercises and manoeuvres, including the firing of weapons, in the exclusive economic zone of another country? The text of the 1982 United Nations Law of the Sea Convention addresses this question in Article 58 (1):

In the exclusive economic zone, all States, whether coastal or landlocked, enjoy, subject to the relevant provisions of this Convention, the freedoms referred to in Article 87 of navigation and overflight and of the laying submarine cables and pipelines, and other internationally lawful uses of the sea related to these freedoms such as those associated with the operation of ships, aircraft and submarine cables and pipelines, and compatible with the other provisions of this Convention.

Article 87 recognizes the freedom of navigation for all states in the high seas, and Article 58(1) thus confirms that this same right also exists in the exclusive economic zone, subject, however, to the qualifications found in Article 58(3):

In exercising their rights and performing their duties under this Convention in the exclusive economic zone, States shall have due regard to the rights and duties of the coastal State and shall comply with the laws and regulations adopted by the coastal State in accordance with the provisions of this Convention and other rules of international law in so far as they are not incompatible with this Part.

When Brazil signed the Convention on December 10, 1982, it issued a Declaration containing the following language:

(3) The Brazilian Government understands that the provisions of Article 301, which prohibits "any threat or use of force against the territorial integrity or political independence of any State, or in any other manner inconsistent with the principles of international law embodied in the Charter of the United Nations", apply, in particular, to the maritime areas under the sovereignty or the jurisdiction of the coastal State.

(4) The Brazilian Government understands that the provisions of the Convention do not authorize other States to carry out in the exclusive economic zone military exercises or manoeuvres, in particular those that imply the use of weapons or explosives, without the consent of the coastal State.

Is Brazil's "understanding" of the Convention correct?[53] Since then similar declarations have been filed by Cape Verde, India, Malaysia, Pakistan, and Uruguay, and sharply opposing declarations have been filed by Germany, Italy, the Netherlands, and the United Kingdom.[54] What is the effect of these "declarations" and "understandings"? Article 309 of the Convention prohibits ratifying countries from filing reservations that would have the effect of opting out of any of the Convention's obligation, but Article 310 does permit states to make declarations explaining the relationship of the Convention's provisions to their own laws "provided that such declarations or statements do not purport to exclude or to modify the legal effect of the provisions of this Convention in their application to that State."

Also relevant to the analysis of what military activities are permissible near the coasts of other countries is Article 2(4) of the United Nations Charter[55] which says that: "All members shall refrain in their international relations from the threat or use of force against the territorial integrity or political independence of any state, or in any other manner inconsistent with the Purposes of the United Nations."[56] This limitation is reinforced by Article 88 of the Law of the Sea Convention which says that "[t]he high seas shall be reserved for peaceful purposes," and which explicitly applies to the exclusive economic zone pursuant to Article(2).[57]

Are there some military activities in the coastal areas that would be viewed as inherently threatening? Are there some that would threaten the marine environment and offshore resources in the exclusive economic zone, which the coastal state is obliged to protect and authorized to exploit? Could a coastal state rightly require that it be notified prior to military manoeuvres occurring in its EEZ pursuant to the overarching international-law obligation to consult with affected states prior to engaging in activities that might threaten their interests?[58]

During the negotiations, some countries expressed strong opposition to military activities in the exclusive economic zone, because of the threats such activities present to coastal communities and marine resources. Delegates focused particularly on military activities that involved the use of weapons, the launching of aircraft, espionage, interference with coastal communications, and propaganda aimed at the coastal communities. Among the nations that expressed concern were Peru, Brazil, Albania, the Khmer Republic (Cambodia), North Korea, Costa Rica, Ecuador, El Salvador, Pakistan, the Philippines, Portugal, Senegal, Somalia, and Uruguay.[59] The delegate of China said "freedom of scientific research in the past has meant espionage" and sought clarification about what activity would be considered legitimate scientific research in the EEZ.[60] The United States took the consistent position during these negotiations that military activities on the high seas and in the EEZ were consistent with the "peaceful purpose" requirement if they were conducted in a nonthreatening fashion in order to prepare for legitimate self-defecse.[61]

Governing principles of international law emerge from multilateral treaties and from state practices undertaken with a sense of legal obligation which provide evidence of an international consensus that certain behaviour is required. Where the text of a governing treaty leaves certain matters ambiguous or unresolved, the subsequent practices of states become particularly important to determine the proper interpretation of the treaty's provisions.[62] One commentator has concluded that "[i]n the case of military exercises in the exclusive economic zone no prevailing orientation or trend can be inferred from present States practice."[63]

This topic, which has been examined in detail elsewhere,[64] thus remains controversial. Do maritime nations have unlimited authority to engage in all variety of military activities in the exclusive economic zones of other coastal states, or does the duty of "due regard" impose limits on such activities, particularly with regard to the launching of missiles and other weapons?

The Disagreements Regarding Hydrographic Surveys

The issue regarding whether hydrographic surveying to aid navigational safety is "marine scientific research"[65] continues to fester. In December 2002,

China announced that it had enacted a new law explicitly requiring Chinese approval of all survey and mapping activities in China's EEZ, and stating that unapproved ocean survey activity will be subject to fines and confiscation of equipment and data.[66]

The Proliferation Security Initiative

In a speech delivered in Poland on May 31, 2003, US President George W. Bush outlined the (Proliferation Security Initiative, whereby the United States is trying to mobilize "like-minded states" to prepare for and participate in naval intercept operations designed to inspect ships thought to be carrying nuclear materials to or from "rogue" states, notably North Korea and perhaps also Iran. The countries most actively supporting this US-initiative are Spain, France, the United Kingdom, Portugal, Australia, Germany, Italy, Japan, the Netherlands, and Poland.

The countries coordinating efforts met several times during 2003 and held a number of joint exercises to practice interdiction techniques. Related to these efforts were the seizure by Taiwan of 150 barrels of dual-use chemicals from a North Korean freighter when it stopped in Kaohsiung to refuel,[67] the confiscation of 22-tonnes of ultra-strong dual-use aluminum tubing bound for North Korea on the French-flagged vessel Ville de Virgo when it was about to enter the Suez Canal on April 12, 2003,[68] and Japan's searches of the cargoes of North Korean ferries when they are in Japanese ports.[69]

After numerous meetings, the concerned countries issued a "Statement of Interdiction Principles" in September 2003 including the following:

- Countries agree to inspect suspicious vessels flying their own flag and will consider allowing other countries to inspect suspicious vessels flying their flag.
- Countries agree to stop and search suspicious vessels in their internal waters, territorial seas, or contiguous zones.
- Countries agree to require suspicious vessels entering or leaving their ports, internal waters or territorial seas to be boarded and searched for such cargoes prior to entry.

Although the public statements have said that these endeavours would be undertaken in a manner that is consistent with international law, it is also clear that the United States and its allies are seeking to expand international law to permit more active interception when warranted. President Bush's National Security Advisor Condoleezza Rice explained recently that:

While all actions will be taken consistent with existing national and international legal authorities, we are also seeking ways to expand those authorities. And it is for this reason that the President proposed in his September address to the United Nations that the Security Council adopt a resolution calling on all states to criminalize proliferation activities, establish effective export controls, and ensure the safety and security of sensitive materials and technologies.[70]

Australia's Foreign Minister Alexander Downer also has expressed support for changing the law permitting free navigation on the high seas in order to stop North Korea' shipping of missiles, nuclear materials, and drugs to its allies or customers.[71]

Balancing Navigational Freedom with Environmental and Security Concerns

The break up of the oil tanker Prestige off the coast of Spain in November 2002 provided a defining moment that appears to have changed perceptions and the governing law. Spain refused to permit the crippled tanker to come into a Spanish port for "safe haven," and then when the vessel was towed out into the open ocean it broke apart causing a dramatic and destructive spillage of its cargo. After huge amounts of oil washed up along the beautiful and resource-rich coasts of Spain, Portugal, and France, France and Spain issued a decree that said:

A. All oil tankers traveling through these two countries' EEZs will have to provide advance notice to the coastal countries about their cargo, destination, flag, and operators.
B. All single-hulled tankers more than 15 years old traveling through the EEZs of Spain and France will be subject to spot inspections by coastal maritime authorities while in the adjacent EEZs and will be expelled from the EEZs if they are determined, after inspection, to be not seaworthy.[72]

Shortly after the Spanish-French decree, Portugal announced that it would also take the same position on this issue.[73] And then Morocco announced that single-hull oil tankers more than 15 years old carrying heavy fuel, tar, asphaltic bitumen or heavy crude oil would be subject to the requirement that they provide prior notification and adhere to strict safety regulations.[74]

Also in the spring of 2003, the European Union banned large single-hulled tankers carrying heavy grade oil from coming into any European ports, and on April 3, 2003, the French National Assembly unanimously adopted a new law asserting the right to intercept ships out to a distance 90 miles from its Mediterranean coast that release polluting ballast waters and also imposing stricter controls on transient oil tankers.[75] Captains of vessels violating these new French rules can be sentenced to up to four years in prison and fined up to $600,000.[76] About this same time, Spain, France, and Portugal were joined by Belgium and the United Kingdom in submitting a petition to the International Maritime Organization (IMO) to declare virtually their entire EEZs to be "particularly sensitive sea areas" that would be completely off-limits for single-hulled oil tankers and other cargo vessels transporting dangerous cargoes.[77] Although the IMO has not yet approved this initiative, this effort by five maritime countries to protect their own coastal resources provides strong support for the view that it is legitimate to restrict maritime freedom in order to protect the resources of the EEZ.

Even the United States has imposed some restrictions on navigational freedoms to protect its environmental and security interests. In December 1998, for instance, the International Maritime Organization (IMO) approved a US proposal to require ships transiting through the northeast and southeast coasts of the United States to report their locations and travel plans in order to protect the northern right whale from being hit by ships.[78] This whale species was hunted almost to extinction because of its oil, and is now thought to be the rarest whale species in the world. This mandatory ship reporting area joins nine others that have been established by IMO to protect other fragile environmental areas.[79]

Although it is not yet clear how all these conflicts will be sorted out, it seems that we are in a period of reassessment and transition regarding how to strike the balance between navigational freedoms and the right of coastal states to limit navigation to protect their environment and security. The law of the sea has always been created through the give-and-take process of states make conflicting claims, which are ultimately resolved through negotiation, a decision rendered by a tribunal or international organization, military force, or a pattern of practice that emerges and is accepted as obligatory by those concerned about the issue.[80] We are in a particularly active law-making period at present regarding navigational rights and responsibilities, and it appears that the law that will emerge will be different than the law that had existed previously

Use of Low Frequency Sonar[81]

On July 15, 2002, the U.S. National Marine Fisheries Service (NMFS) exempted the US Navy's Low Frequency Active Sonar (LFAS) program from the requirements of the Marine Mammal Protection Act after determining that its operation would have a "negligible impact" on any species.[82] NMFS thus authorized the Navy to use two ships to transmit low frequency active sonar in about 75 per cent of the world's oceans (exempting the polar extremes). Ten weeks later, in late September 2002, fifteen Cuvier's beaked whales beached on the Canary Islands at the same time the U.S. destroyer Mahan was manoeuvering in the area with ships from nine other members of the North Atlantic Treaty Organization.[83] Autopsies of the whales revealed brain damage consistent with an acoustic impact. This mass stranding followed similar incidents near the Bahamas in March 2000,[84] near Greece in 1996,[85] and in the Canaries between 1985 and 1989.[86] The U.S. Navy's Surveillance Towed Array Sensor System (SURTASS) Low Frequency Active Sonar (LFAS) will employ very loud low-frequency sounds (less than 500 Hz with intensity levels as great as 230 dB re: 1μPa at 1 m), posing a significant threat to the safety and welfare of marine mammals, and possibly to other forms of marine life as well.[87] The transmitted sound will be about 215-dB at its source, arrayed in a manner to have "an effective source level" of 230-240-dB.[88] According to the Navy's environmental impact statement (EIS), the sound would be at the 180-dB level one kilometre from the source, at 173-dB two kilometres from the source, about 165-dB 40 nautical miles from the source, at the150-160-dB level up to 100 miles from the source, and some 140-dB 400 miles from the source vessel.[89] (Decibel levels are logarithmic in nature, so that a sound of 180-dB is ten times as intense as one of 170-dB.) The sounds are not transmitted uniformly in all directions from the source, but travel in a beam that is a few hundred feet in width.[90] These sounds are the loudest ever put into the world's oceans by humans, with the possible exception of underground explosions. They are designed to travel great distances and are audible by humans 1000 kilometres away without any signal processing.

In October 2002, federal Magistrate Judge Elizabeth D. LaPorte determined that the Navy's use of low frequency active sonar was likely to violate four US statutes and to cause irreparable injury to ocean creatures, and she thus issued a preliminary injunction restricting the Navy's actions, but allowing further testing and training of personnel regarding this system.[91] The court explained: "It is undisputed that marine mammals, many of whom depend on sensitive hearing for essential activities like finding food and mates and avoiding predators, and some of whom are endangered species, will at a minimum be harassed by the extremely loud and far traveling LFA sonar."[92] The subsequent agreement between the parties allowed the Navy to test its sonar in an area of the Western Pacific extending from Saipan, in the Commonwealth of the Northern Mariana Islands, to Japan's Bonin Islands, south of Tokyo, pending the hearing for a preliminary injunction.[93] About the same time, another federal judge in Northern California issued a temporary restraining order blocking geographers from the National Science Foundation, Columbia University, and the Georgia Institute of Technology from mapping the sea floor with 220-dB sound blasts which had killed at least two beaked whales.[94]

In January 2003, U.S. District Judge Samuel Conti of the Northern District of California made an additional ruling against sonar use, blocking experiments (authorized by NMFS) that were to be conducted by Woods Hole Oceanographic Institution scientist Dr. Peter Tyack to determine the effect of the sound on the gray whales migrating along the West Coast of California to their winter grounds along the coast of Mexico.[95] Judge Conti ruled that because the permits involved "major amendments" to the original project, which had generated "public controversy", it was necessary to conduct a proper environmental impact assessment under the National Environmental Protection Act before undertaking the experiments. In the process of "balancing" the "harms" to determine whether to issue an injunction, Judge Conti noted that the population of gray whales had been dropping since 1984 (from 21,942 individuals to 17,414) and that "Dr. Tyack's proposed experiments might inflict unacceptable levels of harm on the gray whales". [96]

If US judges eventually allow the Navy and other researchers to proceed with this powerful new sonar, this activity is sure to be challenged at the international level. The unusually loud sounds emitted in the LFAS process would certainly be considered "pollution" under Article 1(1)(4) of the Law of the Sea Convention, which is defined as: the introduction by man, directly or indirectly, of substances or energy into the marine environment, including estuaries, which results or is likely to result in such deleterious effects as harm to living resources and marine life, hazards to human health, hindrance to marine activities, including fishing and other legitimate uses of the sea, impairment of quality for use of sea water and reduction of amenities. (Emphasis added)

Sound is a "form of energy manifested by small pressure and/or particle velocity variations in a continuous medium."[97] "While the definition of [pollution in the Law of the Sea Convention] was...not drafted with acoustic pollution in mind, the inclusion of 'energy' implies that noise can be a form of pollution under the terms of the LOS Convention."[98] Although the US Navy did prepare an EIS, the scientific tests it relied upon were woefully inadequate because they did not test the effects above 155-dB and, even so, these tests demonstrated that LFAS will have significant negative impacts on marine mammals.[99]

Claims to an Extended Continental Shelf

The Law of the Sea Convention allows countries to claim a continental shelf beyond their 200-nautical-mile EEZ, to a line 350 nautical miles from their coastal baselines, if they can establish that their continental shelf meets the complicated formula found in Article 76. This provision may be of substantial importance in the Arctic, now that the ice in that region is breaking up, as exemplified by Russia's planting of a flag on the sea floor of the North Pole on August 2, 2007. Russia was not claiming the North Pole, but was exploring the seabed to see whether it could justify a claim to an extended continental shelf under Article 76. The United States may also be able to make an extended continental shelf claim in the Arctic region, perhaps claiming "more than 200,000 square miles of additional undersea territories,"[100] but its ability to make such a claim credibly will be substantially weakened if it remains outside the Law of the Sea Convention.[101]

Allocation of High Seas Fishing Resources

As living resources become increasingly scarce, it has become clear that Grotius' vision of freedom to fish on the high seas is no longer realistic and that the fish stocks of the high seas will have to be allocated among those nations seeking to harvest them. The initial allocations will be very important, because countries will come to see their allocations as a "property right" and will expect to receive at least the same allocation in future years. What criteria can be used to conduct this allocation process?

Everyone who has ventured an opinion about the challenge of allocating fish agrees that such allocations should be both "equitable" and "efficient," but giving meaning to those terms remains elusive. One typical well-meaning but vague pronouncement on this topic provides the following language:

Equity in the allocation of both rights and obligations. Regimes that balance the competing interests of all participants are likely to be perceived as the most legitimate, which should in turn promote higher levels of compliance with agreed fishing rules. Among the many balances to be found are: those that have historically participated vs. new entrants; coastal States vs. distant water fishing States; developed States vs. developing States.[102]

Conservation is Paramount

Michael W. Lodge and Satya N. Nandan have made the important point that "allocation rights, both in the EEZ and on the high seas, are subordinate to the obligation to conserve."[103] At the present time, they note, "neither UNFSA, nor the decision rules of many existing RFMOs, provide mechanisms for allocation that balance conservation interests with the economic and social interests of states. In fact, within many RFMOs, negotiated criteria for catch allocations are often based on the notion of historical catch, which is a powerful incentive to indulge in a race to fish."[104] And, they add, the problem of overfishing may be exacerbated by "adding developing state fishing capacity to existing overcapacity, especially where this operates simply as a mechanism to support reflagging and transfer of effort by distant water fishing nations (DWFNs)."[105]

Professor Ted L. McDorman has noted that "the setting of the total allowable catch (TAC)" and "quota allocation decisions...are inevitably the most controversial" for regional fishery management organizations (RFMOs).[106] He suggests looking to the considerations listed in Article 11 of the Straddling and Migratory Fish Stocks Agreement governing the participation of new members of fishery organizations for guidance regarding allocation rights within the fishery—"the status of the stocks and existing fishing efforts; existing fishing patterns (historic fishing activity); economic need and coastal state dependence; and contribution to conservation."[107] He stresses that consensus is important to ensure support for the allocation decisions, and suggest that to promote consensus "in years, and for stocks where consensus cannot be reached, that the quotas for each member decline by a pre-set amount (e.g. 20%) for each year non-consensus prevails."[108]

"Equity" is a complicated and multifaceted concept, with different applications in different contexts. It certainly includes the concept of being "fair," but just as certainly it does not inevitably mean that everyone should receive an equal amount. In the maritime boundary context, Articles 74 and 83 of the Law of the Sea Convention require opposite and adjacent states to reach an "equitable solution", language was chosen instead of phrasing that would have stated that boundaries should be drawn along the "median" or "equidistance" line separating the land areas of the countries. The concept of an "equitable solution" in the boundary context has generated a series of specific rules, including, for instance, that the boundary that would exist if the equidistance line were utilized should be adjusted in light of the length of the coastlines of the competing countries, because the coastlines provide some rough indication of the relationship between the country and the adjacent waters.[109]

Should Allocation be Based on Population? Or On a State's "Dependence" on Fish for Food Security?

If the focus remains on "equity," then obviously some attention to the numbers of mouths that need to be fed is relevant to any allocation decision. Some may argue that a fish-per-capita allocation system, perhaps with some modifications for unique "equitable" considerations, makes sense and offers some elegant simplicity. Others would point out that some communities "depend" on fish or enjoy eating fish more than others, and would argue historical fishing practices should be recognized as the baseline from which allocations should be made. Still others[110] might suggest that utilizing historical fishing practices will inevitably reward the more developed countries, which have been able to finance large fishing operations, and will once again disadvantage developing countries. Basing allocations on historical fishing activities will tend to reward those countries that have overcapitalized and subsidized their fishing fleets, thus giving benefits for activities that have distorted the market and which would be punished in other economic sectors.

The Importance of "Contiguity" or Geographical Proximity

A system focused on population would allow the populated nations to come into all regions with priorities to harvest the fish, and would ignore the link between the residents of the area and the nearby fish. Any equitable system of allocation will have to recognize the importance of geographical proximity, or contiguity, to the allocation choices that must be made. Especially since regional fishery management organizations frequently have responsibilities over fish within exclusive economic zones as well as fish on the high seas, the allocation decisions made by the organizations must recognize the "sovereign rights" that states have to the fish in their EEZs, which gives them a substantial priority in any allocation scheme. In the Pacific, the Pacific Island communities must have a priority to the fish in their region because of their geographical proximity and because they are developing nations that are entitled to assistance and priorities under both the Law of the Sea Convention and the Straddling and Migratory Fish Stocks Agreement.

How Should States be Rewarded for Good Behaviour?

Careful management of fish stocks is expensive and challenging, and countries that make financial sacrifices to monitor and maintain threatened fish stocks should receive some reward for their actions. This principle forms the basis of Article 66 of the Law of the Sea Convention, which says that "[s]tates in whose rivers anadromous stocks originate shall have the primary interest in and responsibility for such stocks." Because the spawning habitat of salmon and other anadromous species must be maintained carefully to enable them to reproduce successfully, it has been recognized that the countries that maintain their river systems to permit successful spawning should be able to reap the bounty of the salmon harvest. This principle means that even when the salmon are in the high seas, they cannot be caught without explicit permission of the country of origin. If we extrapolate from this principle, we should find ways of rewarding countries that invest in the monitoring and maintenance of fish stocks by giving them allocation bonuses.

How Should States be Punished for Using Selfish and Destructive Fishing Practices?

Another aspect of "equity" is that countries must be held accountable for taking more than their share and engaging in destructive fishing practices. The highly destructive high seas bottom trawling, for instance, is an unsustainable practice that does "major damage" to biodiversity and destroys "resources that should be available to all states."[111] Other examples of selfish and unacceptable activities include providing a flag to vessels that engage in improper fishing activities and distorting the market by subsidizing fishing vessels.

Controlling IUU Fishing

Obviously, any solution to the overfishing of high seas fisheries must involve true cooperation and transparency, which must include bringing the practice of "illegal, unregulated, and unreported" (IUU) fishing under control. This effort will require revisions to the flag-of-convenience system that allows many fishing vessels to operated with limited regulation. It will also require use of modern satellite-based vessel-monitoring-system (VMS) technology, on-board independent observers, and detailed boarding and inspection programs to increase monitoring and thus permit active enforcement of regulations.[112]

Flags of Convenience

The problem of IUU fishing is directly related to the extensive use of flags of convenience: there has to be a collective effort to deal with the related and urgent problems of IUU fishing and free riders. The problem is that, despite the advances made by the 1995 Agreement and the various measures adopted through the FAO, not all flag states are able or willing to exercise effectively their responsibilities for fishing vessels flying their flags on the high seas. Urgent action is needed to address this problem. It is a matter of great concern that seven out of the 11 cases before the International Tribunal for the Law of the Sea related to the activities of fishing vessels flying so-called flags of convenience, or flags or non-compliance.[113]

Numerous strategies have been proposed to deal with the flag-of-convenience conundrum, such as "co-ordinating global and regional high seas vessel registers, vessel monitoring systems, port state measures, the use of trade measures and so on," but the essential answer is that states must "take full responsibility for the activities of their nationals, regardless of the flag of the fishing vessel concerned."[114]

Evolving into a Rights-Based System

The allocation decisions that will be made by regional fishery management organizations in the next few years are extremely important, because it is almost inevitable that the allocation schemes will evolve into something akin to a "rights-based" system, and that countries will view their allocation quotas as a vested property right that they are entitled to maintain in future years. Professor McDorman seemed to recognize this phenomenon, when he proposed that countries' quotas from last year be automatically cut 20 per cent for the current year if they cannot reach a consensus on the allocation for the current year.[115] In other words, he appeared to accept the idea that last year's quota would be the starting point for any discussion about allocation for this year and coming years. Each allocation will thus have importance not just for the current year, but because it will set a baseline for future years, and states will seek to maintain and increase their allocation. States will make investments in reliance on the allocations given to them, and they will insist that they are entitled to continue fishing at the rate that they have fished in previous years.

Summary

The decisions made by the regional fishery management organizations allocating fish must be "equitable" and "efficient". Translating such vague terms into actionable criteria is one of the major challenges of our generation. The analysis presented above suggests that these criteria must include the following elements:

- Conservation values must be paramount and the precautionary approach must be utilized to ensure that fish stocks remain bountiful for future generations. Countries must share data regarding their fishing activities and must support scientific research to understand the life cycle of each species and its relationships with other species in its ecosystem.

- Developing countries must be given priorities in the allocation of stocks and must be given assistance so that they can utilize their allocations effectively.
- Geographical proximity to the fish stocks must be recognized as an important element of any allocation scheme. When the stocks straddle EEZs of states, those states have a particularly strong claim to a substantial share of the allocation quota, but even for stocks outside the EEZ, the countries in the region should have a priority over those outside the region.
- Countries that make expenditures to monitor and maintain the fish stocks should be rewarded with enhanced allocations.
- Those countries that misbehave by abusing the flag-of-convenience system, by permitting IUU fishing, by allowing their vessels to engage in destructive high-seas bottom trawling, and by subsidizing their fishing industry should be punished by having their allocations reduced.
- The population of a country, its historical dependence on the fisheries in question, and its historical consumption of sea food and need for it as "food security" are also relevant considerations, although of less importance than those listed above.

Decisions must, of course, be made through a transparent process, and by consensus whenever possible. The process of allocation will be one of trial-and-error in the early years, and, because we still know so little about many species and many ocean area, precaution must always guide the allocations.

Conclusion

The 1982 Law of the Sea Convention has served to regulate ocean activities for a quarter of a century and will continue to be the main document utilized to guide conduct and resolve disputes. This carefully-crafted treaty includes many compromises and leaves some issues unresolved or ambiguous, but it will be the starting point that officials and scholars turn to when conflicts arise. It has brought substantial stability, has allowed countries to utilize ocean resources cooperatively, and will be viewed in coming generations as one of the international community's crowning achievements.

But where should we go from here? Should we undertake the ambitious task of negotiating a new treaty, or should we address individual problems with individual solutions? Would an attempt to negotiate a new treaty lead to new solutions, or just a reiteration of the ambiguous language used in past efforts? Probably, given the deep divisions among countries at the present time, it is best to focus on specific issues to try to provide specific solutions through new directed instruments and protocols rather than try to revise the entire document at this point. ■

Notes

1. United Nations Convention on the Law of the Sea, Dec. 10, 1982, U.N. Doc. A/CONF.62/122, reprinted in 21 I.L.M. 1261 (1982) and The Law of the Sea: Official Text of the United Nations Convention on the Law of the Sea with Annexes and Index, UN Sales No. E.83.V.5 (1983).
2. Chronological Lists of Ratifications of Accessions and Successions to the Convention and the Related Agreements as of 1 February 2008. <http://www.un.org/Depts/los/convention_agreements/convention_agreements.htm> (last visited Feb. 4, 2008).
3. Presidential Proclamation No. 2667, 10 Fed. Reg. 12303 (1945), 4 Digest of International Law 756-58 (Margery Whiteman ed. 1965); see 2 Foreign Relations of the United States, 1945, at 1502.
4. Convention on the Territorial Sea and Contiguous Zone, April 29, 1958, 516 U.N.T.S. 205, 15 U.S.T. 1606; Convention on the High Seas, April 29, 1958, 450 U.N.T.S. 82, 13 U.S.T. 2312; Convention on Fishing and Conservation of Living Resources of the High Seas, April 29, 1958, 17 U.S.T. 138, 599 U.N.T.S. 285; Convention on the Continental Shelf, April 29, 1958, 499 U.N.T.S. 311, 15 U.S.T. 471.
5. In 1967, Ambassador Arvid Pardo of Malta told the U.N. General Assembly that vast riches lay scattered across the floor of the deep seabed in the form of exploitable, softball-sized rocks and offered the "Pardo proposal" urging that they be viewed as the "common heritage" of humankind. (This idea was also developed in John Mero, The Mineral Resources of the Sea (1965).) Within three years of Ambassador Pardo's speech, an international consensus developed that these nodules should be viewed as a "common heritage" resource, that national claims of exclusive rights to seabed resources must be prohibited, that exploitation should take place pursuant to an international legal regime, and that developing nations should share genuine benefits from seabed exploitation. The key international document recognizing this consensus was the U.N. General Assembly's 1970 Declaration of Principles Governing the Seabed and the Ocean Floor, and the Subsoil Thereof, Beyond the Limits of National Jurisdiction. U.N. General Assembly's 1970 Declaration of Principles Governing the Seabed and the Ocean Floor, and the Subsoil Thereof, Beyond the Limits of National Jurisdiction, G.A. Res. 2749 (XXV), 25 U.N. GAOR, Supp. No. 28, at 24, U.N. Doc. A/8028 (1970).
6. George Galdorisi, *The United States and the Law of the Sea: Decade of Decision* in The United States and the 1982 Law of the Sea Convention: The Cases Pro and Con7, 16-17 (George Galdorisi, Doug Bandow, and M. Casey Jarman eds., Law of the Sea Institute Occasional Paper No. 38, 1994).
7. See, e.g., Jon M. Van Dyke, *The Disappearing Right to Navigational Freedom in the*

Exclusive Economic Zone, 29 Marine Policy 107-21 (2005).

8. Law of the Sea Convention, *supra* note 1, Article 246.
9. See generally Freedom for the Seas for the 21st Century 72 (Jon M. Van Dyke, Durwood Zaelke & Grant Hewison eds. 1993).
10. *Fisheries Case*, (United Kingdom v. Norway), 1951 I.C.J. 116.
11. Agreement for the Implementation of the Provisions of the United Nations Convention on the Law of the Sea of 10 December 1982 Relating to the Conservation and Management of Straddling Fish Stocks and Highly Migratory Fish Stocks, UN Doc. A/CONF.164/37, 34 I.L.M. 1542 (1995). See generally Jameson E. Colburn, *Comment, Turbot Wars: Straddling Stocks, Regime Theory, and a New U.N. Agreement*, 6 J. Transnat'l Law & Policy 323 (1997); Derrick M. Kedziora, *Gunboat Diplomacy in the Northwest Atlantic: The 1995 Canada-EU Fishing Dispute and the United Nations Agreement on Straddling and Migratory Fish Stocks*, 17 Northwestern J. of International Law and Business 1132 (1996-97); Moritaka Hayashi, *The 1995 Agreement on the Conservation and Management of Straddling and Highly Migratory Fish Stocks: Significance for the Law of the Sea Convention*, 29 Ocean and Coastal Management 51 (1996); Moritaka Hayashi, *Enforcement by Non-Flag States on the High Seas Under the 1995 Agreement on Straddling and Highly Migratory Fish Stocks*, 9 Georgetown International Environmental Law Review 1 (1996); David A. Balton, *Strengthening the Law of the Sea: The New Agreement on Straddling Fish Stocks and Highly Migratory Fish Stocks*, 27 Ocean Development & International Law 125 (1996); Julie R. Mack, Comment, *International Fisheries Management: How the U.S. Conference on Straddling and Highly Migratory Fish Stocks Changes the Law of Fishing on the High Seas*, 26 California Western International Law J. 313 (1996); Mark Christopherson, Note, *Toward a Rational Harvest: The United Nations Agreement on Straddling Fish Stocks and Highly Migratory Species*, 5 Minnesota J. of Global Trade 357 (1996).
12. Straddling and Migratory Fish Stocks Agreement, id.
13. Law of the Sea Convention, *supra* note 1, Part XI.
14. See generally Jon Van Dyke and Christopher Yuen, "Common Heritage" v. "Freedom of the High Seas": Which Governs the Seabed?, 19 San Diego L. Rev. 493-551 (1982); also published in *The Law of the Sea and Ocean Development Issues in the Pacific Basin, 206-76* (Law of the Sea Institute, E. Miles and S. Allen eds., 1983).
15. Agreement Relating to the Implementation of Part XI of the United Nations Convention of the Law of the Sea of 10 December 1982, U.N. G.A. Res. 48/263 (28 July 1994).
16. Section 1 of the Annex to the Part XI Agreement says, for instance, that "all organs and subsidiary bodies to be established under the Convention and this Agreement shall be cost-effective" and that the creation of such organs (shall be based on an evolutionary approach." Section 2(3) states that "[t]he obligation of States Parties to fund one mine site of the Enterprise...shall not apply." Other provisions in the Annex state that the provisions of Articles 151(1-7) and (9), 155(1) and (3-4), 161(1), 161(8)(b) and (c), 162(2)(j) and (q), 165(2)(n), and Annex III, Articles 5, 6(5), and 7 of the Law of the Sea Convention "shall not apply."
17. Nihan Unlu, The Legal Regime of the Trukish Straits 74 (2002).
18. The Turkish scholar Nihan Unlu lists the countries that "consider the regime of transit passage as an exclusive part of the UNCLOS" as Chile, Denmark, Egypt, Greece, Iran,

Indonesia, Italy, Japan, South Korea, Malaysia, the Netherlands, Oman, and Spain. Id. at 75.

19. Tullio Scovazzi, The Evolution of International Law of the Sea: New Issues, New Challenges 174 (The Hague: Martinus Nijhoff, 2001) (reprinted from Recueil des Cours, Volume 286 (2000)). Nihan Unlu agrees that "a general right of transit passage has not yet been established in customary law." Unlu, supra note 17, at 75.
20. See, e.g. George P. Politakis, The Aegean Dispute in the 1990s: Naval Aspects of the New Law of the Sea Convention, in Greece and the Law of the Sea 291, 303 (Theodore C. Kariotis ed. 1997) (similar to George P. Politakis, The Aegean Agenda: Greek National Interests and the New Law of the Sea Convention, 10 International Journal of Marine & Coastal Law 497 (1995)) (summarizing scholarly discussion that indicates that all aspects of the transit passage regime have not yet crystallized into customary international law), and Anastasia Strati, Greece and the Law of the Sea: A Greek Perspective, in The Aegean Sea After the Cold War 89, 94 (Aldo Chircop, Gerolymatos & Iatrides, eds., 2000) (it is highly questionable whether the LOS Convention provisions on transit passage in all their detail reflect customary law, thereby entitling Turkey to benefit from them").
21. Scovazzi, Evolution, supra note 19, at 174-75.
22. Id. at 175-77.
23. Id. at 177-87 (providing examples from the Strait of Malacca, the Canadian Arctic Straits, the Russian Arctic Straits, and the Turkish Straits).
24. Tullio Scovazzi, Management Regimes and Responsibility for International Straits, in The Straits of Malacca: International Co-operation in Trade, Funding & Navigational Safety 344 (Maritime Institute of Malaysia, Kuala Lumpur: Pelanduk Publications, Hamzah Ahmad ed., 1997). See also Hamzah bin Ahmad, Global Funding for Navigational Safety and Environmental Protection, in Straits of Malacca, supra, at 125, 131 ("the concept of transit passage is relatively new and cannot be said to have acquired the status of customary international law").
25. Bernard H. Oxman, Transit of Straits and Archipelagic Waters by Military Aircraft 21-22 (paper delivered at Third International Law Seminar, Singapore, August 28, 1999, scheduled for publication in 4 Singapore Journal of International and Comparative Law (2001)).
26. Id. at 22.
27. Id. at 27.
28. Satya N. Nandan, *Legal Regime for Straits Used for International Navigation*, in The Proceedings of the Symposium on the Straits Used for International Navigation 1,6 (Bayram Ozturk & Resat Ozkan eds., Turkish Marine Research Foundation, Istanbul, Nov. 16-17, 2002).
29. Japanese Cargo Ship Foils Attack, Honolulu Advertiser, July 5, 2006, at A14, col. 3.
30. Marcus Hand, Joint Radar System for Singapore Straits, Lloyd's List, February. 6, 2005.
31. Mary George, The Regulation of Maritime Traffic in Straits Used for International Navigation, in Oceans Management in the 21st Century: Institutional Frameworks and Responses 19, 22 (Alex G. Oude Elferink & Donald R. Rothwell eds. 2004) (citing Tullio Treves, Navigation, in 2 A Handbook on the New Law of the Sea 950 (R.J. Dupuy & D. Vignes eds. 1991).
32. Id. See, e.g., Wan Awang bin Wan Yaacob, Regional Co-Operation and the Straits of Malacca, in Straits of Malacca, supra note 24, at 15, 21 (citing Article 26(2) of the Law

of the Sea Convention for the proposition that " [t]herefore international law does indeed provide for riparian states situated along straits to impose charges on foreign ships, but for specific services rendered only").

33. Nandan, supra note 28, at 8.
34. 2 United Nations Office of Legal Affairs, Division for Ocean Affairs and the Law of the Seas, The Law of the Sea: Straits Used for International Navigation: Legislative History of Part III of the United Nations Convention on the Law of the Sea 75, draft art. 11(3) (New York: United Nations, 1992). In 1973, Ecuador, Panama, and Peru submitted a paper that suggested that strait states should be allowed to establish an "equitable charge" that would be administered by the (international ocean space institutions" to finance dredging, to promote navigational safety, and to compensate strait states for damage caused by passing vessels. Id. at 102, art. 40(2)-(3).
35. Id. at 85.
36. Bernard Oxman, Observations on the Interpretation and Application of Article 43 of the United Nations Convention on the Law of the Sea with Particular Reference to the Straits of Malacca and Singapore 6 (paper presented at Conference on Navigational Safety and Control of Pollution in the Straits of Malacca and Singapore: Modalities of International Co-operation, sponsored by the IMO and the Institute of Policy Studies, Singapore, Sept. 2-3, 1996, Singapore) [hereafter cited as Oxman, Observations on Article 43].
37. Satya N Nandan & David H Anderson, *Straits Used for International Navigation: A Commentary on Part III of the United Nations Convention on the Law of the Sea 1982,* 1989 BRITISH YEAR BOOK OF INTERNATIONAL LAW 159, 193 (1990).
38. Id. at 193-94 (citing Amendment C2/22 offered by Morocco in 1978 that would have substituted "shall" for "should").
39. Nandan, supra note 28, at 7-8.
40. Id. at 7.
41. Id. at 8.
42. IMO Resolution MSC 52(66) (May 30, 1996).
43. IMO Doc. MEPC 49/8 (submitted by Australia and Papua New Guinea).
44. MSC, 79/23.
45. MEPC, 49/22.
46. See, e.g. G Naidu, *The Straits of Malacca in the Malaysian Economy* in Straits of Malacca, supra note 24, at 33-60.
47. See Nandan, supra note 28, at 8.
48. A distinguished Malaysian author has asserted this equitable perspective in stronger terms, noting that (maritime nations are concerned about collisions, pollution liability, higher navigational safety standards, low-level threats to navigation, such as piracy and thefts" and they "have demanded that navigational aids, charts and other services be secured for them to ensure the continued freedom of navigation," but "they are not prepared to contribute to the cost of providing all these public good in the straits. They insist on a free ride." Hamzah bin Ahmad, supra note 24, at 132-33.
49. Nandan, supra note 28, at 8.
50. Id.
51. Id. at 8-9. Professor Oxman agrees that the term 'user state' includes "those whose trade is carried through the straits" and includes both the purchasers and sellers of

the goods. Oxman, Observations on Article 43, supra note 36.

52. Some of the material that follows is updated from Jon M. Van Dyke, Military Ships and Planes Operating in the Exclusive Economic Zone of Another Country, 28 Marine Policy 29-39 (2004).

53. In November 1990, a Brazilian judge ordered a US submarine out of Brazil's EEZ, ruling that it posed environmental danger because it was nuclear powered. Judge Orders US Sub Out of Brazilian Waters, Honolulu Advertiser, Nov. 5, 1990, at D1, col.1.

54. When Germany ratified the Convention in 1994, it filed the following declaration: "According to the Convention, the coastal State does not enjoy residual rights in the exclusive economic zone. In particular, the rights and jurisdiction of the coastal States in such zone do not include the right to obtain notification of military exercises or manoeuvres or to authorize them." Italy, the Netherlands and the UK filed similar declarations.

55. Charter of the United Nations, June 26, 1945, 59 Stat. 1031, T.S. No. 993, 3 Bevans 1153.

56. Article 103 of the UN Charter says that if a country's obligations under the UN Charter are inconsistent with its obligations under any other treaty, the "obligations under the present Charter shall prevail."

57. Also relevant is Article 301 of the Law of the Sea Convention which says that: "In exercising their rights and performing their duties under this Convention, State Parties shall refrain from any threat or use of force against the territorial integrity or political independence of any State, or in any other manner inconsistent with principles of international law embodied in the Charter of the United Nations."

58. The duty to consult is a seminal principle of international law found, for instance, in Principle 19 of the Rio Declaration on Environment and Development, June 14, 1992, UN Doc. A/Conf.151/5/Rev.1 (1992), 31 I.L.M. 874 (1992), which says: "States shall provide prior and timely notification and relevant information to potentially affected States on Activities that may have a significant adverse transboundary environmental effect and shall consult with those States at an early stage and in good faith." See also Lac Lanoux Arbitration, 24 I.L.R. 101 (1957) (requiring France to consult in good faith with Spain over riparian rights); Mox Plant Case (Ireland v. United Kingdom), Int'l Tribunal for the Law of the Sea (December 2001) (requiring the United Kingdom to consult in good faith with Ireland over the pollution issues created by the Sellafield nuclear reprocessing plant, including the exchange of information about the risks, monitoring the emissions and their effect on the marine environment of the Irish Sea, and working together to reduce these risks).

59. See Michele Wallace, *The Right of Warships to Operate in the Exclusive Economic Zone as Perceived by Delegates to the Third United Nations Law of the Sea Convention,* in International Navigation: Rocks and Shoals Ahead? 345, 346-47 (Jon M. Van Dyke, Lewis M. Alexander, and Joseph R. Morgan eds. 1988).

60. Id. at 347 (citing Third United Nations Conference on the Law of the Sea, 2 or (3d Sess. Geneva)(30th mtg.) 28 (1975)).

61. See, e.g., id. (quoting U.S. delegate T. Vincent Learson who said " [t]he term 'peaceful purposes' did not, of course, preclude military activities generally. The United States had consistently held that the conduct of military activities for peaceful purposes was in full accord with the Charter of the United Nations and with principles of international law." Third United Nations Conference on the Law of the Sea. 5 OR (4th Sess. New York)(67th mtg.) 62 (1976)).

62. See, e.g., Vienna Convention on the Law of Treaties, May 23, 1969, UN Doc. A/Conf. 39/27, art. 31(3)(b), recognizing the importance of "any subsequent practice in the application of the treaty which establishes the agreement of the parties regarding its interpretation."
63. Scovazzi, Evolution, supra note 19, at 162, 163-64.
64. See, e.g., Van Dyke, *Military Ships and Planes Operating in the EEZ of another Country,* supra note 52.
65. See, e.g. id.
66. *PRC Seeks Control Over Coastal Exclusion Zone,* China Post, Jan. 29, 2003. China appears to be particularly concerned that its "interests in and jurisdiction over [its] exclusive economic zone should be fully respected." In March 2002, Chinese Foreign Minister Tang Jiaxuan expressed continued concern about the Japanese vessel that chased the North Korean "mystery ship" into China's EEZ in December 2001. *China's Interests in Exclusive Economic Zone should be Respected,* Xinhua News Agency, March 6, 2002.
67. Christopher Cooper, *Taiwan Seizes North Korean Cargo,* Asian Wall Street Journal, August 13, 2003, at A4.
68. These incidents are discussed in detail in Mark J. Valencia, The US Proliferation Security Initiative: Legal and Political Implications (paper delivered at Honolulu Meeting, December 9, 2003, and published on numerous websites).
69. See, e.g., James Brooke, *Japan Detains 2 North Korean Ships, Part of Pressure Strategy,* New York Times, June 11, 2003, at 13.
70. Speech by Condoleezza Rice to the National Legal Center for the Public Interest, Waldorf Astoria Hotel, New York City, November 2, 2003 (emphasis added).
71. Lincoln Wright, *Change to High Seas Law Sought,* Canberra Times (Australia), June 12, 2003, at 5.
72. See, e.g. Emma Daly, *After Oil Spill, Spain and France Impose Strict Tanker Inspections,* New York Times, November 27, 2002, at A5, col. 3. Earlier, France had banned vessels over 1,600 tons from coming within seven nautical miles of the coast around Cherbourg and Brest, to protect the fragile coastal environment. Robert Nadelson, After Mox: The Contemporary Shipment of Radioactive Substances in the Law of the Sea, 15 International J Marine & Coastal L 193, 224 n. 189 (2000) (citing Joint Prefectorial Decree 326 Cherbourg/18/81 Brest of May 13, 1981).
73. Interview with Kristina Gjerde, Paris, November 12, 2003.
74. Press release from Government of Morocco, January 23, 2003.
75. Marlise Simons, *France Clamps Down on Shipping Pollution,* New York Times, April 7, 2003, at A8, col. 1.
76. Id.
77. Interview with Kristina Gjerde, Paris, November 12, 2003.
78. IMO Resolution MSC.85(70) (Dec. 3, 1998), discussed in Lt. Rachel Cantry (US Coast Guard), *The Coast Guard and Environmental Protection,* 52:4 Naval War College Rev. 77 (Autumn1999).
79. IMO Resolution MSC 52(66) (May 30, 1996) (Torres Strait between Australia and Papua New Guinea, the inner route of Australia's Great Barrier Reef, and the area adjacent to France's Ouessant (Ushant) islet); IMO Resolution MSC.63(67) (Dec. 3, 1996) (Denmark's Great Belt Traffic Area, the Strait of Gibraltar, and the area off of

Finisterre on the Spanish coast); IMO Resolution MSC.73(69)(May 29, 1998) (the Strait of Bonifacio between Corsica (France) and Sardinia (Italy) and also through the Straits of Malacca and Singapore); IMO Resolution MSC.85(70) (Dec. 3, 1998) (the Strait of Dover/Pas de Calais).

80. See, e.g. Myres McDougal and Norbert Schlei, *The Hydrogen Bomb Tests in Perspective: Lawful Measures for Security,* 64 Yale L.J. 648, 659-60 (1955).

81. Some of the material that follows is updated from Jon M Van Dyke, *Balancing Navigational Freedom with Environmental and Security Concerns,* 15 Colo. J. Envtl. L. & Pol'y 2003 Y.B. 19-28 (2004).

82. Kenneth R. Weiss and Tony Perry, "Navy's Use of Sonar OK'd Despite Risk to Whales," Los Angels Times, July 16, 2002, at A1; Marc Kaufman, "Navy Cleared to Use a Sonar Despite Fears of Injuring Whales," Washington Post, July 16, 2002, at A3, 2002 WL 23853879.

83. Nine Cuvier's beaked whales were found dead on September 24-25, 2002 on the Canary Islands of Fuerteventura and Lanzarote. Six beached whales were pushed back into the sea, and another two were seen floating lifeless in coastal waters. Ships from Belgium, Canada, France, Germany, Greece, Norway, Portugal, Turkey, the United Kingdom, and the United States were conducting a multinational exercise known as Neo Tapon 2002 designed to practice securing the Strait of Gibraltar. The Cuvier's beaked whale is a toothed cetacean that ranges from five to eight metres in length. Jerome Socolovsky, (Investigation Points to NATO Exercise in Mass Whale Beaching, Associated Press, October 10, 2002, <http:/www.enn.com/news/wire-stories/2002/10/10102002/ap_4866>.

84. Seventeen whales of four different species, including Cuvier's beaked whales, two minke whales, and a dolphin stranded in the Bahamas in March 2000 as a result of tactical mid-frequency sonar transmitted from US Navy vessels, which were thought to have reached the whales at the 165 decibel level. Scientists found hemorrhaging around the brain and ear bones of the beached cetaceans, injuries consistent with exposure to extremely loud sounds. The US Navy admitted that these strandings "were most likely caused by its [mid-range] sonar transmissions." Center for Biological Diversity v. National Science Foundation, No. C02-5065, 2002 WL 31548073 (N.D. Cal. Temporary Restraining Order, 30 October 2002), slip op. at 8.

85. Twelve Cuvier's beaked whales stranded in the Mediterranean near Greece at a time that coincided temporally and geographically with "sound detecting system trials" of LFAS by the NATO research vessel Alliance. The whales were exposed to sound transmitted from at least 25 kilometers away, which was determined to have reached them at the level of 150-160 decibels after 238 four-second pings of sound were released, which caused severe tissue damage to their ear cavities. US Department of Commerce and Secretary of the Navy, Joint Interim Report Bahamas Marine Mammal Stranding Event of 15-16 March 2000 (Dec. 2001), <http://www.nmfs.noaa.gov/prot_res/overview/Interim_Bahamas_Report.pdf>.

86. MP Simmonds and LF Lopez-Jurado, *Whales and the Military,* 351 Nature 448 (June 6, 1991).

87. Although the Navy refuses to release the maximum source level of Surtass LFA, claiming it to be classified information, reports indicate the maximum source level to be 230 dB re 1 uPa. "Quiet Please. Whales Navigating," The Economist, March 7, 1998, at 85, 1998 WL 8884376; Alexandros Frantis, Does Military Testing Strand Whales? 352 Nature 29 (March 5, 1998).

88. Because of the way sound is measured and the different speed that sound travels through water, as compared to land, it is estimated that "underwater sound pressure levels numerically are about 61.5 dB greater than sound pressure levels in air for an equal intensity." Robert C. Gisiner, *Proceedings, Workshop on the Effects of Anthropogenic Noise in the Marine Environment,* 10-12 February 1998 (Marine Mammal Science Program, Office of Naval Research, 1988) 24, <http://www.onr.navy.mil/sci_tech/personnel/cnb_sci/proceed.pdf>. In other words, sound measured at 131-dB in water would have the same pressure impact as sound measured at 70-dB on land. 60-dB on land is the sound generated by freeway traffic. Continuous exposure above 85-dB (on land) is likely to degrade the hearing of most humans. "Deafening" noise (on land) begins at 110-dB, with 120-dB measuring a hard rock band, 130-dB being the point at which pain is registered, and 140-dB being the point adjacent to a jet engine. The 180-dB (in water) figure said by the Navy to be "safe" for cetaceans would thus affect them at about the same extent as human hearing would be affected by standing next to a hard rock band at a rock concert, if we can assume that the hearing system of cetaceans is roughly comparable to ours.

89. *See Natural Resources Defense Council v. Evans,* 232 F. Supp. 2d 1003, 1021, 1033-34 (N.D. Cal. 2002) (Opinion and Order Granting Plaintiffs' Motion for a Preliminary Injunction).

90. Id at 1033-34.

91. *Natural Resources Defense Council v. Evans,* 232 F.Supp.2d at 1053. The four statutes are the Marine Mammal Protection Act of 1972, 16 U.S.C. sec. 1361 (2003), the National Environmental Protection Act of 1969, 42 U.S.C. sec. 4332 (2003), the Endangered Species Act of 1973, 16 U.S.C. sec. 1531 (2003), and the Administrative Procedure Act of 1940, 5 U.S.C. sec. 551 (2003).

92. Id. Although Magistrate Judge LaPorte found that the Navy's activities violated four federal statute, she accepted the testimony of the NMFS experts regarding the impact of LFAS on marine mammals over the sharply conflicting testimony presented by the Natural Resources Defense Counsel. Judge LaPorte wrote that: "The law is clear...that when qualified experts on both sides reach carefully reasoned but different conclusions, the Court must defer to the agency's experts..." Id. at 1017. Other US courts dealing with ocean environmental issues have taken a more skeptical view of the scientific opinions offered by US agencies. See, e.g., Natural Resources Defense Counsel v. Daley, 209 F.3d 747, 755, 754 (D.C. Cir. 2000) (explaining that courts "do not hear cases merely to rubber stamp agency actions" and criticizing the agency's scientific conclusions as ones that could only be correct in "Superman Comics' Bizarre world, where reality is turned upside down"); *Greenpeace v. National Marine Fisheries Service,* 106 F.Supp.2d 1066 (W.D. Wash. 2000) (where the court treated the views of the two sides' experts as having equal credibility and issued the injunction sought by plaintiffs despite the contrary testimony of the agency's experts).

93. David Kravets, U.S. Navy Agrees to Temporarily Limit Testing of New Sonar System Amid Marine Life Concerns, Associated Press, November 18, 2002, <http://www.planetsave.com/ViewStory.asp?ID'3299> (March 2, 2003).

94. *Court Order Blocks Whale Killing in Gulf of California,* October 29, 2002), <http://www.endangeredearth.org/alerts/result.asp?index'1210> (November 2, 2002) (summarizing issuance of temporary restraining order by Magistrate Judge

James Larson in the case of Center for Biological Diversity v. National Science Foundation, No. C2-5065 JL (N.D.Cal. Oct. 31, 2002).

95. *Hawaii County Green Party v. Evans,* No. C-03-0078-SC (N.D. Cal., Order Granting Permanent Injunction, Jan. 24, 2003).
96. Id. slip op. at 24.
97. WJ Richardson, et al., Marine Mammals and Noise (1995) 544.
98. HM Dotinga and AG Oude Elferink, *Acoustic Pollution in the Oceans:* The Search for *Legal Standards,* 31 Ocean Development and International Law 151, 158 (2000).
99. See Christopher W Clark, Peter Tyack, and William T Ellison, Quicklook, Low-Frequency Sound Scientific Research Program, Phase I: Responses of Blue and Fin Whales to Surtass LFA, Southern California Bight, 5 September–21 October, 1997 at 30-31 (February 27, 1998), Figure 28; Peter Tyack and Christopher Clark, Quicklook Phase II, Playback of Low-Frequency Sound to Gray Whales Migrating Past the Central California Coast, January 1998 at 22-25 (June 23, 1998).
100. Neil King Jr., *US Resistance to Sea Treaty Thaws,* Wall Street Journal, August 22, 2007, at A6, col. 1.
101. Id. ("Without being a party to the treaty, the US has no clear way (short of threatening force (to assert its claims").
102. See David A. Balton and Dorothy C. Zbicz, *Managing Deep-Sea Fisheries: Some Threshold Questions,* 19 International Journal of Marine and Coastal Law 247, 257 (2004).
103. Michael W. Lodge and Satya N. Nandan, *Some Suggestions Towards Better Implementation of the United Nations Agreement on Straddling Fish Stocks and Highly Migratory Fish Stocks of 1995,* 20 International Journal of Marine and Coastal Law 345, 374 (2005).
104. Id.
105. Id.
106. Ted L. McDorman, *Implementing Existing Tools: Turning Words Into Actions (Decision-Making Processes of Regional Fisheries Management Organizations* (RFMOs), 20 International Journal of Marine and Coastal Law 423, 425 (2005).
107. Id. at 438.
108. Id. at 440 (noting that the quota reductions "can be justified on the basis of precaution" and that this procedure would provide (an important incentive to agree on allocations").
109. See, e.g., Jon M. Van Dyke, *The Aegean Sea Dispute: Options and Avenues,* 20 Marine Policy 397, 398-401 (1996).
110. Lodge and Nandan note that "neither UNFSA, nor the decision rules of many existing RFMOs, provide mechanisms for allocation that balance conservation interests with the economic and social interests of states. In fact, within many RFMOs, negotiated criteria for catch allocations are often based on the notion of historical catch, which is a powerful incentive to indulge in a race to fish." Lodge & Nandan, supra note 103, at 374.
111. Lee Kimball, *Deep-Sea Fisheries of the High Seas: The Management Impasse,* 19 International Journal of Marine and Coastal Law 259, 273 (2004).
112. See Balton and Zbicz, supra note 102, at 249-50.
113. Michael W Lodge, *Improving International Governance in the Deep Sea,* 19

International Journal of Marine and Coastal Law 299, 307 (2004).

114. Id. at 308.

115. McDorman, supra note 106, at 440.

PAPER 2

Maritime Capacity Enhancement: The Case of the Gulf States and Beyond

Mustafa Alani*

The Gulf region contains no less than 60 per cent of the world's oil reserves and some 40 per cent of the world's natural gas reserves. Almost all the region's energy products (oil, gas, and petrochemical products) are transported by sea to the world markets; equally the major bulk of this region's requirements of essential goods are transported by sea. Therefore, the security of this region is paramount for the entire world, and maritime capacity and maritime security are crucial issues for the Gulf States.

There is a number of factors to consider with regard to the enhancement of maritime capacity. The first is the need and the justification for the enhancement; second, the availability of financial resources to meet the related costs; and third, the availability of technical and professional expertise/resources to manage such expansion or enhancement.

The paper attempts to look at these issues and identifies the problems that hinder the much-needed maritime capacity-building in the Gulf States and beyond. It examines the main requirements for maritime capacity building process or strategy. The paper also tries to examine the perceived state of inadequate maritime capacity in the region that undermines the littoral states' ability to deal effectively with the emerging challenges.

---

* Senior Adviser and Director of Security and Terrorism Department, Gulf Research Center (GRC), UAE

Maritime Capacity Development is About Change

Change involves individuals and institutions. Developing maritime capacity needs leadership and commitment, in particular, where major policies and institutions are involved directly or indirectly. It means that we may have to change the way we do things and interact. Political commitment is required to introduce change, clarify goals and develop national and regional frameworks for change. The process of change is often costly, complex and even unpredictable. Development and change requires resources, human and financial. Developing capacities requires adequate financial resources to support the expansion of the intellectual and physical infrastructure, undertaking capital investment and meeting recurring costs. All these factors are critical when we speak about maritime capacity enhancement too. Flexibility and the ability to respond to changing circumstances are an essential requirement, as is continuous learning and feedback. Further, adequate timing and managed expectations, improved access to information, and coordination of resources to maximise their impact remain key factors in the success and sustainability of any maritime capacity-building process. Thus maritime capacity development is both a means and an end for sustainable human development. However, unfavourable policies in many countries have not made it easy for the promotion of the task of capacity development.

The existing maritime capabilities are very limited in many regional states. The objective of the capacity-building strategy must be to achieve long-term development which can be sustained. The policy needs to comprise a number of different but interrelated components. To mention some of them:

- The awareness component
- The assessment component
- The planning component
- The finance component
- The management and implementation component
- The education and training component

What we need in the Gulf region and beyond is to support a maritime capacity-building strategy, collectively or individually, that could guarantee and provide the required support by providing for the growing maritime economy and the rapidly expanding regional and global trade activities. Thus any maritime capacity-building programme must focus on the efforts to create a conducive environment to support this objective. Indeed, one can see a strong link between maritime capacity building and the implementation of an effective maritime policy. Traditionally, political objection has constituted a major obstacle hindering the efforts at maritime capacity enhancement. Political support is necessary to secure funding and to facilitate the administrative and legal changes which could provide the catalyst to embark on the capacity enhancement process.

Viewed from a wider angle, it is hard to imagine that a successful national maritime policy could operate in isolation, as the basic requirement of any effective, sustainable policy will be the promotion of the concept of maximum integration with the maritime policies of other states.In fact, achieving a high degree of coordination with other nations' maritime policies needs to be considered as the ultimate objective. Indeed, by combining efforts and resources, a regional capacity could be built, leading to an enhancement of maritime security. However, this would require the countries to set aside their political disagreements.

The task of maritime capacity enhancement or development has many requirements, but I will highlight the four main or core demands, which are:

An Effective Assessment Mechanism: A Key Requirement

An essential step in planning of a maritime capacity-building process is to focus on identifying a suitable development strategy that takes the enabling environment into consideration.

Thus, the planning and the management of any maritime capacity-building strategy require an effective mechanism for "capacity assessment". The main task of such a mechanism would be to identify and determine the main components of the capacity-building project assess basic needs, define priorities and, at the same time, prevent duplication at all levels, regional and local.

Capacity assessment would also address the question of how to make more effective use of existing resources and capabilities, and how these resources could be integrated within the new capacity-building strategy. In fact, identifying the available capacity will help in determining what is needed and in directing the limited financial resources to meet the needs according to the priorities.

Before initiating an assessment, it is important to define the scope of the capacity-building project, which should be based on the ability to manage and absorb change and the political will and resources behind it. The size, scope and duration of the programme must be designed to reflect the country's situation and capabilities.

Human Resources Development

The availability of skilled human resources is a basic requirement of any plan for maritime capacity enhancement. Indeed, the task could not be achieved without highly qualified and highly trained cadres or a workforce that enables the planning and implementation of the required capacity-enhancement projects. Any human resource development plan needs to be comprehensive in order to cover the entire spectrum of maritime jobs such as ports managers, shipyard managers, safety inspectors, officers, pilots, engineers and technicians, all of whom are professionally trained and have the necessary maritime knowledge and skills. In the Gulf region, and in the wider Middle East, currently we cannot find great interest in choosing a maritime-related career. Indeed, finding nationals with training in maritime skills is considered a major challenge facing any national maritime enhancement or expansion strategy. For the small states in the Gulf region, while financial resources do not constitute a problem, the scarcity of skilled human resources is a major challenge that could hinder any maritime capacity-building process. But, at the end of the day, we know that the sailor is a citizen of the world and a capacity-building plan could utilise other nations' human resources.

Structural Development

This part of the requirement covers the need to encourage the maritime-related institutional development in order to provide the much-needed legal, administrative, and technical framework for capacity-building process. Besides creating new institutions, as the process requires, the strategy must aim to achieve institutional improvement. This would require regulatory changes which enable the existent organisations and institutions to develop reform and enhance their capacities. One of the main objectives of any plan must be to deal with the competing and non-coordinated institutional structures.

While talking about the need to create new institutions and reform the existing ones, no effective capacity-building policy could progress without promoting the area of research activities in all fields related to the task of maritime capacity building, including natural science and social science by encouraging the research facilities in the universities and research institutions. Research work related to maritime activities is often done without much interaction, cooperation, and coordination between local, regional, and international research institutions. Research in the maritime field, as with most research in other fields, has to cope with a lack of funding.

In our region, there are several dimensions regarding institutional development: one at the Gulf Cooperation Council (GCC) level, and the other at the national/state level. The progress on maritime institutional building is very slow and is not considered as a top priority.

Realisation of the Need to Enhance Maritime Capacity and for Political Support

Maritime capacity enhancement is a complicated, costly and time-consuming process. Decision makers need to take greater interest in the process of maritime capability enhancement. Members of the society need to realise the importance of the oceans in their lives and the contribution of the oceans in the welfare and the development of all nations, as well as in the overall development of humankind. As part of an awareness strategy, it is important to develop education and training programmes; information about the oceans should be a part of the school curriculum and interest should be generated at different levels of the society regarding the importance of maritime activities.

On the other hand, the oceans belong to all mankind and therefore require universally applicable rules and the development of a common vision. However, such universally applicable rules should come with adequate room for flexibility to accommodate and cater for the more specific rules that have been framed in keeping with the different management requirements of each part of the oceans and seas.

The task of maritime capacity building cannot be achieved without political support. Although the basic nature of the task appears mostly technical, the final decision and the essential funding will have to come from the political leadership.

Finally, I would like to draw attention to the impact of the vast advances in the field of information technology. The information revolution has important implications for the task of maritime capacity building. Traditional technical cooperation has relied on training and expert assistance as the main way to transmit technical information. The global information and communications revolution has altered traditional approaches to technical cooperation and capacity development in all fields. Now, closer communication links which have enabled better coordination, regional maritime organisations will be able to become part of larger transnational systems. ■

PAPER 3

Operationalising Regional Maritime Cooperation Towards Ensuring Collective Maritime Security for the Indian Ocean RIM Association for Regional Cooperation

Bernard H Teuteberg*

Introduction

Observable in the challenges of post-Cold War and post-9-11 security paradigms, is the fact that states are continuing to group themselves together, and shifting alliances in order to achieve mutual security, at economic, social and military levels. Some have, over the past decade plus, adopted new forms (such as the European Union), while there are a number of new institutions, such as NAFTA, APEC, IOR-ARC, SADC, ECOWAS, Mercosur,[1] the Andean Community, the Black Sea Economic Cooperation Forum, etc. There is a number of influencing factors, not least of which is the absence of a need for states to identify with either of the erstwhile bipolar political fundamentals, which constitutes an inferred greater freedom of choice.[2] These factors include intense and increasing pressure on resources, increased interdependence of nations, globalisation of markets and economies, increasing burdens on national budgets and the need for nations to direct their budgets towards economic growth and development.[3]

A common denominator among the newly formed and extant regional economic communities noted above, is that geographical proximities of member nations facilitate interaction at regional cooperative levels. A notable exception appears to be the Indian Ocean Rim Association for

* Chief Director Maritime Strategy (CDMS), South African Navy.

Regional Cooperation (IOR-ARC), where nations are, first, at far-flung distances on the littoral rim of the vast Indian Ocean—thereby making co-lateral interaction problematic—and second, nations belong to other regional economic groupings; such as ASEAN, GCC, SADC and EAC[4] in the first instance; and only then—in a tiered approach—are members of the IOR-ARC. This appears to have an operationally inhibitory effect in the Indian Ocean Rim, where evidence abounds of maritime cooperation sub-regionally (i.e. within SADC, EAC, GCC and ASEAN regional economic communities), but very little cooperation in the larger IOR-ARC region. Hence, as the title of the paper indicates, maritime cooperation in the

IOR-ARC region is in a state of dormancy, and would require energisation.

Aim

Accordingly, based on an analysis of IOR-ARC joint and individual countries' capabilities and limitations, this paper will have as its aim the mooting of efficient and effective methodologies to operationalise maritime regional cooperation by the Indian Ocean Rim littoral states.

Scope

In order to achieve its aim, the paper will briefly lay out the drivers of foreign policy initiatives, as underscored by the various applicable theories of international relations, followed by related conceptual analyses. Thereafter, regional cooperation in the area under survey will be analysed, first as noted in terms of international law, and the United Nations organisation; and also in terms of nations, associated regional economic communities within the Indian Ocean Rim region. A short review will be conducted to confirm that maritime cooperation exists in the area, but only at a sub-regional level, and not at the level of IOR-ARC supra-regional level; and the rationale will be analysed as a delta inactivity. Thereafter, a short objective analysis will be conducted delineating individual countries' navies, utilising an existing ranking system. At this point, some deductions will be required, in order to focus on the 'operationalisation' challenges that lie ahead. This would be best achieved by compiling a SWOT[5] analysis, as this will enable the paper to overcome identified lacuna through opportunities, a plan to be put forward (tactics) to set about the operationalisation of maritime cooperation in the area. A process, based on nations' common denominators, to operationalise the Indian Ocean Region will be proposed; and importantly, the paper will suggest way in which to address national sensitivities and sovereignty concerns of states that may arise in pursuance of some of the regional objectives set out above, or for overcoming asymmetric maritime challenges. Based on these, conclusions will be drawn, and recommendations made so as to achieve operationalisation of maritime cooperation in the area.

Theories of International Relations: An Overview

In this process of regional groupings, it is general consensus that the development of nations' economies does not occur in isolation; further that the "... route to global integration ... runs through regional consolidation ...".[6] Regional maritime cooperation involves the adoption, whether stated or not, of an international relations approach by the various nations of that region, that is underpinned by a theoretical approach. It would serve the aim of this paper to briefly and cursorily examine appropriate theories of international relations. Over the years, there has been a number of traditions in the interpretation of international relations, and at the certain risk of oversimplification, the four main theories follow, with an indication of which may be an apposite approach with respect to regional cooperation.

One tradition emphasises such ideas as the autonomous actions of sovereign states, the anarchy of international relations, the importance of national power, and the pursuit of national realism. It is less likely that regional cooperation, except for parochial attainment of national goals, will be a driving force for nations that embrace the realist approach to international relations.

Yet another tradition emphasises such ideas as the necessity for States to engage in international cooperation, the harmony of interests, the importance of international economic exchanges, and the erosion of the nation-State. For the past quarter century, this perspective has been known as liberalism, which was founded on idealism.

A third perspective, forms part of the so-called Radical Theories (Orthodox Marxism, Neo-Marxism, Structuralism, World-System and Constructivist Theories of International Relations), perceives the existing system of states with disfavour, combined with an understanding that radical progress of the human condition towards a more desirable state of affairs is possible, if not the only way out. They often view the world in largely economic terms, from the less-developed countries' perspective; emphasising core-periphery relationships, underdevelopment, colonialism and imperialism concepts as foundational argumentation. International relations processes are seen as designed to perpetuate inequality and ensured dominance by richer nations. However, the narrowed economic view that Structuralists have of international relations, and devolved national security is not shared in a world that is increasingly defining security in terms of a holistic or systemic approach.

There is also a fourth perspective that we should consider. It is not yet really a great tradition in the interpretation of international relations, but rather a major tradition in the study of comparative politics. In the future, however, it may prove to be the most useful, even if the most demanding, perspective from which to view their role in the world. It emphasises the distinctive cultural characteristics of different societies, as they are expressed by different kinds of states in the international arena. Many of these cultural characteristics derive from the great religions, a few of these societies are nation-States, while others are multicultural states, yet others are entire civilisations largely under the rule of one government. "The Clash of Civilizations" by Samuel Huntington[7] epitomises this approach to understanding international relations.[8]

Thus each nation adopts a theoretical foundation, which informs its foreign policy approach and develops instruments (including navies) to deal with other nations at the regional, continental and international level.

Conceptual Analysis

Security and its conceptual variants—national security, international security, global security, collective security, cooperative security, comprehensive security, human security, and so forth—are characterised by murky conceptual parameters. This makes analytic delineation problematic, both for scholars but more so for policy functionaries, who have to formulate and implement policy. It is against this background that, for the purposes of this paper, comprehensive and cooperative security, as sub-sets of human security will be defined as they pertain to the focused aim of the paper. Accordingly, the United Nations Development Programme (UNDP) defined "human security" as "the sense that people are free from worries, not merely from the dread of a cataclysmic world event, but primarily about daily life."[9]

Thus, human security is not conceptualised as a process, but an ideal to which states aspire and that has to be pursued at global level. It impacts both domestic and foreign policies, and hence requires concerted effort to harmonise such programmes that collectively and directly benefit humanity, here with reference to the Indian Ocean Rim region. This approach calls for "de-nationalisation" of issues and harmonisation of policies across territorial boundaries.

The broadening of the concept of security incorporates non-military aspects such as socio-economic development, environment and politics. Security has become more comprehensive. Complementary to this, the notion of cooperative security approach, based largely on regional systems, emphasises the significance of cooperation rather than competition. The cooperative approach emphasises and promotes "consultation rather than confrontation, reassurance rather than deterrence, transparency rather than secrecy, prevention rather than correction, and interdependence rather than unilaterism."[10]

For states, these infer numerous actions at domestic and international levels, for which nations must have traits, one of the most important attributes of states being credibility. Achieving credibility through the maintenance of domestic stability, democratic governance and a resilient and robust economy is one durable and internationally laudable way. From a national security perspective, this is also achieved by by exhibiting a high degree of control over its professional military force. While these forces are predominately defensive in nature, the states 'devive' strategic (and political) mileage through ambitions to regional, continental and international security and stability.[11]

It is here that navies feature for a number of reasons. Globally, over centuries, the relationship between sea power and foreign policy has been "... one of the most inveigling".[12] The phrase "defence diplomacy" is not an oxymoron; instead, it is the collateral use of navies in operations-other-than-war. Navies possess a range of attributes that lend themselves to naval diplomacy; they are remarkably flexible, they are relevant to any kind of international, continental or regional order being created, they operate in international space, navies are perceived as significant diplomatic assets in a world where, often, it is important to avoid coercive use of military force. Navies have a global acceptance as "... a potent military move, but one far short of war and essentially non-provocative". [13]

Singly or combined, maritime forces have positive effects with respect to maritime security, disaster management, humanitarian assistance as well environmental management challenges and a host of other functions. Most states that possess naval forces use these assets as enablers of regional, continental and international stability and security. It is in this context that the operationalisation of the Indian Ocean Rim region should be viewed.

Maritime Cooperation in the Indian Ocean Rim: Review, Principles, Objectives and Status

Cooperation among regional organisations is therefore a force multiplier, and is often most desirable—especially in this vast, relatively unpoliced, area of the world. The United Nations provides for the eventuality where such a function is required to be performed and where it does not have the capacity, resources or expertise which have strong regional imperatives and implications. Accordingly, Articles 33 and 52 of the UN Charter state:

Article 33

The parties to any dispute, the continuance of which is likely to endanger the maintenance of international peace and security, shall, first of all, seek a solution by negotiation, enquiry, mediation, conciliation, arbitration, judicial settlement, resort to regional agencies or arrangements, or other peaceful means of their own choice.

The Security Council shall, when it deems necessary, call upon the parties to settle their disputes by such means.

Article 52

Nothing in the present Charter precludes the existence of regional arrangements or agencies for dealing with matters relating to the maintenance of international peace and security as are appropriate for regional action provided that such arrangements or agencies and their activities are consistent with the Purposes and Principles of the United Nations.

Having been 'mandated' by the aforementioned United Nations Articles, the phenomenon of regionalism has found expression at many levels and in most regions of the world. One of the latest to be formed is the Indian Ocean Rim Association for Regional Cooperation.

Review of the Indian Ocean Rim

The Development of the Indian Ocean Rim

For many centuries, the countries, economies and peoples of the Indian Ocean have been bound together in an informal cooperative economic community. Traders, seamen, fishermen, and pilgrims traversed the Indian Ocean and its numerous ports, enabling a vibrant trading network to emerge.

After the Second World War, the decolonisation process ended British hegemony in the Indian Ocean. Superpower rivalry in the region escalated due to the strategic importance of the area. The common historical experience of European imperialism had left a lasting impression on the leaders of states in the Indian Ocean region—a sense of shared identity. The rediscovery of the past littoral economic, social and cultural community, of an ocean-centric regional cooperative grouping serving as a bridgehead among Africa, Asia, and Australasia, seemed only natural.

In 1995, during a visit to India, then South African President Nelson Mandela stated that "the natural urge of the facts of history and geography...should broaden itself to include the concept of an Indian Ocean Rim for socio-economic co-operation and other peaceful endeavours. Recent changes in the international system demand that the countries of the Indian Ocean shall become a single platform".[14]

After a number of preparatory meetings, the Indian Ocean Rim Association for Regional Co-operation (IOR-ARC) was formed in Mauritius on 6-7 March 1997, through its adoption of IOR-ARC Charter. The IOR-ARC comprises 18 member states; being Australia, Bangladesh, India, Indonesia, Iran, Kenya, Madagascar, Malaysia, Mauritius, Mozambique, Oman, Singapore, South Africa, Sri Lanka, Tanzania, Thailand, the United Arab Emirates, and Yemen. The Seychelles announced its withdrawal from the Association in July 2003.

China, Egypt, France, Japan, and the United Kingdom are dialogue partners of the IOR-ARC. At present, only the Indian Ocean Tourism Organisation (IOTO) has observer status.

IOR-ARC Member States and Dialogue Partners[15]

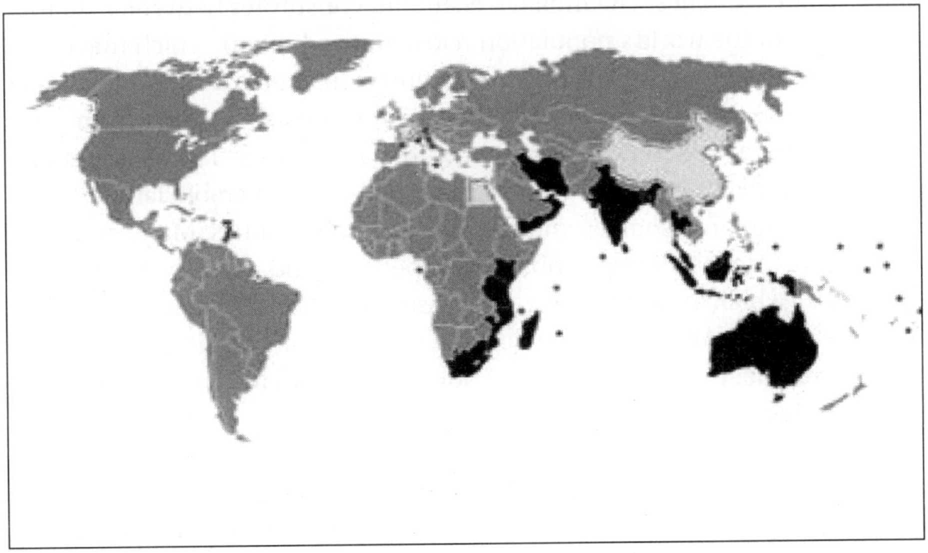

Geo-Strategic Aspects of the Indian Ocean Rim

The Indian Ocean Rim defines a distinctive area in international politics consisting of coastal states bordering the Indian Ocean. It is a region of much diversity, in culture, race, religion, economic development, and strategic interests; with forty-seven countries that have the Indian Ocean on their shores. The countries vary in the size of their populations, economies, trade, and technological development and in the composition of their gross domestic product. A number of sub-regions is evident, for example, Southern and Eastern Africa, the Horn of Africa and the Red Sea, South Asia, South-east Asia, and Australasia. It also includes a number of regional organisations, such as ASEAN, GCC, SAARC,[16] and SADC.

"The first and most obvious light in which the sea presents itself from the political and social point of view is that of a highway; ...over which men may pass in all directions, but on which some well-worn paths show that controlling reasons have led them to choose certain lines of travel rather than others. These lines of trade are called trade routes; and the reasons which have determined them are sought in the history of the world."[17] This is possibly even more so the case with the Indian Ocean, the world's third largest Ocean.[18] The Indian Ocean occupies 20 per cent of the world's ocean surface—it is nearly 10,000 kilometres wide at the southern tips of Africa and Australia and its area is 68.556 million square kilometres. It carries half of the world's container ships, one-third of the bulk cargo traffic, two-third of the world's oil shipments. It is a lifeline of international trade and economy. The region is interlaced, woven together by trade routes and commands control of the major sea-lanes. The Indian Ocean Rim constitutes between a quarter and a third of the world's population (close to two billion), which makes it a massive market. It is rich in strategic and precious minerals and metals and other natural resources, valuable marine resources, ranging from food fisheries to raw material and energy for industries. It has abundant agricultural wealth in terms of the variety and mass of arable land and has significant human resources and technological capabilities. Many countries of the Rim are becoming globally competitive and are developing new capacities, which can be jointly harnessed through regional cooperation efforts. Economically, the Indian Ocean is economically crucial to Africa, Asia and Australasia, the three continents bordering it, and the world at large.

Increasing globalisation, specifically economics, today dominates strategic considerations. This has led to enhanced maritime security concerns, since most regional trade is sea-borne. Despite "maritime bonding",[19] this region has unfortunately not seen the emergence of a vibrant trans-oceanic community.

This may be rooted in regional countries' wide dissimilarities and divergent interests, which have prompted each country to pursue economic linkages with the other major powers, rather than with each other. This has inevitably limited the region's economic growth.

The Indian Ocean Rim contains a number of the world's maritime choke points, which "... implies that at such points there is the opportunity for closure, or at least restriction, of the flow of ocean-borne traffic and/or overflight which are critical to the well-being of a particular state or group of states."[20] These include the Cape Sea Route, the Mozambique Channel, the Straits of Hormuz, Strait of Malacca, Lombok and the Sunda Straits. Any disruption in traffic flow through these points can have disastrous consequences. The disruption of energy flows in particular is a considerable security concern for littoral states, as a majority of their energy lifelines are sea-based. Since energy is critical in influencing the geopolitical strategies of a nation, any turbulence in its supply has serious security consequences. Given the spiraling demand for energy from developed and developing countries in the Rim, it is inevitable that these countries are sensitive to the security of the sea lines of communication (SLOCs) and choke points of the region.

The member nations of the IOR-ARC have direct access to the sea, giving associated extensive and increasing maritime interests. With notable exceptions and as a generalised observation, very few have a direct, imminent maritime threat on their sovereign territory projected, yet all view actual and potential conflict arising in the maritime domain in an operations-other-than-war scenario. These threats, which have been described as a situation akin to "anarchy at sea"[21] arise from a variety of sources, unsecured or ungoverned seas as havens for transnational threats that provide relatively inexpensive and inconspicuous movement, including illegal use of high seas by transnational crime syndicates, commercial opportunists, increasing incidences of organised piracy that plagues and endangers maritime traffic, human traffickers, polluters, "...the continued existence of territorial disputes and ethnic conflicts in the region with long historical roots,"[22] terrorism, that continues to thrive in the region and world-wide, despite ongoing counter-terrorism actions; while a further factor ".... is the confrontational posture adopted by regional states to resolve conflicting ocean interests and how naval power is used to assert rights over the disputed areas."[23]

The response by most states has been to shift their defence emphasis in the direction of their maritime resources so as to utilise them as flexibly as possible.[24] The challenge for the 18 nations of the Indian Ocean Rim Association for Regional Cooperation is to focus their collective maritime forces symbiosis in order to ensure permanent maritime security in this principal maritime arena.

Principles

The Charter declares that the IOR-ARC seeks to build and expand understanding and mutually beneficial co-operation through a consensus based, evolutionary and non-intrusive approach. There are no laws and binding contracts. Compliance with consensus-based decision remains without any rigid institutional structure to specify any rules and regulations.[25]

The IOR-ARC is based on the principles of open regionalism, which is a flexible arrangement that is more member-friendly than other neo-liberal regional arrangements such as preferential trading arrangements, free trade areas, customs unions, common markets, etc., as encouraged by the World Trade Organisation.[26]

Objectives of The IOR-ARC

The main focus of the IOR-ARC is on economic cooperation, particularly on trade and investment. It is primarily an outward-looking forum for economic dialogue and cooperation.[27] The open regionalism of the IOR-ARC has four components:

Trade Liberalisation

Non-discriminatory basis towards members. A 2020 deadline to reduce tariffs to zero for all member countries of the IOR-ARC has been set.

Trade and Investment Facilitation

Sharing of information on trade finance, investment regime, intellectual property, procurement procedures, customs regulations and quarantine requirements as well as the harmonisation of standards.

Economic and Technical Cooperation

Identifying specific areas for economic and technical cooperation. Building capacity for trade and investment cooperation.

Trade and Investment Dialogue

Develop shared strategies and take common positions on trade and investment issues.

It is apparent that the 'open regionalism' cornerstone of the IOR-ARC has an Achilles' heel, in that it does not (yet) address defence and security cooperation in a direct manner at IOR-ARC level, given that the very tenets of the numerous references to 'trade', above, are founded upon maritime security. There is some irony in this oversight.

Status

In the past few years, many of the countries in the IOR-ARC have made improvements in their economic policies, though they may still differ widely with respect to the policy instruments used and the magnitude of reform. These changes include reductions in tariff rates, removal of exchange controls, implementation of market-oriented economic policies, and removal of price controls. These have provided an impetus for intra-regional trade cooperation within the region.

There is a large degree of variation in the levels of economic development among the member countries. While Australia and Singapore rank among the high-income category countries of the world, Malaysia, Mauritius, Oman and South Africa are normally classified as middle-income countries. Moreover, the IOR-ARC encompasses a number of low-income countries like Mozambique, Kenya, Madagascar, Tanzania, Sri Lanka, and Yemen. Trade statistics reinforce this view. Close on 77 per cent of average world exports and imports of the IOR-ARC involve Australia, Indonesia, Malaysia, and Singapore. The other countries make up for the remaining percentage.

During the past four years, the Association has been putting its house in order. It has been dealing with internal issues such as formulating rules of procedure, an Instrument of Accession for new members, a Headquarters Agreement with the Government of Mauritius, formulating criteria for membership, Dialogue Partner and Observer Status, establishing a Coordinating Secretariat and determining its yearly budget. The decision therefore by the Committee of Ministers to appoint a High-Level Task Force seems most appropriate and timely. The mandate of the HLTF was broad and inclusive of most of the teething problems being experienced by this youthful Regional Association.[28] These proactive plans and management initiatives will bode well for the establishment and later operationalisation of maritime co-operation within the IOR-ARC region.

Maritime Capabilities at Sub-Regional Level

As noted earlier, all IOR-ARC member states are also member states of other, more geographically or culturally-identified proximate regional economic communities (for the purposes of this paper, called 'sub-regional economic communities'), with some even having dual sub-regional membership. At the same time, it needs to be noted, and for the purpose of this paper it is cardinal, that each of the IOR-ARC member States is an island or littoral State; which in turn infers a degree of maritime, naval or coastguard capability. This section of the paper will give a brief overview of the regional economic communities to which IOR-ARC countries belong in the first instance; and also analyse the individual nations' regional maritime capabilities in this regard, simultaneously noting regional maritime cooperation levels. In clockwise order, starting from the Southern African Development, the countries and their maritime capabilities are:

Southern African Development Community (SADC)

The predecessor to the SADC, the Southern African Development Co-ordinating Conference (SADCC) was formalised by means of an MoU on the Institutions of the Southern African Development Co-ordination Conference, dated 20 July 1981. In 1992, the SADCC transformed itself into the Southern African Development Community (SADC). The SADC Treaty was signed in Windhoek on 17 August 1992 and entered into force on 30 September 1993. Of the 14 member states, the following are also members of the IOR-ARC—the Republics of South Africa, Mozambique, Madagascar, Mauritius, and the United Republic of Tanzania.[29] Concerning maritime cooperation, the SADC has an active Standing Maritime Committee; its vision being to promote peace and prosperity in the SADC region through maritime military cooperation. The three main objectives are: the provision of mutual maritime security in order to ensure the freedom of sea lines of communication, the development and maintenance of maritime capability in the region; and the development of maritime capacity to meet contingencies that require quick response. Naval cooperation plans are assigned as follows: Angola: Search and Rescue, Mozambique; Force Support, South Africa: Naval Training, Multinational Force Preparation and Naval Co-ordination and Guidance of Shipping (NCAGS) and Naval Hydrography.

East African Community (EAC)

The East African Community is the regional inter-governmental organisation of the area, with its headquarters in Arusha, Tanzania. The EAC aims at widening and deepening cooperation among the five member states, in among others, political, economic and social fields for their mutual benefit, while at the same time constructing a powerful and sustainable bloc. The ultimate aim is a political federation of the East African States. Only the Republic of Kenya and Tanzania are also members of the IOR-ARC, Tanzania in addition to being a member of the SADC.[30] The dormant state of

Somalia, on the north-east African coast, represents an area of instability in this region, yet is not represented on the IOR-ARC (see Pakistan, further). Maritime security off Somalia is an increasing problem, with the International Maritime Bureau labelling Somalia as one of the top risk countries for shipping, and piracy is common.[31] Maritime coordination activities between Kenya and Tanzania appear to be limited, and information not in the public domain.

The Arab League

Also called the League of Arabian States, the League is a regional organisation of Arab states in the Middle East and North Africa, formed in Cairo in March 1945, with membership currently standing at twenty-two, with Iran and Yemen also being members of the IOR-ARC. The main aim of the League is "... draw closer the relations between member states and coordinate collaboration between them, to safeguard their independence and sovereignty, and to consider in a general way the affairs and interests of the Arab countries."[32] The signing on April 13, 1950, of an agreement on Joint Defence and Economic Cooperation also committed the signatories to coordination of military defence measures. All Arab League members are also members of the Organisation of the Islamic Conference. In turn, the memberships of the smaller Gulf Co-operation Council (see further) and the Arab Maghreb Union are subsets of the League. Maritime cooperation has been delegated to the subordinate regional economic communities.

The Organisation of the Islamic Conference (OIC)

Between 1969 and 1972, the Organisation of the Islamic Conference was founded by its thirty member states. Only the Islamic Republic of Iran and the Republic of Yemen are also IOR-ARC affiliates.

The objectives of the Islamic Conference are: to promote Islamic solidarity among member states; to consolidate cooperation among member states in the economic, social, cultural, scientific and other vital fields of activities, and to carry out consultations among member states in international organisations; to endeavour to eliminate racial segregation, discrimination and to eradicate colonialism in all its forms; to take necessary measures to support international peace and security founded on justice; to coordinate efforts for the safeguarding of the Holy Places and support of the struggle of the people of Palestine, to help them regain their rights and liberate their land; to back the struggle of all Muslim people with a view to preserving their dignity, independence and national rights; to create a suitable atmosphere for the promotion of cooperation and understanding among member states and other countries.[33] Information regarding any maritime cooperation is not in public domain.

The Gulf Co-operation Council (GCC)

The Gulf Co-operation Council was established in 1981, and was created in response to the outbreak of the Iran-Iraq war. The GCC seeks to strengthen cooperation (in areas such as agriculture, industry, investment, security and trade) among its member states. Progress towards economic integration has been slow during the 1980s economic downturn in the region.[34] Of the six GCC states, only the Sultanate of Oman and the United Arab Emirates are also member states of the IOR-ARC. The GCC member states have been aiding and supporting all regional and international counter-terrorism efforts, while stressing at the same time the need to differentiate between terrorism and the legitimate right of the people to struggle against occupation. Military and maritime cooperation among the GCC States is characterised by a serious effort to create and develop a GCC defence force. The GCC States signed a Joint GCC Defence Pact, ratified during the 21st session on 31 December 2000. The Pact was guided by the principle of collective, integrated and mutually guaranteeing defence force based on the Muslim faith first, and then on the individual capacities of each state. The objective is to protect the interests of the member states and to defend the land, air and the regional waters belonging to them. The pact was the culmination of several years of military cooperation.

The GCC Supreme Council approved the studies as well as the steps for the implementations of two projects; the first of which aims at the automatic interlinking of the air force and air defence operation centres of the GCC countries; as well as a secured (fibre optic) communications network. It became operational in June 2000).

In addition, the standardisation of fundamentals and concepts have received ab initio attention, the objective being to raise mutual support, facilitate support exchange, and to derive mutual benefit from the available capacities in the GCC States. It comprises two major components. The first is joint exercises that began with dual and triple naval and air exercises, and culminated in annual joint air and naval exercises with the participation of all GCC States. The second is the 'unification' of manuals, where more than a hundred military manuals have been standardised. Also, more than a hundred curricula of various training courses have also been standardised for military training schools and colleges.

Other fields of military cooperation have been expanded to include military intelligence, military survey, medical services, weapon systems, communications, airforce, environment security, defence against chemical weapons, naval forces, electronic warfare, and defence against ballistic missiles.[35]

The South Asian Association for Regional Cooperation (SAARC)

The South Asian Association for Regional Coöperation (SAARC) was established when its Charter was formally adopted on December 8, 1985 by the Heads of State or Government of Bangladesh, Bhutan, India, the Maldives, Nepal, Pakistan and Sri Lanka. SAARC provides a platform for the peoples of South Asia to work together in a spirit of friendship, trust and understanding. It aims to accelerate the process of economic and social development in member states.[36] Of the seven SAARC states, only three—the People's Republic of Bangladesh, the Republic of India, and Democratic Socialist Republic of Sri Lanka are also members of the IOR-ARC, with Pakistan being a notable omission (effectively inducing a gap in the IOR-ARC's coverage of the Indian Ocean Rim). Maritime cooperation, if any, is not within the public domain; indeed, given the latent degrees of difference between India and Pakistan, military and maritime cooperation of any nature appears unlikely in the short to-medium term.

The Association of South-east Asian Nations (ASEAN)

The Association of South-east Asian Nations or ASEAN was established on 8 August 1967 in Bangkok by the five original member countries, namely, Indonesia, Malaysia, the Philippines, Singapore, and Thailand. The objectives of ASEAN are contained in its Declaration, which states the aims and purposes are twofold: to accelerate economic growth, social process and cultural development in the region; and also to promote regional peace and stability through abiding respect for justice and the rule of law in the relationship among countries in the region and adherence to the principles of the United Nations Charter. Interestingly, from a military maritime viewpoint, in 2003 the ASEAN leaders resolved that an ASEAN Community shall be established comprising three pillars, the primary one being the ASEAN Security Community (followed by the ASEAN Economic and Socio-Cultural Communities). The Republics of Indonesia and Singapore, Malaysia, and the Kingdom of Thailand are also IOR-ARC member states. Based on the Declaration, above, maritime co-operation is not a core function of ASEAN per se, but has been devolved upon the ASEAN Regional Forum (see next).

The ASEAN Regional Forum (ARF)

The ARF is the principal forum for security dialogue in Asia (whereas the

Asia-Pacific Economic Cooperation, or APEC,[37] is the premier forum for facilitating economic growth, cooperation, trade and investment in the Asia-Pacific region). The ARF comprises 27 countries; the 10 ASEAN member states, 10 ASEAN dialogue partners (including the Commonwealth of Australia and India, being IOR-ARC member states) plus seven nations (including Pakistan, Bangladesh and Sri Lanka, who are also IOR-ARC member states).

The ARF "... provides a setting in which members can discuss current regional security issues and develop cooperative measures to enhance peace and security in the region. In areas of defence and security, relationships among ARF nations appear to be '... strong and diverse. Counter-terrorism cooperation, in particular, has expanded significantly since 11 September 2001 and the Bali bombings of October 2002."[38]

In terms of maritime cooperation, the outlook is very positive. Research indicates that the ARF, in a number of respects, is pursuing an excellent course of action towards achieving and maintaining maritime cooperation for this reason. In March 2005, Singapore's Defence Minister proposed that Asia's only security forum move beyond dialogue and hold maritime security exercises to improve its ability to deal with terrorist and other threats. At a seminar on maritime security cooperation, he said that Asian militaries and their counterparts outside the region collectively address security threats in the region's waters. ARF military officials and security analysts had called for increased patrols in the area amid fears that ships passing through the straits are vulnerable targets for terrorists bent on crippling world trade. A maritime security exercise involving 22 navies in the Western Pacific region was carried out in May 2007.[39] "These are all very positive developments that build confidence, enhance capabilities, and also create a framework for inter-operability that can be useful for future contingencies. By bringing the frontline agencies together to tackle and promote maritime security, ARF demonstrates that it has gone beyond being a forum for confidence building into an inter-governmental framework pursuing common security. Activities like this demonstrate ARF's relevance in responding head-on to the current security issues of the day."[40]

The author would suggest that the documentation which relates to the ARF's inclusive and tactful management for maritime security participation would be a model for the IOR-ARC to emulate.[41]

The Five Power Defence Arrangements (FPDA)

The FPDA is a series of defence relationships established by bilateral agreements between the United Kingdom, New Zealand, Australia, Malaysia, and Singapore (the latter three countries also being IOR-ARC member states), signed in 1971, whereby the five nations will consult one another in the event of external aggression or threat of attack against Malaysia or Singapore. The FPDA replaces some of the United Kingdom's former defence obligations.

The FPDA provides for defence cooperation, and for an Integrated Air Defence System (IADS) for Malaysia and Singapore based in Malaysia, but hosts rotating detachments of aircraft and personnel from all five countries. In 2001,the headquarters of IADS was redesignated Headquarters Integrated "Area" Defence System.

In 1981, the five powers organised the first annual land and naval exercises. Since 1997, the naval and air exercises have been combined. It now has personnel from all three branches of the armed services, and coordinates the annual five-power naval and air exercises, while moving towards the fuller integration of land elements.[42] In March 2005, the Defence Minister of Singapore acknowledged that the Five Power Defence Arrangements, an alliance involving Malaysia, Singapore, Australia, New Zealand and Britain, had already begun conducting maritime security drills in the previous year.[43]

IOR-ARC Individual Countries' Maritime Capabilities: An Overview

A note was made earlier in this paper about the vast stretch of ocean enclosed by the Indian Ocean. The Indian Ocean part of the world's extensive 'highway', as Admiral A.T. Mahan termed it,[44] poses significant time-space management and associated maritime resource challenges for the Indian Ocean Rim nations; in order to "operationalise" it. Reverting to the title of this paper, this would be the verb to bring the Indian Ocean region under fulltime positive control; specifically in this case, by the maritime forces of the IOR-ARC, for as the adage goes, "to patrol is to control"—to provide continuous maritime safety and security in the region.

IOR-ARC countries' maritime capabilities need to be viewed within the paradigm of their foreign policy responsibilities. Without the necessary capacity to interact constructively with IOR-ARC partners and unable to assist those in the Rim that are virtually devoid of maritime capabilities in the attainment of ensuring maritime security in the area, countries may not be able to meet their responsibilities.

The maritime forces of the IOR-ARC display a range of maritime capabilities that cover the continuum from those states that have extensive and indeed impressive maritime capabilities, to those navies that have adequate medium capabilities; right down to others that have limited resources coupled with significant challenges. The information regarding individual states' maritime, naval or coast guard capabilities is readily available in the public domain. What is apparent generally, is that there is a direct correlation between each state's designation as a developed, developing or even heavily-indebted poor nation; and their maritime prowess.[45] To derive a typology of navies which would assist in ranking them in terms of their abilities to perform a dedicated task, such as maintaining maritime security in the Indian Ocean Rim region beyond the confines of states' standard maritime operations, the Royal Canadian Navy has developed a useful classification instrument.[46] What follows is for purposes of argumentation only, yet will tend to indicate the desires of states to utilise their maritime power in a set strategic direction.[47] For all the caveats listed in the footnote, and because it is not within the aim of this paper, nations will not be listed in the last column, but only the author's subjective indication of how many nations' navies qualify per ranking, as they apply within the IOR-ARC.

Table 1: Ranking Navies according to their Maritime Security Capabilites

Rank	Description	Possible IOR-ARC Navies
1: Major Global Force Projection Navy (Complete)	This is a navy capable of carrying out all the military roles of naval forces on a global scale. It possesses the full range of carrier and amphibious capabilities, sea control forces, and nuclear attack and ballistic missile submarines, and all in sufficient numbers to undertake major operations independently.	Nil
2. Major Global Force Projection Navy (Partial)	These are navies that possess most, if not all of the force projection capabilities of a "complete" global navy, but only in sufficient numbers to undertake one major "out-of-area" operation.	1
3. Medium Global Force Projection Navy	These are navies that may not possess the full range of capabilities, but have a credible capacity in some of them and consistently demonstrate a determination to exercise them at some distance from home waters, in cooperation with other Force Projection Navies.	1

Rank	Description	Possible IOR-ARC Navies
4. Medium Regional Force Projection Navy	These are navies possessing the ability to project force into the adjoining ocean basin. While they may have the capacity to exercise these further afield, for whatever reason, they do not do so on a regular basis.	3
5. Adjacent Force Projection Navies	These are navies that have some ability to project force well offshore, but are not capable of carrying out high-level naval operations over oceanic distances.	2
6. Offshore Territorial Defence Navies	These are navies that have relatively high levels of capability in defensive (and constabulary) operations up to about 200 miles from their shores, having the sustainability offered by frigate or large corvette vessels and (or) a capable submarine force.	2
7. Inshore Territorial Defence Navies	These are navies that have primarily inshore territorial defence capabilities, making them capable of coastal combat rather than constabulary duties alone. This implies a force comprising missile-armed fast-attack craft, short-range aviation and a limited submarine force.	4
8. Constabulary Navies	These are significant fleets that are not intended to fight, but to act purely in a constabulary role.	2
9. Token Navies	These are navies that have some minimal capability, but this often consists of little more than a formal organisational structure and a few coastal craft. These states, the world's smallest and weakest, cannot aspire to anything but the most limited constabulary functions.	3

Indian Ocean Rim Maritime Cooperation and Capabilities at Sub-Regional Level: Deduction in Terms of Strengths and Weaknesses

The previous section has dealt with the countries of the IOR-ARC at sub-regional level and endeavoured to determine the level of interaction at maritime cooperation level. In addition, countries' naval and maritime capabilities were cursorily examined.

Both these elements would have provided an overview, first, of the level and degree of success that the IOR-ARC member states have experienced thus far in terms of integrative cooperation, if at all, at sub-regional level. Second, by gaining an insight into individual states' naval and maritime capabilities (and by inference, their limitations, as indicated by the ranking system employed, above); an idea can be obtained about what each member state can contribute towards establishing and maintaining the operational state of the Indian Ocean Rim region.

It would be appropriate to list these two attributes, i.e. maritime cooperation at sub-regional level, together with nations' naval and maritime capabilities in terms of the perceived and deduced strengths and weaknesses.

Strengths

The following strengths are perceived:

From Present Institutional Resource—Progression to the IOR-ARC

All the IOR-ARC member states belong to one (or, frequently, more than one) regional economic community, which—as pointed out above—includes maritime cooperation at varying levels of intensity. This infers a number of issues that may be included as strengths. First, that the political desire exists at individual states' level to cooperate for reasons of own national interest, that the cooperation will bring about enhanced status, economic and developmental benefits of long-term duration, together with lasting improvements in maritime security. In addition, this means that member states possess the institutional and bureaucratic capacity and related embedded experiential value to perform these tasks; and that it may be transferred to another (in this case the IOR-ARC) collective cooperation organisation. This bodes well for any progression towards maritime cooperation and the operationalisation of the Indian Ocean Rim region.

Common Denominator—States' Goodwill The IOR-ARC is relatively unique in the sense that its common denominator is the rim of a vast oceanic area, and that the importance of the values of the common denominator were deemed sufficiently important to set aside differences that lie within the IOR-ARC states. In a number of ways, it represents sub-sets of differing civilisations, yet with a common goal within the IOR-ARC. The widely disparate nature of the member states' gubernatorial composition, and the fact that each member state is aware of the fact that its formation represents, in essence, a comity of nations, and should generate sufficient goodwill to allow for bonafide integrative activities—states want to be seen to succeed. Therefore, the IOR-ARC's heterogenic composition should be viewed as a definite strength, a potent source of wide-ranging effort into the initiation and solving the complex maritime security challenge of the region.

Impressive Military Maritime Resources of the Region

The maritime, naval and coast guard resources of the IOR-ARC nations are, collectively, inspiring. Together, they represent the entire scope of maritime operations, which would include good radar and satellite surveillance. Most nations have, over the past decade, prioritised their new vessel acquisitions, upgraded interactive intelligence at sub-regional level and have ensured good support systems and infrastructure. Different platforms, systems, and support infrastructure may serve to complement various capabilities. With proper planning and proactive utilisation, the instruments of the maritime, naval and coast guards of the Indian Ocean Rim region may be focused, and the region placed under positive control.

Weaknesses

The following weaknesses are appreciated, and if not managed well, could serve to undermine the achievement of lasting maritime security in the Indian Ocean Rim.

The maritime forces, navies and coast guards of the Indian Ocean Rim are vastly dissimilar, not only size, but also origin of platforms, weapons, doctrine, tactics, surveillance and reconnaissance, and maritime air assets.

In addition, the IOR-ARC nations are founded on different political and governing systems; which range from a Commonwealth state, a People's Republic, a Sultanate, an Islamic Republic, a Democratic Socialist Republic, a Kingdom; to standard Republics. There may be difficulties in achieving common ground with respect to the initiation, operationalisation and subsequent management of the Indian Ocean Rim region, particularly as seen from maritime military cooperation perspectives.

These two aforementioned disparities present challenges, which are not insurmountable and should not present disjunctive propositions; yet it does infer a laboriously extended challenge to align maritime attributes and processes.

The sheer size of the Indian Ocean presents massive challenges in terms of ensuring continuous security, it will tend to place pressure on member states' maritime, naval and coast guard resources, many of which are already buckling under the strain. It may be a prudent strategy to secure the region from a maritime perspective in two or more phases, with the first covering states' littoral areas as well as established trade routes; and the second phase moving toward full coverage.

Indian Ocean Rim: Future Maritime Cooperation: Conclusions and Recommendations in Terms of Opportunities and Tactics

Having briefly analysed the IOR-ARC's strengths and weaknesses with respect to cooperation and capabilities, and mindful of the aim of this paper, namely the operationalisation of the Indian Ocean Rim region, this paper will conclude with two final aspects. First, the concept of broadening the Objectives of the IOR-ARC, so that it may be underpinned by an operationalised maritime security system, presents exciting opportunities, and these will be listed. Then, a course will be plotted to provide guidelines and recommendations in terms of a proposed plan of action, tactics if you will, which may aid the process of establishing an operational maritime security system in the IOR-ARC.

Opportunities to Enhance Military Maritime Cooperation in the Indian Ocean Rim Region

Opportunities for cooperation in the Indian Ocean Rim region are manifold, some of which follow:

> Sailors who become diplomats can fulfill important functions in the region through "enlargement and engagement".[48] This concept would include military training (including agreed doctrine and tactics), multinational maritime exercises, supply military aid and equipment (a process which may contribute directly to inter-operability and standard operating practices), and support towards integration at IOR-ARC maritime level. Professional and organisational skills inherent in the maritime forces, navies and coast guards of the IOR-ARC member states can be used constructively in the field of humanitarian aid (with the South-East Asian tsunami of December 2004 being a case in point). Maritime military groups can give protection from hostile and criminal forces, which may exploit an institutional vacuum that may develop in the period directly after the catastrophe, and, in addition can render aid in terms of logistics, transportation and distribution in terrain difficult to access; all of which can be non-offensive. Often, "goodwill" or "showing the flag" visits are precursors to improved trade, with diplomacy having paved the way, following the adage that "trade follows flag". Also, navy ships are often used to promote visitors' defence industry, helping to market and promote systems and products. The differences between IOR-ARC maritime forces, navies and

coast guards' capabilities, technical and operational competencies ought to be handled with sensitivity, whereby cooperative strategies are formulated and agreed to in sync. In this regard, "... naval forces are often the best forces to use for coalition building because of their utility for development with limited commitment".[49] The greatest opportunity that maritime cooperation in the IOR-ARC presents, is that of bringing about maritime security through the operationalisation of region. As a first step, the increasing use of the expanded term "maritime safety and security" by the IOR-ARC forum may signal the convergence of regional views on maritime security.[50] This is a sine qua non condition for effective and enhanced trade for the region, a critical foundation that will see the realisation towards improved stability, associated development and increased trade within, and for, the region.

A Plan of Action: Towards a Maritime Coalition of the Indian Ocean Rim

How should this "maritime coalition" in the Indian Ocean Rim be formed? Given the (prima facie) incongruent nature of the IOR-ARC's member states, it would be apparent that any envisaged formation would have to be operative at the political level. It is submitted that the most critical important fundamental measure would be to establish consensus in peacetime to cope with non-military threats. This would be an easier task for states to resolve in practice and it would also produce less angst (in terms of perceived potential breaches of sovereignty, territorial integrity, etcetera)—thoughtful management of perceptions would be crucial. This would explore regional confidence and security-building initiatives in ways that are non-threatening to all IOR-ARC member states, where significant success may be anticipated.

More sensitive issues that contribute to inter-state conflict could be examined once confidence in the resolution of peacetime issues is developed. The focus will need to shift to more extensive maritime cooperation to counter growing threats to maritime security, noted above. This requires added emphasis on operational cooperation, where the focus is more coordinated, more multilateral and with greater inter-operability. In this respect, several measures can be taken to enhance maritime security in the region.[51]

There are five convergent strategies and measures that may contribute to maritime security in the region.

First, given the current economic growth rates and reliance on maritime trade in the region, there is an urgent need to build a regional consensus over "maritime coalition" to provide maritime safety and security for the SLOCs. The United Nations and the IMO have an excellent track record in facilitating such initiatives. In this respect, three issues are critical:

Building a maritime coalition will best be served by working through an existing, functional and institutionalised structure, and it is submitted that the IOR-ARC is the most suitable regional economic vehicle.

Second, the mandate of the IOR-ARC must be expanded to include security, and specifically maritime security cooperation; as a matter of collective resolve.

Further, and this is a critical point, the membership of the IOR-ARC needs to expanded significantly to include most—if not all—the Indian Ocean Rim countries; as this will extend its mandate and strengthen its cooperative hand.

Then, two options for the development of a regional 'security framework' are: either to expand on any one of the existing REC maritime cooperation frameworks (one that is verifiably operational), or to establish a "binding security structure" out of the web of existing bilateral and alliance relationships.

Third, in order to proceed down either of the two tracks, IOR-ARC regional nations must discard the notion of "... 'security only during emergencies' and instead work to build common values, based on consensus to ensure 'maritime safety in peacetime, full-time'".[52] Similar to the Five Power Defence Arrangements (FPDA) noted above, and over time (with proven confidence-measures as a function of time) an IOR-ARC multinational maritime headquarters should be established to coordinate the development, implementation, operationalisation and continued operational status of maritime safety and security in the region.

Fourth, it may be easier initially to develop maritime coalitions based on responses to emergencies that could then be expanded to other peacetime areas once confidence over cooperation has increased.

Last, developing and sharing common values with respect to the management of the regional maritime domain would benefit both the individual nation and the region as a whole.[53]

Conclusion: Indian Ocean Maritime Secusity on the Horizon

For geo-strategic reasons, IOR-ARC countries' national interests can be served by this outward-looking and foreign security approach, for at least two reasons: one is a redefinition of what sort of country each state perceives itself to be, including their public's view of what sort of people they are; the other is to recognise and accept the fact that a very significant part of each IOR-ARC country's destiny lies across the oceans.[54]

Thus, each IOR-ARC country needs to look beyond its own littoral and contribute to international organisations, structures and processes; making realistic and practical contributions—for the betterment of the Indian Ocean Rim region at large. ■

Notes

1. North American Free Trade Agreement (NAFTA), Asia-Pacific Economic Cooperation (APEC) forum, Indian Ocean Rim Association for Regional Cooperation (IOR-ARC), the Southern African Development Community (SADC), Economic Community of West African States (ECOWAS), Southern Cone Market (Mercosur).
2. Mills, G. *The Wired Model. South Africa, Foreign Policy and Globalisation.* Published jointly by the South African Institute of International Affairs, Jan Smuts House, Johannesburg and Tafelberg Publishers Ltd, 28 Wale Street, Cape Town. © Greg Mills, 2000; p.72.
3. "Joint Approaches to Peacekeeping Missions and Conflict Resolution in the Indian Ocean Rim", by Pradeep Kaushiva, in *South Africa and Naval Power at the Millennium,* edited by Martin Edmonds and Greg Mills, South African Institute of International Affairs, July 2000; p.59 et seq.
4. ASEAN—Association of South East Asian Nations, SADC—Southern African Development Community, GCC—Gulf Co-operation Council, EAC—East African Community.
5. Strengths, Weaknesses, Opportunities and Tactics (SWOT).
6. Mills, supra; p.73.
7. *The Clash of Civilizations and the Remaking of World Order,* by Samuel P. Huntington. Simon & Schuster UK Ltd, Africa House, London, Touchstone paperback, 1998.
8. "Inside the Cave: The Banality of I.R. Studies", article by James Kurth. *The National Interest.* Issue 53, published Fall 1998, p29 et seq. © 1998 The National Affairs, Inc.; © 2002 Gale Group.
9. United Nations Development Programme (UNDP), 1994, *Human Development Report.*
10. Snyder, C.A. "Regional Security Structures", in Snyder, C.A. (ed) Contemporary Security and Strategy. London: Macmillan Press, 1999; p.114.
11. "International and Regional Naval Capabilities", by Martin Edmonds and Greg Mills, *Beyond the Horizon: Defence, Diplomacy and South Africa's Maritime Opportunities,* published by the South African Institute of International Affairs and the Centre and International Security Studies, June 1998; pp.51–67.
12. *The Historical Journal,* 21, 4 (1978), p.973.
13. Ken Booth, *Navies and Foreign Policy.* Croom Helm, London, 1977; p. 285.
14. http://www.dfa.gov.za/RECs/IORARC/IOR-ARC.DFA.mht—Republic of South Africa's Department of Foreign Affairs' website, accessed 27 November 2007.

15. Ibid.
16. Association of South-East Asian Nations (ASEAN), South Asia Association for Regional Co-operation (SAARC), Gulf Co-operation Council (GCC).
17. A.T. Mahan, *The Influence of Sea Power upon History,* quoted in Felipe Fernández-Armesto *Civilizations,* Pan Books, an imprint of Pan Macmillan Ltd, 20 Wharf Road, London NI 9RR, paperback edition 2001; p. 324.
18. The Indian Ocean includes Andaman Sea, Arabian Sea, Bay of Bengal, Flores Sea, Great Australian Bight, Gulf of Aden, Gulf of Oman, Java Sea, Mozambique Channel, Persian Gulf, Red Sea, Savu Sea, Strait of Malacca, and Timor Sea. The decision by the International Hydrographic Organisation in the spring of 2000 to delimit a fifth ocean, the Southern Ocean, removed the portion of the Indian Ocean south of 60 degrees south latitude.
19. International Relations in an Emerging Multilateral World: The Indian Ocean Region: A Story Told with Pictures; collated and sequenced by Nadesan Satyendra.
20. Alexander, Lewis M, 'Choke points of the world ocean' in The Development of Integrated Sea-Use Management. Contributors: Smith, H.D.; Vallega, A. (editors). New York, 1991; p. 99.
21. "Maritime Security in the Asia-Pacific". Report of a Conference Organised by the Institute of Defence and Strategic Studies (IDSS), 20-21 May 2004, Marina Mandarin Hotel, Singapore, pp. 6-7.
22. Ibid, comments by Lee Seo Hang (Institute of Foreign Affairs and National Security, South Korea).
23. Ibid.
24. Edmonds & Mills, supra.
25. Cooperation is based on principles of sovereignty, equality, territorial integrity, political independence, and non-interference in internal affairs, peaceful coexistence, and mutual benefit.

    Membership is open to all sovereign states of the Indian Ocean Rim willing to subscribe to the principles and objectives of the Charter. The IOR-ARC is firmly based on the principle of open regionalism, as encouraged by the WTO.

    Decisions on all matters and issues and at all levels, will be taken on the basis of consensus. The IOR-ARC explicitly excludes bilateral relations and other issues likely to generatecontroversy and be an impediment to regional cooperation.

    Cooperation within the Association does not prejudice the rights and obligations of the member states within the framework of other economic and trade cooperation arrangements and will not apply automatically to member states of the Association. It does not seek to be a substitute for, but to reinforce, be complementary to and consistent with, the bilateral, plurilateral and multilateral rights and obligations of member states.

    Within the framework of the Association, member states will pursue measures to promote the achievement of its objectives, and will not take any action likely to prejudice its objectives and activities. The work programmes of the Association will be undertaken by member states on a voluntary basis. Ibid.
26. Ibid.
27. According to its Charter, the objectives of the Association are:

    To promote the sustained growth and balanced development of the region and of the

Member States and to create common ground for regional economic cooperation; To focus on those areas of economic cooperation which provide maximum opportunities to develop shared interests and reap mutual benefits. Towards this end, to formulate and implement projects for economic cooperation relating to trade facilitation, promotion and liberalisation; promotion of foreign investment, scientific and technological exchanges, and tourism, movement of natural persons and service providers on a non-discriminatory basis; and development of infrastructure and human resources, as laid down in the Work Programmes of the Association; To identify other areas of cooperation as may be mutually agreed; Towards promoting liberalisation, to remove impediments to, and lower barriers towards, freer and enhanced flow of goods, services investment and technology within the region;

To explore all possibilities and avenues for trade liberalisation with a view to augmenting and diversifying trade flows among Member States; To encourage close interaction of trade and industry, academic institutions, scholars and peoples of the Member States, without discrimination among Member States and without prejudice to obligations under other regional economic and trade cooperation arrangements; and To strengthen cooperation and dialogue among Member States in international fora on global economic issues, and, where desirable, to develop shared strategies and take common positions in the international fora on issues of mutual interest: and To promote cooperation in development of human resources, particularly through closer linkages among training institutions, universities and other specialised institutions of the Member States. Ibid.

28. Ibid.
29. http://www.iss.org the (South African) Institute for Security Studies, accessed 5 December 2007.
30. http://www.eac.int/about_eac.htm the website of the East African Community, accessed 4 December 2007.
31. http://www.iss.org the (South African) Institute for Security Studies, accessed 10 January 2008.
32. http://www.arableagueonline.org/las/english/details_en.jsp?art_id=8538level_id=11, accessed 14 January 2008.
33. Ibid.
34. http://www.arab.de/arabinfo/gcc.htm, accessed 4 December 2007.
35. http://www.gcc-sg.org/English/EPicShow.asp? mycover=40.html, accessed 8 January 2008.
36. http://www.saarc-sec.org/main.php, accessed 08 January 2008.
37. http://www.apec.org.
38. http://www.dfat.gov.au/arf/ index.html.
39. However, he emphasised that much more could be done through the ARF. Senior officers from the navy, coast guard, port authorities, shipping lines and law enforcement agencies from the ARF member nations are attending the two-and-a half-day conference in Singapore this week, most of which will be held behind closed doors. The head of the ARF unit at ASEAN's Jakarta-based secretariat, M.C Abad, who was attending the conference, told AFP the gathering was a positive step in improving regional maritime security. http://www.aseanregionalforum.org/News/tabid/59/newsid399/25/Default.aspx, accessed 18 January 2008.
40. Ibid, accessed 18 January 2008.

41. For example, the Co-Chairs' Report Pursuant to the decision of the 11th ASEAN Regional Forum on 2 July 2004 in Jakarta, an ARF Confidence-Building Mechanism seminar on "Regional Cooperation in Maritime Security" in Singapore from 2 to 4 March 2005, also the "MARITIME THREATS WORKSHOP" United States Army Pacific's: Defense Environmental and International Cooperation (DEIC) Workshop, by Commander Robert Wohlschlegel, Lieutenant Colonel Curtis W. Turner, and Dr. Kent Butts in Issue Paper, Center for Strategic Leadership, U.S. Army War College, October 2004, Volume 09-04.
42. http://www.wikipedia/wiki/Five_Power_Defence_Arrangements
43. http://www.aseanregionalforum.org/News/tabid/59/newsid399/25/Default.aspx, accessed 18 January 2008.
44. Felipe Fernández-Armesto, *Civilizations,* supra.
45. However, historically, there have been examples where this was not necessarily the case. For instance, the 'great' continental power of the 17thcentury Chinese Qing Dynasty chose to employ only a limited navy; whereas a 'lesser' power exerted disproportionate influence because of the vivacity and related national interest imbued in its Navy (the Dutch Republic, also of the 17th century). Noted in "Leadmark: The Navy's Strategy for 2020", Chapter 3 Gathering the Instruments. Directorate of Maritime Strategy, National Defense Headquarters/Chief of the Maritime Staff, Major General George R. Pearkes Building, 101 Colonel By Drive, Ottawa, Ontario, Canada K1A0K2, published 18 June 2001, ISBN 0-662-30934-0 Cat. no. DB3-22/2001E, p. 43.
46. Ibid, pp. 43-45. In turn, this was from a model described in Eric Grove, The Future of Sea Power, pp. 236–240. Grove built upon previous works by other authors, notably M.A. Morris, *Expansion of Third World Navies* (London: Macmillan, 1987).
47. Further caveats—"Leadmark" supra, notes that "...because each state defines its naval requirements in its own terms, any attempt at ranking involves a complex matrix of circumstances particular to a state's defence and foreign relations, modified by its economic well-being and dependence upon the sea, all qualified by some assessment of actual operational capabilities. Moreover, a simple quantitative ranking based on absolute aggregate numbers of hulls must be tempered by some qualitative analysis as to how the fleets are employed. It has been further suggested that the distinction between rankings is a function of the ability to act independently across the spectrum of naval roles and functions, and at some range from home waters ("out of area" operations)." Ibid, pp. 44. Haydon, Peter T. *Sea Power and Maritime Strategy in the 21st Century: A "Medium" Power Perspective.* Halifax, NS: Dalhousie University Centre for Foreign Policy Studies, Maritime Security Occasional Paper No 10, 2000 pp. 75–81 offers this alternative typology.
48. George Robertson, *Building European Security and the Role of Defence Diplomacy.* Speech given before the English Speaking Union, 4 September 1997. Quoted in Edmonds & Mills, supra.
49. Eric Grove, "Sea Power in the 21st Century", *Journal of the Australian Naval Institute,* Vol. 21, No. 3 (August/October 1995), p.11.
50. Maritime Security in the Asia-Pacific" supra., adapted from a presentation given by Hideaki Kaneda, (The Okazaki Institute, Japan).
51. First, each regional country would have to tighten up the security of its port facilities, as required by the new International Ship and Port Facilities Security (ISPS) Code. Second, the littoral states responsible for the maritime security of the region, should

take unified and concerted action to enhance the security of its strategic waterways. Third, there is a need to involve key international players like the International Maritime Organisation, an organ of the UN. Multilateral cooperation and diplomatic initiatives like maritime security conferences, all contribute to the discussion on maritime security. From "Maritime Security in the Asia-Pacific" supra.

52. Maritime Security in the Asia-Pacific" supra., adapted from a presentation given by Hideaki Kaneda, (The Okazaki Institute, Japan).

53. Ibid.

54. Adapted from Edmonds & Mills, supra. p.122.

CONCLUDING SESSION

Commonality of Maritime Challenges and Options for a Cooperative IOR Maritime Security Structure

Arun Prakash*

I feel privileged to be here this afternoon, to deliver the closing address for the maiden gathering of the Indian Ocean Naval Symposium organised by the Indian Navy. The fact that the distinguished leaders of 27 Indian Ocean navies have gathered in New Delhi at Admiral Mehta's invitation is a matter of great satisfaction not only for us in India, but for everyone in this neighbourhood.

In the list of hazardous occupations in the world, I would venture to suggest that delivering the closing address in a symposium of this nature should be right up there amongst the more dangerous activities. One has to be either brave or foolhardy to follow in the wake of erudite speakers who have already said everything that was worth saying on the subject.

When faced with a difficult situation, one can only seek guidance from another sailor, similarly placed. I refer to Admiral Farragut's famous order to his fleet during the American Civil War: "Damn the torpedoes and full speed ahead".

Introduction

History and geography are two immutable factors which offer themselves as promising catalysts when we seek commonality and cooperation between nations in an environment of diversity. At the risk of causing offence to some, I have to say with regret that people who live on the shores of the Indian Ocean traditionally, have not been inclined to reflect on their past.

* Former Chief of the Naval Staff, Indian Navy.

For all of us therefore, George Santayana's aphorism, that "those who fail to learn from history are doomed to repeat it", bears poignant significance at this juncture.

Since the inhabitants of these countries have been remiss in neither researching the past, nor adequately documenting their own history, it was often left to colonial administrators, and European missionaries and scholars to record their rich past. However, those who write history also enjoy the licence of imparting it the kind of slant they wish to, even at the cost of objectivity.

Almost all works on maritime history from Western sources start with a description of the seafaring tradition of the Mediterranean basin around 2500-2000 BCE, and dwell on the sea power of Crete, Phoenicia, Greece, Carthage and Rome. Rarely do Western historical accounts, make even a passing mention of the seafaring skills of people of the East: the ancient Arabs, the Chinese, or Indians.

So much so that one wonders: is there an Indian Ocean maritime tradition?

An Indian Ocean Maritime Tradition

For an answer we have to turn to the lonely voice of Sardar KM Pannikar, an Indian historian and visionary. He expresses the firm conviction that because of the strong and steady seasonal monsoon winds, and also because of the earlier growth of civilisations on its shores, it was the Indian Ocean, and specifically the lands washed by the Arabian Sea, which saw the first oceanic sailing activity.

European writers, mostly ignorant about Asiatic history, have, according to Pannikar, erred seriously in assuming that navigational tradition first grew around the inland Aegean Sea. We also have a new thesis now, which says that Magellan, Columbus and Prince Henry were only following in the wake of the Chinese Admiral Cheng Ho, whose fleets actually discovered much of the New World, with the active assistance of Indian mariners.

Notwithstanding the early Indian Ocean maritime tradition, certain breakthroughs made by seafaring European nations around the 15th century, in the fields of shipbuilding, navigation and gunnery equipped their sailors not only to undertake long-distance voyages, but also gave them the means of overwhelming races less advanced in these fields.

European Domination of the Indian Ocean

On the 20th of May 1498 the Portuguese frigates San Gabriele and San Rafael anchored off the Malabar Coast, and Vasco da Gama landed on Indian soil. This date signifies a defining moment in the history of the IOR, because it marks the start of a new era of European domination.

The discovery of sea routes to the Indian Ocean made it, for the next five hundred years, virtually a European monopoly. As historian Paul Kennedy says: "Once the Portuguese and Spanish fleets had demonstrated the ease of conquest over others, and the financial benefits to be gained, the race was on; with Dutch, French, and English adventurers joining in what was to become a scramble for loot, trading links, and political advantage". As the largest colonial power, no nation demonstrates these aspects of commercialism better than Britain.

The period of about 60 years, after the final defeat of Napoleon in 1815, is often termed as an epoch of "Pax Britannica". The industrial revolution transformed Britain from a "nation of shopkeepers" into the "workshop of the world," and it now suited British interests to propagate the new concept of "free trade" whereby they could dominate markets worldwide, and flood them with their produce.

With the change from sail to steam and the imperial contest between European powers being played out at sea, the Royal Navy became a critical instrumentality of Britain's colonial and commercial ambitions. It had two essential requirements: bases in strategic maritime key points to command the sea-lanes, and an excuse to sail warships into areas of interest.

Accordingly, Britain occupied strategic locations like Singapore, Ceylon, Aden, Mombassa, Zanzibar, Mauritius, the Seychelles, and Cape Town; which converted the Indian Ocean virtually into a British lake. In the 19th century, the Royal Navy assumed the role of self-appointed international policeman for the suppression of piracy and slave trade, and thereby found legitimate cover for the presence of its warships wherever commercial or other interests dictated. This was the origin of the infamous "gunboat diplomacy", which underpinned British influence worldwide, and resulted in huge economic spin-offs.

Through this brief historical overview, I have attempted to make four points:

- Colonialism was an expression of the theory of political realism, which postulates that the international community is essentially anarchic and self-seeking, and that morality and law may not be binding beyond one's own national boundaries.
- The Indian Ocean colonies were therefore kept in a state of

impoverishment and industrial backwardness, and exploited economically to enhance the prosperity of their colonial masters.

- While colonialism may have become an anachronism, exploitation remains extant in many other manifestations. Having learnt from history, the inhabitants of the Indian Ocean littoral nations should resolve never to allow themselves to be exploited again.
- And last, shared history could be the glue that binds the diverse and varied nations of the Indian Ocean, in their quest for a secure, stable and prosperous future.

The Post-Colonial Era

In the post-colonial era, the main concern of major maritime powers remained the safety of the international sea-lanes traversing the Indian Ocean, and perhaps the deployment of their ballistic missile submarines in secure havens. Their navies hastened to fill the so-called "power vacuum" resulting from the withdrawal of the British from east of Suez.

The preoccupations of most newly independent countries, on the other hand, were domestic, and this tended to make them inward looking and insular in their vision. Some, like India, sought in vain to become autarchic and only succeeded in isolating themselves. Others, like Sri Lanka, ignored maritime security only to find that they had allowed the monster of separatism to breed with impunity.

As a consequence of this introversion, discourse as well as cooperation on security and other issues of maritime significance has remained relatively low key and muted in the IOR.

Maritime Security Discourse

In 1992, at a symposium held in Delhi, an interesting, if somewhat radical, concept of a "Panchayat" for naval cooperation in the Indian Ocean was mooted by the then Indian Chief of Naval Staff (CNS). A Panchayat is the local council for governance in an Indian village, and forms the basic building block of democracy in India. While this concept aroused considerable interest in academic circles, it was an idea whose time perhaps had not yet come, and it petered out for lack of official interest.

A decade later, an academic group of the Heidelberg University undertook an analytic study of Indian Ocean security. While endorsing the old Panchayat concept as well as the idea of a regional security regime, they also recommended enhancement in the range, scale and scope of security cooperation in the Indian Ocean, mainly through non-governmental activity.

In discussions such as these, one can find some common and recurrent themes, of which I will mention three that appear most germane:

- First, that the Indian Ocean is not seen as a distinct "region" in the perception of many outsiders as well as littoral nations themselves.
- Second, that any initiatives of this nature by India tend to be seen as a cloak for attaining regional hegemony or establishing domination over others, become unwelcome to her neighbours and hence are unlikely to succeed.
- And finally, that Track II initiatives have a distinct but vital supporting role to play in maritime discourse, but the barriers that are erected between governmental diplomacy and non-official Track II, often make the latter infructuous.

I consider the end of this symposium an apt juncture to throw up these issues, so that you can take home some thoughts to mull over later. But let me address them briefly here.

First; is the IOR a region?

Is the IOR a Region?

The states around the Indian Ocean, ranging in size from small island nations to continents, today find themselves at various levels of economic development. They also follow diverse methods of governance, and often differ in their political beliefs. The existence of the IOR as a regional entity is also questioned because some observers see it as a "kaleidoscope of crisis": one big jumble of military, economic, and racial turmoil and strife.

Such a detached outlook ignores the fact that the Indian Ocean has been one of the strongest unifying factors in history. For centuries, the waters of this ocean have carried religions, cultures, languages, traditions, and indeed people, across thousands of nautical miles from one shore to another.

It is an unfortunate fact that turmoil and disruptions, natural or man-made, have a cascading effect, and when we lend a hand to a neighbour; we may actually be helping ourselves. Common threats, challenges and opportunities confronting us, thus have the potential to become catalysts for fusion in the IOR. Let us examine this aspect very briefly.

Catalysts for Fusion

Even as Iraq continues to smoulder, the Persian Gulf remains tense, and Afghanistan's future remains uncertain, there are many other areas in our region where the seeds of historical conflict lie just beneath the surface, and bilateral tensions could escalate into shooting wars, with a distinct spillover potential. The spectre that haunts most nations in this context is that of external intervention.

Just a little lower in magnitude are the threats emanating from the hydra-headed monster of fundamentalist militancy, and from other non-state organisations, which now seem to be quite ready and willing to take on nation states. Any major conflagration in the IOR would have a serious impact on the movement of trade and energy resources through the sea lanes, with resultant repercussions on world economy.

At the next level, we are faced by numerous challenges; natural as well as man-made. Approximately 60 per cent–70 per cent of the world's natural disasters strike this part of the world, with catastrophic consequences. Nonmilitary challenges with trans-national dimensions include gunrunning, drug trafficking, piracy and poaching. More often than not, these activities are underwritten by terrorist organisations or crime syndicates.

As far as opportunities are concerned, the Indian Ocean is endowed with plentiful natural resources, including fish, oil, gas and many strategic materials. We could create multinational fishing fleets, we could pool technology to extract resources and undertake other commercial activity on and beneath the seas. Relaxation of trade barriers would be of immense benefit because of enhanced inter-dependence all round. One of the region's major assets is its population with a youthful profile, an abundance of intellectual assets, and the ability to work hard.

Let me next come to what I term as the "India Factor".

The India Factor

No matter how modest or unassuming one may consider oneself, size does matter in perceptions as well as in geopolitics. Many analysts delight in exploiting this issue, and play on the worst fears of our neighbours by evoking fanciful images of India as an aspiring regional hegemon. Perhaps we ourselves are partly to blame for not being forthcoming enough, and I will make a modest attempt to offer clarifications on two issues which appear to worry people.

First; what is the Indian Navy all about?

Two hundred years of foreign rule, which left India impoverished and underdeveloped, resulted from invasion over our shores. This was followed by four decades of Cold War, during which we witnessed the enactment of deadly power play in the Indian Ocean; often coercive in intent. All this has left an indelible mark on the Indian psyche, accompanied by a resolve never to let our sovereignty or independence be threatened from the seas again.

Today our national interests, our growing economy and our stakes in the seas around us are such that a capable maritime force is essential to safeguard them. If an Indian speaks of a maritime "security perimeter", it is only in the limited context of a secure and stable regional environment, insulated from external intervention, which will permit the social and economic uplift of our struggling masses.

Gentlemen; countries, like individuals, conform to behaviour patterns, and India's 5,000-year history bears witness to the fact that she has never been an aggressor, and her only conquests have been cultural. In the past 50 years, our naval forces have crossed foreign shores three or four times, but on each occasion it was in response to specific appeals for help from neighbours, or to render humanitarian aid. In each case, our forces, having completed their task, returned home without delay.

Yes, the Indian Navy is growing at this moment, but the numbers are unlikely to increase significantly, and its strength will stabilise in a few years, because it is a force committed only to peace, tranquillity and stability in the region. In any case, I would suggest that hegemony in the context of a developing nation like India is an oxymoron, and we need to beware of mischief makers who spread such canards.

The second issue that causes a degree of disquiet is that of India's nuclear deterrent.

At Independence, Prime Minister Nehru's vision was to launch a large-scale nuclear power-generation programme, which would accelerate the country's economic development, and in 1948 he set up an Atomic Energy Commission (AEC) followed a few years later, by the Department of Atomic Energy under a brilliant young scientist named Dr. Homi Bhaba.

Our first reactor went critical in 1956, followed by a second one in 1960, and a plutonium extraction plant became operational in 1964. There were suggestions from scientists and others, that we should undertake nuclear weapon research, but Nehru being a strong votary of universal disarmament, abhorred the idea, which he firmly rejected.

China exploded her first nuclear device in 1964, but despite renewed domestic pressure, India steadfastly denied herself the nuclear option. It was a full ten years later, after Prime Minister Indira Gandhi reluctantly accorded approval, that our scientists could conduct a peaceful nuclear explosion in 1974.

Thereafter, for 24 long years, a full-fledged public debate, unprecedented anywhere in the world, raged within the nation, with government after government declining to take the weaponisation route. However, while our democracy was openly discussing the pros and cons of nuclearisation, an astonishing conspiracy, unparalleled in the history of international relations, was unfolding in our close vicinity, in a most surreptitious manner.

One of our neighbours had, over the years, transferred not just the plans, material, and know-how of nuclear warheads to a close neighbour, but had also helped to carry out hot tests, and supplied missiles to deliver them. It now transpires that this activity was in full knowledge of many members of the Nuclear Suppliers Group, but they neither spoke about it, nor intervened to stop this flagrant nuclear and missile proliferation.

The nation felt that our security was in grave peril and we had no choice but to go nuclear in May 1998.

Today, Indian statesmen still regard our small weapon stock with some distaste, and would happily discard it if the nuclear five showed the slightest inclination to discard their huge arsenals. India is committed to "no first use", but it is our sincere hope that we will never have to use our nuclear weapons at all.

Indian Ocean Collective Initiatives

It is a regrettable fact that quite a few collective initiatives in the Indian Ocean have either been stillborn or had very short life-spans. The leadership of the Indian Navy therefore needs to be warmly felicitated for this bold new venture. The foundation of a forum such as IONS will fulfill two long-standing and vital needs: the creation of a distinct Indian Ocean identity, and the provision of an avenue for regional navies to engage each other and promote new avenues of friendship and cooperation.

I am not going to dwell on IONS because this forum is in the capable hands of regional navies, who have models like the Western Pacific Naval Symposium, and the ASEAN Regional Forum before them to examine, and create a new template to meet their specific needs.

I would instead, like to direct the attention of this audience to a related area, where a parallel initiative would be of great significance at this juncture.

A Body for Indian Ocean Maritime Initiatives

The expression "naval" relates to navies and warships, and thus has certain restrictive connotations. Moreover, navies the world over, are instruments of the state's sovereign power, and therefore remain circumscribed in their freedom of action to a considerable extent.

We also need to face squarely that in the IOR nation states, while equal in status, are as widely divergent in size, as in the nature of problems and issues confronting them. The large disparity in the strength of their naval forces would also be a factor inhibiting free intercourse at the navy-to-navy level. In any collective organisation, it is therefore possible that certain types of issues or even certain members may not receive the attention they deserve, leading to a degree of dissatisfaction.

In order to plug this loophole, we need to seriously consider the feasibility of evolving a less formal, non-governmental, Track II body to facilitate interaction within a "maritime" rather than "naval" rubric. I use the term "maritime" deliberately because it is far more relaxed in its scope, and encompasses virtually every issue that is sea-related. Composed of sailors, academics, scholars and former diplomats, such a body would have much more flexibility and freedom of action, and it could take initiatives denied to navies.

I therefore propose for the consideration of this audience, that a body possibly bearing the name: Forum for Indian Ocean Maritime Initiatives, be launched as soon as possible after IONS.

The name eventually given to such a body is not important. What really matters is the need to ensure that it will remain linked to IONS in the closest possible manner, in order to guarantee mutual support as well as synergy. In fact, this Forum must be the alter ego of IONS, and complement all its activities. If at all there has to be a wall between them, it must be as thin and as porous as possible, so that intellectual osmosis can take place continuously.

This is just a thought for all of you to take back; and if acceptable, the IONS secretariat could progress it.

Conclusion

In conclusion, let me hark back to 1890, when Captain Mahan sought to change the world's perception of sea power. His prescriptions regarding battle-fleets, sea control, and the climactic naval clash, survived two global wars, and the advent of air power as well as of nuclear weapons. Exactly a century later, the end of the Cold War forced a rethink amongst major navies.

It brought about a reorientation away from the sea towards the littoral and even further inland; and we have already seen its manifestations in the form of naval intervention in the Balkans, the Persian Gulf and Afghanistan.

In recent years, we have witnessed a new phenomenon in international relations whose ambit is defined by terms like: "fragile states", "failed states" and "regime change". Who makes these classifications, and on what basis? Who decides what is to be done? And on what authority is military action initiated? These are all questions that lurk in the minds of Indian Ocean states. Everyone believes that after making due allowances for globalisation, trade and international laws and treaties, national sovereignty must continue to be the cornerstone of the international order.

As maritime neighbours we, who live on the shores of the Indian Ocean, are duty bound to create and foster a fraternal spirit. If security and prosperity is assured only for some, it would be worse than meaningless—it could well prove counter-productive for everyone else. A collective system like IONS has to be based on common interests of the regional community; cooperation for collective benefit and conflict-prevention must remain its primary aims.

Gentlemen, there is no doubt that IONS is surely an institution whose time has come; and as a final exhortation, I can do no better than to offer a quote, couched totally in nautical language, from Shakespeare's "Julius Caesar":

> "...There is a tide in the affairs of men,
> Which taken at the flood leads to fortune,
> Omitted, all the voyage of their life
> Is bound in shallows and miseries,
> On such a full sea are we now afloat,
> And we must take the current when it serves,
> OR LOSE OUR VENTURES." ■

Conclusion

The seminar provided an opportunity for free discussions on contemporary issues. The commonalities in maritime perception amongst the littorals were evident from the papers presented and from the subsequent discussions that ensued.

The inaugural address was delivered by the Prime Minister, who highlighted the importance of the Indian Ocean Region and spoke of the necessity of stronger maritime linkages in the region. Speaking on the occasion, the Chief of Naval Staff underlined the inclusive nature of the proposed forum. He emphasised that while other forums talked of being exclusive, the IONS would be uniquely "inclusive" in that it would welcome all littorals. Thus the forum mandated an all-encompassing participation without the taints that usually affect membership of such initiatives. In his address, the Defence Minister reiterated its importance and timeliness.

The first session had two speakers and was mainly aimed at painting the background scenario. The first speaker provided the statistics of the Indian Ocean Region, stressing on its political, cultural and economic diversity. He felt that the pronounced sub-regional personalities subsumed the overarching regional identities. Contextually, he also questioned the efficacy of having such a forum in a region that had a fissiparous set of littorals with differing maritime objectives. The second speaker of the session presented an overview of the shipping and trade in the region. He unequivocally stressed on the necessity of structuring greater cooperation amongst the littorals for economic reasons. The emerging Asian and African markets, the growth of manufacturing hubs and their inter-linkages to the enhancing shipping trade in the region were also highlighted.

The second session focused on identifying transnational maritime threats prevalent in the region. The reasons for a mixed bag of successful and unsuccessful operations in controlling such organised criminal activity were outlined. The important issues of emerging terrorist linkages and operation of phantom fleets as sustaining operations towards maritime terrorism was also flagged by the first speaker. Issues related to the UNCLOS and the necessity of introducing changes in the monumental achievement were dealt with in depth by the second speaker of the session. He debated the need for tailoring the existing Laws of the Seas towards countering the evolving maritime asymmetric challenges. He opined that national enforcement and international dispute resolution procedures needed strengthening. The applicability of the Convention in durations of armed conflict remained a grey area and needed greater clarity and focus.

Synergising approaches in enhancing Maritime Cooperation was the focus of the third session of the seminar. Talking of cooperative approaches, the first speaker dealt with various aspects of technological cooperation amongst the littorals while stressing the need for information sharing. He also dwelt at length on various aspects of Maritime Domain Awareness (MDA), its applicability and its feasibility in the regional context, given the high density of shipping and technological capabilities of concerned states. On the other hand, the second speaker chose to highlight aspects of intra-regional trade in the IOR, stressing on the issue of Asian energy imports from the region of the Persian Gulf. He stressed upon the importance of maintaining stability in global trade flows while maintaining the integrity of the supply chain dynamics. The safety issues connected to maritime trade also found mention in his presentation.

The second part of this session, held on the subsequent day, had the presenter speaking on Maritime Capacity enhancement. Taking the case of the Gulf region, he methodically analysed the requirement of maritime capacity enhancement, the ability to meet financial resources and the availability of technical expertise to manage such enhancement. Given the vulnerability and importance of the maritime shipping emanating from the Gulf, the pros and cons of enhancing capacity were discussed in his paper. The next speaker concentrated on analysing and highlighting the inadequacies in the existing multilateral fora, like the IOR-ARC. The speaker's paper carried out a structured analysis of three interconnected issues relating to international protocols, and sub-regional economic communities juxtaposed against the background of maritime capability of the respective navies/maritime forces.

The short concluding session had only one speaker, who reiterated the diversity of the Indian Ocean littorals and summarised the commonalities in "maritime outlook" and priorities amongst the littorals. Ending on a recommendatory note, and stating that while the IONS would necessarily be a forum to address "naval" issues of importance, he suggested a parallel Track II initiative called "**Forum for Indian Ocean Maritime Cooperation**"

(FIOMC). He suggested that this initiative would draw its sustenance from the Track II processes and would work in tandem with IONS with a broader maritime charter.

The seminar concluded with an address by the erudite Rajya Raksha Mantri, Shri MM Pallam Raju, who outlined the commonalities of the littorals and therefore strongly supported the necessity of having such an initiative.

The floor discussions were extensive and covered an entire gamut of areas. Some of these were not necessarily confined to the Indian Ocean. However, the main strands of thought revolved around the following:

- Some delegates questioned the efficacy of launching such an initiative considering that there were numerous dissimilarities amongst the littorals, especially when similar initiatives earlier had been given a quiet burial.
- Other participants and speakers contested this claim and felt that the maritime thread was the main binding factor irrespective of the size and economic clout of the concerned states and that the time for the idea had come.
- The definitional aspects of identifying asymmetric threats were questioned and the "western" labelling of Hamas as a terrorist organisation was also objected to. However, there was little disagreement on the issue of rise of asymmetric threats as a whole, particularly in the Indian Ocean Region.
- The turbulent situation in the Persian Gulf region and the role of the western nations in the region as well as the entire Indian Ocean littoral was discussed at length. Some views were rather critical.
- The need for maritime capacity building, especially for smaller littorals was highlighted and cooperation was seen as perhaps the only workable solution.
- The need for certain changes in UNCLOS was expressed by many. Undoubtedly participants were of the view that the LOS needed to adapt itself to the changing geopolitical and economic trends.

Overall, given the overwhelming response of the participants and the visiting dignitaries, the seminar proved to be an unqualified success. The IONS initiative has got off to a resounding start. ■

SPEECHES

Address by the Honourable Prime Minister of India

Honourable Minister of External Affairs, Honourable Defence Minister, my other esteemed Cabinet colleagues, Excellencies and honourable members of the Diplomatic Corps, Admiral Sureesh Mehta, Chief of the Naval Staff of the Republic of India, Chiefs of Navy and Heads of Maritime Security Organisations of the littoral States of the Indian Ocean Region, Chief of the Army Staff and Chief of the Air Staff of the Republic of India, Flag Officers, General Officers, Air Officers, Commanders and Senior Officers from India and abroad, Chairman of the National Maritime Foundation, Vice Admiral KK Nayyar, distinguished speakers and panellists of the 'IONS Seminar 2008'.

As I stand before you today, to deliver the inaugural address of the seminar of the newly-launched regional initiative, the 'Indian Ocean Naval Symposium', aptly abbreviated to the acronym IONS, I can feel the 'ionisation' of the very air around us—it is positively crackling with the hope and excitement inherent in the great changes that this initiative portends within the maritime domain of our region. That the launch of so important a regional initiative is able to meet with such wide acceptance across the length and breadth of the 28 million square kilometres of the Indian Ocean is in itself a unique phenomenon. It is a phenomenon that is representative of a region that has come into its own and is ready to evolve a broad consensus in facing the myriad security challenges that face it within the maritime domain.

We live in a state of constant change and it ought to come as no surprise that the concept of security, too, has changed steadily over the years. Traditionally, security used to be thought of only in terms of the defence of territory within a state system, whose defining characteristic was an incessant competition for military superiority with other nation-states, all lying, without superior or governing authority, within a classic state of anarchy. Yet, for most people of the world, threats to individual security, such as disease, hunger, inadequate or unsafe water, environmental contamination, crime are far more immediate and significant. Consequently, new terms such as 'Non-Traditional Security' and 'Human Security Issues', drawn from the 1994 Report of the UNDP, have made their way into our contemporary security-lexicon and established themselves within our individual and collective security-consciousness. By the last couple of decades of the twentieth century, security was well established within a new construct that incorporated military, political, economic societal and environmental dimensions, and recognised the many linkages between them.

Many of you will recall that it was in 1980 that the late Prime Minister of Sweden, Mr Olaf Palme, chaired the "Independent Commission on Disarmament and Security Issues", which authored the famous "common security" report that emphatically drew attention to alternative ways of thinking about peace and security, by formally acknowledging that common security requires that people live in dignity and peace, that they have enough to eat and are able to find work and live in a world without poverty. Apart from military security, which does, of course, continue to enjoy prominence if not primacy in a world-system defined by the comity of nations, the UNDP lists as many as seven components of Human Security: Economic Security, Food Security, Health Security, Environmental Security, Personal Security, Community Security, and, Political Security. These issues have risen in importance within the security-matrices of nations and, especially since the end of the Cold War, this shift in importance is to be found even in military-based multi-national or regional groupings. Today, threats to human security, such as religious extremism; international terrorism; drug and arms smuggling; demographic shifts—whether caused by migration or by other factors; human trafficking; environmental degradation; energy, food and water shortages—all figure prominently as threats that are inseparable from military threats.

These have led to the formulation of new concepts, such as "comprehensive security" and "cooperative security" and, indeed, the "Indian Ocean Naval Symposium" is founded upon these new concepts of "cooperative" rather than "competitive" security and "comprehensive" rather than narrowly "military" security. For the sagacity and forward-looking orientation evident in the conceptualisation of the "IONS Initiative," I offer my compliments to all the countries of the Indian Ocean littoral, ably represented here in this gathering by their Chiefs-of-Navy or by the heads of the principal uniformed agency responsible for ensuring maritime security.

We are now well into the closing years of the first decade of the twenty first century and the criticality of the Indian Ocean littoral, with its huge assets including a young and dynamic human resource, vast mineral and energy resources, and burgeoning economies, is now universally recognised and acknowledged. I think it was probably the eminent strategic analyst and prolific writer, Barry Buzan, who in the late 1980s, articulated the concept of a Regional Security Complex to describe "...a group of states whose primary security concerns link together sufficiently closely that their national securities cannot realistically be considered apart from one another". It is probably premature to apply this term in its entirety to the Indian Ocean Region, but we certainly appear to be heading that way, and movements such as the IONS Initiative" might well consolidate the region into what some are already calling a "Maritime Regional Security Complex". This is a noble goal towards which to orient our endeavours and I would commend it for your careful consideration.

I am aware that regional security issues within the maritime domain need to be referenced more towards common interests rather than threats. Our common interests are indeed the Human Security Issues, of which I have already made mention. It is in our common interest to create and consolidate a region in which the comity of nations is both intrinsic and assured.... where every nation, big or small, is treated as an equal... where multiple options of governance are recognised as being functions of the independent choice of the people of each nation-state... where the people of every state of the region can live in dignity and peace... where poverty stands banished and prosperity sits in its place.... where the state protects the individual and the individual preserves the state in a symbiotic relationship designed to establish and spread stability across the region.... where malevolent non-State entities find neither spatial nor temporal room for manoeuvre... in sum, then our common interests are the absence of or freedom from threats.

It is, therefore appropriate that within the maritime domain, the concept of "Maritime Security" is increasingly being described as a condition characterised by freedom from threats arising either in or from the sea. These threats could arise from natural causes or from man-made ones, or from the interplay of one with the other, as in the case of environmental degradation, or, global warming. The threats arising from a lack of maritime security could be faced by individuals themselves or by one or more of the levels by which individuals organise themselves into societies and into nation-states. When these threats address the regional fabric itself, nation-states find themselves increasingly enmeshed in a complex web of security interdependence, which tends to be regionally focused and an initiative such as the IONS is a logical outcome of this regional focus. We are disconcertingly familiar with many of the forms that these threats take. The scourge of piracy has resurfaced from the pages of regrettably romanticised history and, along with the more enduring spectre of maritime crime, mocks the United Nations' "Law of the Sea" that we have so painstakingly formulated. Elsewhere, human traffickers utilise the maritime medium to cruelly exploit economic inequalities and the human yearning for betterment in the quality of life, cramming their hapless human cargo into appalling conditions of deprivation and degradation. Poachers, gunrunners, drug smugglers and a variety of maritime criminals, including terrorists abuse the freedom of the seas, bringing into question the very rationale underlying these historical freedoms.

To find regionally relevant and acceptable responses to these and similar security issues that lie within the maritime domain is the challenge before us. Howsoever desirable, a "one-size-fits-all" omnibus solution appears unlikely. Attempts to force-fit some extra-regional prescription, seem even less likely to succeed and all too often, failures of such prescriptive options are attributed to the regional diversity of the Indian Ocean littoral. Indeed, the tapestry of the Indian Ocean littoral is rich with a diversity that, I grant, might appear bewildering to the uninitiated, incorporating an intricacy of interrelated patterns, much as any oriental carpet might. The threads that represent the political, social, economic and military strains of the regional security loom, with its complex weave of wefts and warps, are varied and multi-coloured. I would, however, recommend that we should not be intimidated by this diversity. Rather, we should luxuriate in the richness and strength inherent in its texture. The interplay of the concepts of "amity" and "enmity" have been seen right through history, but as our region matures, we would do well to promote "amity," at the expense of "enmity". "Amity" is characterised by trust and cooperation amongst states and encompasses a wide range of security interactions, including expectations of capacity-building, capability-enhancement, information-exchanges, the development of inter-operability in doctrinal as well as operational terms, and mutual protection or support. "Enmity", on the other hand, connotes fear and rivalry generated by states and incorporates security relations founded upon mutual suspicion and competition. The launching of the IONS Initiative is an emphatic rejection by our region of security relations that are founded solely upon such negative values as mutual suspicion and military competition. This is not to marginalise the State at the altar of non traditional security. The State remains an important player, if not the principal one, in both, domestic and international intercourse. It is the main referent of security, but the enlightened State recognises that security—whether maritime or land-based, encompasses not just military issues, but social, economic and ecological ones as well.

I see from the programme that you have an impressive agenda chalked out for the IONS Seminar-2008 and I am delighted to find that these issues and concerns will, indeed, form an important segment of your deliberations. I hope that from these deliberations and from the more private deliberations amongst the Chiefs-of-Navy (I understand they will meet in a separate "conclave" tomorrow and the day after) will emerge an action-plan of activities, designed to strengthen the IONS regional construct without seeking to unduly reduce the vibrancy inherent in its diversity.

I would like to conclude by reiterating the support of the Government of India to the IONS Initiative. I wish each one of you a successful and stimulating seminar and look forward to seeing the emergence of a dynamic, purposeful, consensual and positively-oriented set of specific activities to carry the movement into a bright, stable and prosperous future.

Thank you. Jai Hind. ■

Address by the Honourable Defence Minister of India

My other esteemed Cabinet colleagues, Excellencies and honourable members of the Diplomatic Corps, Admiral Sureesh Mehta, Chief of the Naval Staff of the Republic of India, Chiefs of Navy and Heads of Maritime Security Organisations of the littoral States of the Indian Ocean Region, Chief of the Army Staff and Chief of the Air Staff of the Republic of India, Flag Officers, General Officers, Air Officers, Commanders and Senior Officers from India and abroad, Chairman of the National Maritime Foundation, Vice Admiral KK Nayyar, distinguished speakers and panellists of the 'IONS Seminar-2008', Ladies and gentlemen, Good morning.

At the very outset, let me freely admit that the singular ability of the Indian Navy to create an all-pervasive maritime ambience—even in the far northern hinterland of our country—is something that I have always found fascinating and have greatly admired. That this ability should be capable of being replicated with such ease by so many other navies and maritime agencies of our region is even more admirable. It underscores my belief that it is in the maritime domain that our hopes and aspirations of coming together as a strong and united region have their greatest chance of being realised. Today, even though I am physically here in the familiar environs of Vigyan Bhavan, I can still feel the pull and tug of waves far stronger than those that regularly lap the shores of my native state of Kerala. These waves are the result of the winds-of-change and they rock our various ships-of-state, sometimes gently and sometimes violently. As a simple deckhand on board one such ship-of-state of the "Indian Ocean regional fleet," I am suffused with the constancy of movement... of continuous and restless motion.... I am, in a word, experiencing the magic of IONS, for the word itself connotes 'movement' and, as such, is the correct acronym for the Indian Ocean Naval Symposium.

Ladies and gentlemen, as I have publicly stated, the sheer physical dominance of the maritime environment over our planet is such that happenings in the maritime domain, whether natural or man-made, and whether occurring for good or ill, impact man's natural land-habitat, sooner rather than later. As such, the maritime domain is demanding and deserving of continuous study, discussion and debate. Safety, stability and security are an indivisible part of mankind's endeavour to achieve physical, economic and even spiritual well-being and prosperity. The fact that the littoral states of the Indian Ocean Region too, realise this and understand its implications is clearly evident from your presence here at the launch of the Indian Ocean Naval Symposium Initiative.

Every organisation needs strong intellectual underpinnings—and in the National Maritime Foundation, the Indian Navy has its very own "ocean" of maritime wisdom and experience. This is an "ocean" in which all manners of intellect flourish, engaging constructively both within and outside the bounds of "officialdom", whether uniformed or in civilian garb, whether Indian or from abroad. Thus, it is entirely fitting that the Indian Navy and the National Maritime Foundation should have jointly garnered the honour and the privilege of hosting the inaugural activity of the IONS Initiative, namely, the IONS Seminar-2008.

I find IONS to be a uniquely consultative and cooperative initiative.... one that holds so much promise for the future that it already transcends narrow national moorings and the earlier thinking on security, which used to be limited to military and competitive constructs alone. IONS is a robust sign of a paradigm shift from *competitive* security to *cooperative* security within the maritime domain. It encourages us all to view the oceanic expanses of our region, not as obstacles that isolate, but rather, as bridges that integrate nation-states. This is why the Navy's peaceful forays overseas are often described as building *Bridges of Friendship*.

In providing a forum in which the navies and similar maritime-security agencies of the littoral states of the Indian Ocean Region can discuss issues and concerns that bear upon regional maritime security and consensually arrive at solutions based upon common understanding, the IONS Initiative fulfills a long-felt need for cooperative engagement in the face of present-day maritime challenges.

Today we are privileged to sit amongst the assembled Chiefs of Navy of very nearly all the littoral states of the Indian Ocean. I would like to warmly welcome them and the distinguished members of their respective delegations to India. We are also surrounded by an entire galaxy of national and international luminaries, drawn from the strategic community; academia; the diplomatic corps; the political establishment; the bureaucracy; the uniformed and civilian segments of the defence, paramilitary and police establishments of several countries of the Indian Ocean Region and beyond; a host of uniformed and civilian maritime agencies; and, the learned members of the Fourth Estate, representing both, print and electronic media. To all of these worthies, I say that we are here because we have all dared to "....dream the Indian Ocean Dream" —we have come together to share and explore the contours of a grand vision of a coalesced, prosperous and progressive Indian Ocean. This is a vision that is neither diminished nor daunted by our diversity. In fact, as the Chief of the Naval Staff has so forcefully said, we revel in this diversity, recognising that it is precisely this regional diversity that makes for the presentation of multiple solutions to any given problem. It even provides for the problem itself to be presented in more than a single manner, thereby actually increasing the applicability of a variety of possible solutions!

I would like to exhort all present and future members of the IONS Initiative to resist the temptation of trying either to provide a prescriptive set of answers to a prescribed set of problems or challenges. I would caution them against seeking to import extra-regional solutions and force-fitting them on to the regional template. I would, instead, ask them to tap the huge intellectual and innovative resources available within the IOR littoral. I encourage them to explore a variety of regionally-relevant and regionally-sensitive solutions to problems whose very definition is given form and shape-not by extra-regional players often pursuing agendas of their own but by the regional players themselves, acting in close consultation with one another and cooperating freely for the common good of all.

The principal interlocutors of the Indian Ocean Naval Symposium are, of course, the navies of the region. However, I hope that these interlocutors will not remain restricted to the apex levels represented here this morning by the assembled Chiefs of Navy. I, for one, would be extremely happy to see a much wider and more dispersed representation of young or mid-level officers and sailors, engaging and interacting with one another to their mutual benefit. It is, after all, they who will have to face the nebulous but nevertheless deadly threats of the future and it is, consequently, they who must be prepared and armed to face them.

The threats facing present-day law-abiding states are not arising from the territorial or ideological ambitions of other nation-states. They are, instead, a bewildering variety of manifestations of malevolent non-state entities.

Within the maritime environment, thieves and robbers, illegal traffickers in guns, drugs and human beings, poachers, polluters, pirates, warlords, terrorists are establishing pan-oceanic and trans-oceanic connectivities that tend to make a mockery of our boundaries and borders. To these problems must be added natural disasters and man-made catastrophes such as cyclones, earthquakes, landslides, floods, tsunamis, and the very real threat of widespread coastal inundation caused by global warming. These are not threats or challenges that can be met by states acting in splendid isolation, each secure in its military capability. These are "common" threats and demand "common" approaches and "common" solutions.

It is these very solutions and, indeed, this very commonality of approach that this inaugural IONS Seminar and the seminars and other activities that are to follow, must find. In your ensuing deliberations, debates and discussions on these and allied issues, I wish each one of you—speakers, panellists, and listeners alike—every success. My own modest contribution is to assure you of the continued unstinting support of the defence establishment of the Government of India to the Indian Ocean Naval Symposium and all its present and envisaged cooperative and consultative activities.

Thank you. ■

Address by the Honourable Vice President

Once upon a time the commander-in-chief of a rising land power, unfamiliar with seafaring and uneasy about it, asked one of his field commanders to describe the sea and seafarers to him. The officer dutifully reported:

'Verily I have seen a great creature [that is, the sea] ridden by a small one [that is, man]. When it is calm it renders the heart with anxiety, and if it is agitated it leads the mind into confusion. On it certainty shrinks and doubt increases. Those who are on it are like a worm on a twig; if it bends he is drowned, and if he is saved he is astounded'.

In another region of the world, in the island of Bali, the traditional belief considered the sea to be full of demons; hence to be approached with care, if not avoided. In both cases, perhaps, the immenseness of the body of water and the mysteries in its depths acted as a deterrent.

These examples can be multiplied. History is witness to great land powers failing to comprehend the relevance of the sea as an instrument of statecraft. The historian Paul Kennedy attributes the rise of European powers, sixteenth century onwards, to "technological change and military competitiveness"; he may have added, with equal justice, that seafaring was an equally relevant ingredient of promoting trade, competing with rivals, and eventually overcoming them.

The fact nevertheless remains that for a good percentage of humankind, the sea is not in the same category of familiarity as the land. This may be no more than an accident of natural history and the manner in which humans assumed a centrality on this planet. On the other hand, certain facts relating to this planet of ours may suggest correctives to such a slanted approach.

Earth is a planet of oceans. They constitute 71 per cent of its total area. In a very real sense, they sustain life on earth. Cheap transportation is possible through them. They are in increasing measure a source of food, energy and minerals. The Indian Ocean is the third largest ocean in terms of area but unquestionably the first in terms of its impact on human civilisation. The reason for this is obvious; some of the oldest civilisations took shape and blossomed in lands around the Indian Ocean or the seas adjacent to it. They interacted with each other principally through trade. For this reason alone, a gathering of people from Indian Ocean lands would provide a useful collection of perspectives.

Today's conference, I believe, goes beyond an exercise in history and ethnology. Its timing and purpose are sharply focused on the world of today and tomorrow. A look at recent history provides the perspective.

The Portuguese discovery of the sea route to India was of such critical importance that the King of Portugal thought it fit to reflect it in his formal titles. Its wording is to be noted: "Lord of Conquest, Navigation and Commerce, of Ethiopia, Arabia, India and Persia". Their hegemony lasted for two centuries, to be replaced by the British, who followed the pattern and the new jewel in the Crown justified the additional title of Empress of India.

The end of the British era saw the enhancement of the role of the United States. Alongside, the Cold War witnessed super-power rivalry which extended itself in the Indian Ocean littoral. In each of these, the external impulse remained the dominant one. The littoral states themselves had little or no input into it.

Whatever be the past, the imperative today is of a qualitatively different situation in the Indian Ocean littoral. The external impulses have in good measure given way to internal dynamics of individual societies. This, however, is not easily comprehended and older patterns of thinking persist.

A few years back, a scholar in Honolulu delved in futurology pertaining to the Indian Ocean: 'We do not yet understand the political geography of the 21st century. However, no region is likely to feature as prominently in that geography as the Indian Ocean due to its combination of oil, Islam and the likely rise—and probable mutual rivalry of both India and China. Indian Ocean regionalism, or regional integration, remains quite retarded when perceived through an economic lens. Sadly, however, it is the converse conclusion that seems warranted when the region is perceived through the prism of geopolitics and nuclear weapons."

This prognosis, and many other similar ones, is premised partly on the location specifics of the Indian Ocean and partly on the known behaviour pattern of states. It is argued, with regard to the first, that unlike the Atlantic and the Pacific Oceans, the Indian Ocean can be accessed through several choke points and thus necessitates intense policing. With regard to the second, it is asserted that only one-fifth of the total trade flowing through the Ocean is conducted among the countries of the IOR, that 80 per cent of it is extra-regional, and that local conflicts in the Indian Ocean littoral have the potential to acquire international dimensions in view of the need to safeguard the Sea Lines of Communication (SLOCs). These are augmented by actual and potential threats, of varying intensity, from non-state actors. In addition, most of the contemporary international conflicts, from the Iran–Iraq war, to Operation Enduring Freedom and Operation Iraqi Freedom, have taken place in the Indian Ocean Region.

There is merit in both sets of arguments. The quest for security of SLOCs is most vividly demonstrated in the case of Japan where, as shown by Euan Graham in an excellent study published in 2006, it has been the lifeline of the economy and seen as the core security concern. Given the nature of the trade passing through the Indian Ocean, the logic holds good for a great many other regional and extra-regional states.

In this globalised world of today, 95 per cent of world trade is conducted through the sea. Around 100,000 ships transit the expanse of the Indian Ocean annually. Roughly 40 per cent of this sea-borne trade is accounted for by the Strait of Malacca. The Persian Gulf and adjoining region accounts for 50 per cent of the world's containerised cargo and 33 per cent of bulk cargo. Every day, 15.5 million barrels of oil, or 40 per cent of the entire global oil trade passes through the Strait of Hormuz and 11 million barrels of oil pass through the Malacca and Singapore Straits.

At the same time, the argument of securing maritime traffic or lessening the vulnerability of sea-lanes has also been used as a rationale to build up naval capabilities and thus give rise to questions about intentions.

The SLOC argument, valid in itself, is nevertheless reflective of partial reality. The ocean is admittedly a channel of communication; it is also a resource, both for basic forms of existence and for sustaining advanced forms of civilisation. It supports life on earth, regulates temperatures, humidity, rainfall and seasons. It can and does generate catastrophic convulsions affecting the human race.

Any discussion of the ocean therefore, must be multi-dimensional and reflective of four aspects:

- The security paradigm
- Disaster management
- Oceanic resources
- Environmental questions.

Solutions, likewise, would need to be comprehensive and balanced rather than slanted in favour of one aspect, however weighty. Throughout recorded history, maritime security has been the prime concern of states and of their nationals undertaking international trade. In an earlier era, piracy by entrepreneurs for themselves or on behalf of states was common. Then came a time when the balance of advantage was found to lie in the suppression of piracy. The same pattern was followed in regard to slave trade. Economic interests and prevailing moral norms played and continue to play a role in shaping perceptions as is evident by the present-day measures against narcotics. Some would no doubt recall that in another age, a great European power used its military superiority to dump opium on an Asian people in order to correct trade imbalance.

In the past, initiatives for maritime security generally emanated from a strong power driven principally by express or tacit hegemonic perceptions. They received cooperation at times and aroused apprehensions at others.

In conceptual terms, the requirement of maritime security is of necessity linked to threat perception. In the period of the Cold War, security perceptions were based on identified threats and on the need to contain them. The approach, therefore, was cooperative amongst allies and competitive in relation to perceived enemies. In the period after 1990, the focus shifted and attention came to be riveted on questions of common concern. The expectation was that a more comprehensive cooperative approach, on a nondiscriminatory basis, would gradually take shape. It would not dispense with the traditional paradigm of requiring naval power to defend territory or essential national interests but would, instead, add a dimension that would minimise if not eliminate the need to resort to the use of force.

In practical terms, maritime security is to be considered at three levels:

- Measures to create transparency—these include advance notice of exercises and of ship movements.
- Measures to build confidence—these could be undertaken through joint exercises, training, joint naval hydrographic operations, joint task forces for policing and agreement on avoidance of incidents at high sea.
- Measures to build security—regular gatherings of littoral states, user states and other stakeholders to discuss matters of concern and undertaking initiatives to establish regional maritime security mechanisms.

This gathering, I venture to hope, is indicative of a broad acceptance of the need to take these three sets of measures to further maritime security in the Indian Ocean Region. Over time, these may lead to what a distinguished Indian had described many years back as an "Indian Ocean Panchayat," a self-governing council or collective Ombudsman empowered to take decisions on behalf of the community, settle disputes, and suggest ways to prevent disputes.

The voyage even to this point has not been eventless. The recent effort at pursuing security at choke points in the Indian Ocean was highly selective and predominantly extra-regional. It emanated from the Global War on Terror (GWOT) and the Iraq War, and is focused on the western Indian Ocean, the Persian Gulf, Gulf of Aden, Red Sea, Gulf of Oman and the Arabian Sea and extends out to Pakistan's border with India. It functions through a Coalition Task Force known as CTF 150 and includes ships, principally from the navies of the United States, the UK, Australia, Germany, Italy, and France. Its three non-NATO members are Australia, New Zealand, and Pakistan. The Task Force is mandated to prevent terrorist attacks on maritime targets, and disruption of shipment of arms and material to terrorists in Persian Gulf and thereby secure the ocean for use by "legitimate mariners." It is currently led by the Pakistani Navy.

An initiative aimed at the eastern choke point was taken in August 2005 when the governments of Indonesia, Malaysia, and Singapore convened a meeting at Batam for creating a forum for the purpose of making a framework of cooperation to enhance the safety of navigation, environmental protection and security in the Straits of Malacca and Singapore while respecting the sovereignty and sovereign rights of littoral states. In September 2006, the three states convened a larger meeting under the International Maritime Organisation's Protection of Vital Shipping Lanes Initiative. It was attended by 34 countries, including 11 Indian Ocean littoral states.

Also in September 2006, the Regional Cooperation Agreement on Combating Piracy and Armed Robbery Against Ships in Asia (ReCAAP) came into force involving ASEAN, Japan, China, South Korea, India, Bangladesh and Sri Lanka. Subsequent meetings have reinforced the need for cooperation between the littoral states, user states and users of the Straits of Malacca and Singapore. A cooperative mechanism has also been established.

The difference between the two approaches, in respect to the western and the eastern choke points respectively, is significant. The former primarily involves the extra-regional powers and gives the impression of being hegemonic; the latter primarily involves the littoral and user states and is focused on cooperation. This gathering would, undoubtedly, make its own judgements.

Security against anticipated threats is one aspect of the matter. In human terms, situations created by natural disasters and accidents are equally relevant. Tsunamis and cyclones take a heavy toll every year. Seventy per cent of the world's natural disasters take place in the Indian Ocean region. Environmental disasters, oil spills, etc. hold potential for large-scale damage. These happenings do not respect national boundaries. The response, accordingly, has to go beyond national efforts to be meaningful. A very good example of international cooperation is the effort mounted after the December 2004 tsunami. The Indian Navy undertook a commendable operation on that occasion. More recently, the Indian Navy provided help and succour to the victims of the earthquake in Indonesia.

The innate sense of curiosity of the human mind, and the progress of science, has opened the doors on the mysteries of the sea. These, when unravelled, indicate the immensity of resources that the oceans possess. These can be accessed rationally or irrationally. Our generation has not been slow to learn lessons from the past. Hence the comprehensive effort that resulted in the UN Convention on the Law of the Sea and the subsequent Agreement to create the International Seabed Authority charged with the responsibility to organise and control all mineral-related activities in the international seabed beyond the limits of national jurisdiction.

The exercise of regulating the exploitation of the Common Heritage of Mankind has some teething problems that, hopefully, would be overcome. While exploratory ventures have been made, the consensus at this stage is that technology for economic mining of the ocean depths is probably a decade away. This interval is a blessing; deep-sea ecosystems are the main reservoirs of global biodiversity and the scientific and legal framework for protecting them and minimising the potential environmental impact of such mining is yet to be put in place.

Given the diversity of ocean-related activities of humankind, the responsibility of undertaking them is shouldered by various segments of society. Each of these requires an atmosphere of peace and stability. The maintenance of peace is a politico-military exercise necessitating intelligent use of available resources to achieve desired ends. The challenge always is to ensure that contention and cooperation are in harmony. The totality of objectives sought to be achieved in the Indian Ocean region by the littoral, hinterland and user states can only be achieved through a methodology of cooperation.

It has been said, with justice, that the narrative of conflict, as advanced by belligerents, is always one of grievance. The causes, conditions and consequences of conflict almost invariably relate to economic, social and environmental factors. Each of these is better addressed by common endeavour.

The Indian Ocean Region is among the fastest growing regions of the world. The existing structure of cooperation in this broad region is primarily based around five groupings, namely ASEAN, GCC, SAARC, SADC, and SCO. These are not formally linked to each other; their overlapping and overarching framework is an implicit recognition of each other's sensitivities and concerns. It is also reflective of the tenuous equilibrium of the region. An earlier effort, to create an Indian Ocean Rim grouping, did not produce the desired results.

Within the region, and around it, are important political and economic powers that have a stake in peace, stability and progress. They could form the nucleus of an eventual Asian Economic Community.

India is and will remain a maritime nation. In keeping with its maritime heritage, its overseas presence would be based on its soft power and cooperation. With a 7,516 km-long coastline, 27 islands of the Lakshadweep chain and 572 islands of the Andaman and Nicobar chain, 13 major and 185 minor ports and a merchant shipping fleet of over 750 ships, the security imperatives are compelling.

Disaster management in a multilateral framework of cooperation for speedy and effective relief operations is an important element of our maritime approach. India is a UN-recognised pioneer investor in deep-sea mining and has been allotted a mining area of 150,000 sq. km in the central Indian Ocean. In addition, the EEZ of India is set to increase to 2.54 million sq. km. Furthermore, around 20 per cent of our overall petroleum demand is met by offshore production. Environmental issues are now global themes and India has a vital stake in the approaches towards management of global environmental issues.

By disposition, and by inherent capacities, India is well placed to be part of bilateral and non-discriminatory and inclusive regional and multilateral arrangements for maritime security, in consonance with international law and respecting the sovereignty of littoral states. The evolution of perceptions takes time. The key to the future, in the words of Prime Minister Manmohan Singh, is the development of new synergies. This needs to be a comprehensive endeavour. A convergence of interests in the maintenance of peace and in the creation of a co-prosperity area would greatly facilitate the effort. This gathering of the Chiefs of Navies of the Indian Ocean region attends to one aspect of the matter.

I thank Admiral Sureesh Mehta for inviting me to address this distinguished gathering. I am confident that your discussions would further the larger objective of promoting understanding and cooperation among the nations represented here. ■

Valedictory Address of the Honourable Minister of State for Defence of India

Admiral Sureesh Mehta, Chief of the Naval Staff of the Republic of India, Chiefs of Navy and Heads of Maritime Security Organisations of thelittoral States of the Indian Ocean Region,
Excellencies and honourable members of the Diplomatic Corps,
Chief of the Army Staff and Chief of the Air Staff of the Republic of India
Flag Officers, General Officers, Air Officers, Commanders and SeniorOfficers from India and abroad, Chairman of the National MaritimeFoundation, Vice Admiral KK Nayyar, Distinguished speakers andPanellists of the 'IONS Seminar-2008',
Ladies and gentlemen,
Good morning.

Just a few days ago, while I was mulling over what I ought to say at this Concluding Address of the inaugural event of the Indian Ocean Naval Symposium, namely, the 'IONS Seminar-2008', I was struck by an evident paradox. On the one hand, the enormous geo-strategic, geopolitical and geo-economic significance of the Indian Ocean littoral is clearly obvious—especially after the fascinating deliberations that have had us riveted to our seats over the past one-and-a-half days. On the other hand, I have to admit to an uneasy suspicion that despite this blindingly obvious significance, the political leaderships of the clutch of thirty-plus countries that comprise this littoral have clearly had a difficult time in adequately foreseeing the changes being wrought by time, which has made this the moment to seize. In fact, I can share with you that I happened to be glancing through a newspaper at the time—and I came across this little 19th century quote by Sir James Merivale, about that somewhat strange but familiar relative of the lobster, known as the crayfish. I know that the contents are scientifically inaccurate, but they are, nevertheless, entirely appropriate. Let me read out what Sir James wrote:

> "In this small fish I take it that human wisdom is admirably figured and symbolised; for whereas the crayfish doth [pr. 'duth'] move only backward and can have only retrospection, seeing naught but the perils already passed, so the wisdom of man doth not enable him to avoid the follies that beset his course, but only to apprehend their nature afterward".

Now I know that this hall is filled with eminent personages intimately aware of all manners of beings that inhabit the seas and oceans. I am, accordingly, even more delighted than I might otherwise have been, to observe that the Navies of the Indian Ocean Region have consciously chosen to collectively reject the 'retrospective' vision of Sir James Merivale's crayfish. You have, instead, been true to your calling and your chosen profession, in leading from the van, and issuing a clarion call to unite your many individual strengths, capacities and capabilities, in common cause against a common foe.

I have had the great pleasure of going through the excellently prepared papers that have been presented at this Seminar and have been privileged to listen in person to several of this morning's renditions. Within regional geostrategic environment, covered so well by Ambassador Kapil Sibal, lie many challenges and an equal number of opportunities. The management of large maritime zones for resource-constrained states, for example, must necessarily be a cooperative regional endeavour, and is likely to prove to be a litmus test of how nobility of intent is translated into nobility of purpose. It is clear that there are enormous possibilities in terms of both capacity-building in sub-regional as well as regional terms. Dr Alani's excellent paper on maritime capacity enhancement addresses very many core issues.

Yet, I feel that maritime capacity need not be unduly oriented towards hardware. Indeed, the more relevant and, I dare say, the more enduring building blocks of maritime capacity are more likely to be those related to the acquisition, consolidation and sharing of soft-skills. Accordingly, mechanisms such as regionally relevant training through a variety of classroom and ship-borne trainer and trainee exchange programmes, concept-development and doctrine-formulation workshops, simulation processes, personnel exchanges, the free flow of ideas through seminars and symposia, table-top exercises, and so on, are all processes whose realisation and strengthening must define the future agenda of the IONS Initiative. All this must be done within the ambit of the Law of the Sea formulated and established by international consent under the aegis of the United Nations.

Navies have always maintained an intimate relationship with international maritime law and Professor Jon van Dyke's call for choosing dynamism over dogma in matters of international law is well taken. Operating beyond the pale of international law are maritime criminals who take on a number of guises and forms, the most worrisome of which are maritime terrorists. Mr Richardson's view of the future in this regard is both timely and relevant and cannot be taken lightly by any of us, especially not by those of us who have had the misfortune of being at the receiving end of mindless acts of terror that respect neither nationality nor gender nor age nor condition.

The peaceful usage of the sea is centred upon international trade and international shipping. Today we are witness to new trends in shipping whereby the percentage of any given country's overseas trade that is being carried in its own flag-shipping is decreasing exponentially. The implications of this are both nationally and regionally significant, and both, Mr Rajiv Kumar and Mr Andrew Forbes dealt with this and allied issues admirably. The gallop of technology is what most vividly demonstrates the impact of change. Whether and how we can harness changing technology is a fascinating subject, whose outlines were so skilfully sketched by Admiral Shuford, whose vast experience of honing intellect at the US Naval War College, was clearly evident in his paper. The adroitness with which Admiral Teuteberg brought out the linkages between the IOR-ARC construct and the IONS Initiative is laudable and has opened up new vistas of both study and debate. Admiral Arun Prakash, of course, has oratorical and intellectual skills that are well known both in India and abroad, and I agree with his view that there is both intellectual and strategic space available within this new paradigm of cooperative regional security for both, Track-I as well as Track-II initiatives. Much of this constitutes 'virgin fishing grounds' so-to-speak, and there are rich pickings to be had here. These are all weighty subjects, entirely worthy of attention and debate at the very highest levels—of not just the navies of the region, but of the political leaderships as well—in fact, in the latter case, most especially.

The Chief of the Naval Staff of India did make mention of the fact that IONS is the first significant international security-construct of the Twenty First Century. This is a statement of huge import. This, ladies and gentlemen, is the first salvo, the first broadside against those that seek to spread instability, lawlessness and terror either 'in' or 'through' the maritime domain of our region. To them, this assemblage of Chiefs-of-Navy and heads of allied agencies responsible for maritime security is a clear and unmistakable declaration of our intent to uphold the rule of law and assure the dignity, safety and security of our respective people, against the ravages of man and nature alike.

The articulations that have been made over the past day-and-a-half have clearly defined the many and varied contours along which this war will be fought. Make no mistake, ladies and gentlemen, it is a war alright. It is a war against poverty, ignorance and indifference, which are, indeed, the principal weapons of the malevolent non-State actor. It is a war against those entities who seek to terrorise and divide us, against those who seek to destabilise entire regions, unmindful of the human calamities that their ambitions bring in their wake. Like my fellow citizens in every country of our region, and the many seafarers and wayfarers from nations that lie well beyond the geographical bounds of the Indian Ocean, who are anxious to go about their peaceful sea-borne trade, I see in our midst, the able Captains of War of our region and I am encouraged by their enthusiasm and resolve. I am equally encouraged by the weapons that they are being provided with in fora such as these. Burnished steel is being augmented by burnished intellect and sword-edges are being honed by razor-sharp reasoning. The cerebral underpinnings that are so essential for this war to be won are the gifts of academics such as those we have had the pleasure of listening to these past two days. These are master weapon-makers who belong to contemporary 'guilds' such as the National Maritime Foundation and its counterparts in other states of our region and beyond. I join you in echoing a fervent prayer—may their tribe increase.

As I draw this seminar to a close, I would like to once again commend the National Maritime Foundation and the Indian Navy for having so ably organised and conducted this event. On behalf of the Government of India, I would like to thank the Chiefs-of-Navy that have assembled here today for having lent their invaluable support to the IONS Initiative. I am also honoured to be able to stand amongst almost all the ex-Chiefs of the Indian Navy, as also amidst the doyens of the many eminent 'Think Tanks' of our country and those of our friends and neighbours from across the region. Indeed, it would be churlish of me not to acknowledge in the same breath, the enormous contribution made by the serving community of the Armed Forces and the many veterans whose accumulated experience and wisdom is still standing us in such excellent stead and who have gathered in such large numbers, in support of this most excellent of endeavours. ■

Address by Admiral Sureesh Mehta, Chief of Naval Staff

Honourable Defence Minister, Excellencies and honourable members of the Diplomatic Corps, my fellow Chiefs of Navy and Heads of Maritime Security Organisations of the littoral States of the Indian Ocean Region, Chief of the Army Staff and Chief of the Air Staff of the Republic of India, Flag Officers, General Officers, Air Officers, Commanders-in-Chief and Senior Officers from India and abroad, Chairman of the National Maritime Foundation, Vice Admiral KK Nayyar,
Distinguished speakers and panellists of the Indian Ocean Naval Symposium 'IONS Seminar—2008', members of the Fourth Estate, ladies and gentlemen, Good morning.

It is with an abiding sense of honour and very great pleasure that I welcome each one of you to this launch of the Indian Ocean Naval Symposium—which, if I am not mistaken, is the first new and significant international cooperative construct of the twenty-first century.

In a region that has long been dismissed as being too diverse and too insecure to act firmly, cohesively, or collectively, the launch of such an initiative, in the presence of so many of its principal architects, is in itself a matter of enormous regional and global significance. This could not have happened without the active support and the deep and personal commitment of my fellow Chiefs of Navy and Heads of Maritime Agencies across the length and breadth of the Indian Ocean. Today, as the Chief of the Naval Staff of the Republic of India, I am privileged to be able to welcome very nearly all of them amongst our midst and thank them for their unstinting support and encouragement. For the few against whom circumstances have so conspired as to preclude their presence at this inaugural event, I would like to send a message to say, "Rest assured that your places are reserved". I can say this with the confidence born out of certainty, because the 'IONS Initiative' is, at its most fundamental level, all about inclusiveness. IONS, ladies and gentlemen, is a pan-regional construct and we do NOT seek to exclude. There have been initiatives that have lost their acceptance and relevance since their foundations were based upon exclusion as a principle. Also, much of the obsessive focus that some analysts have maintained upon our region's diversities is founded upon 'exclusion' as an axiom. Today, I stand before you, in the august company of my regional peers, to state categorically that we hold such an axiom to be false and that we believe that our diversity is amongst our great strengths. We realise the potential that it has in leveraging the positives to our common advantage. Hence, it is our unshakeable belief in inclusiveness that must be the primary foundation of this initiative.

We live in an age whose most abiding characteristic is the rapidity of change. We are coming to terms with the changes wrought by galloping technology; yet technology is not, by any means, the only target of change. There are enormous changes that are occurring, practically on a minute-to-minute basis, in the mobility of ideas, opinions, people and capital. Our individual countries and our collective region too, are being swept along in the maelstrom of fast-paced change. Old, competitive constructs from across the regional security environment are making place for new cooperative ones, such as the one whose launch we are quietly celebrating today. Indeed, the IONS was conceived of and designed within these very parameters of change. The IONS initiative recognises the strength that can be derived from cooperative engagement in our region. Multi-polarity, much like spring, is breaking out everywhere. As India's Foreign Secretary said just a couple of months ago, "....our shorthand for this phenomenon is the rather inadequate word 'globalisation'...". It is a somewhat inadequate word, because it does not sufficiently capture the enormity and complexity of the changes that are being shaped in our time. Yet, it is a familiar word—'globalisation', and we have a more or less common version of the mental images associated with it. Perhaps the defining characteristic of globalisation has been economic interdependence. Whether economic interdependence actually diminishes the chances of conflict is a view that has equally powerful arguments in favour of and against it, and this is not, perhaps, the most opportune time to get into the merits and demerits of the traditionalist versus the liberal points of view. However, what is certain is that today's world of geo-economics does possess great potential for cooperation. This economic interdependence is creating a new global order by the emergence of multiple economic and cultural 'collectives', in one form or another. The IONS should be seen as a construct in our region that focuses on issues related to, or those which can be influenced through the maritime environment. In doing so, it would perhaps help in creating conditions for regional cooperative efforts to spill over to other fields as well. That would be a welcome spin-off indeed.

Some may argue that collective security constructs preceded all others, but there is an important distinction to be made here between the cooperative groupings that I have mentioned and the competitive alliances that characterised the Cold War. NATO and the Warsaw Pact were competitive constructs that pitted combinations of nation-states against one another. The changed realities of our present time provide both strategic and intellectual space for other forms of collective groupings of states that are arrayed not against one another, but against security challenges and threats that are common to all. This is as true of the Indian Ocean Region (IOR) as of any other.

I grant that each one of us is interested primarily in the well-being and economic prosperity of our respective people. These are our core national interests. Threats to these core interests are likely to produce immediate and robust responses from each one of us. Yet, the economic interdependence that globalisation has brought about means that whatever threatens the economic well-being of one, threatens the economic well-being of all. The responses to collective threats, therefore, need to be equally immediate and robust.

At the high end of such security challenges are issues concerning 'nontraditional security' and 'human security'. These are not obscure concepts that can remain confined to academic interaction in workshops and seminars. None of us in this room can have possibly forgotten the devastation that was wrought by the tsunami of December 2004. Which is the navy that could have stood by and done nothing? Not one. We have all been witness to the human agony and the long-term effects of the Yogyakarta earthquake of 2006 and of the cyclone Sidr that struck the coast of Bangladesh in November of last year. These are instances where 'human security' issues predominate, demanding rapid and comprehensive, yet culturally and territorially sensitive responses, from the region as a whole. Perhaps our greatest asset in such times is our fundamental societal commonality and the strength and tenacity of our family values. These values cause us to respond instinctively.... to bond together in times of familial crisis. The IONS seeks to provide a regionally and culturally sensitive organisational structure to this instinctive reaching out. It seeks to build capacity and enhance capability amongst the individual states of the region, and, in so doing, strengthen the collective IOR as a whole.

As one military professional addressing his peers and colleagues, let me focus attention upon the most immediate of the security challenges that face us, the response to which demands not just the creation, but also the success, of the IONS Initiative. The threat from malevolent non-State actors presents a clear and present danger to not just one or some, but to all of us. The response from us must, therefore, be from not just one or some, but from all of us. This does not mean forging a military alliance of any sort, what it does mean is that we must coordinate our efforts, share experiences and expertise, establish mechanisms for training, for doctrine-development, for ship-design and ship-construction, for cooperative surveillance.... we must allow our young officers to grow and bond together and to be alive and sensitive to the drivers, the strengths and capabilities of their colleagues in other parts of the region. They must be so conditioned by us as to intuitively and instinctively see one another as colleagues and not as competitors. It is critical to ensure that whatever we plan and do, flows from a broad consensus, with political backing, maritime commitment, and naval resolve.

Most of you would agree with me if I said that we in the IOR live in a 'fragile' neighbourhood. A look at the region will depict a mosaic of crises in different shades and hues. The threats of 'intra-State' turmoil as well as a variety of security threats that are short of State-on-State conflict, remain a grim reality, presenting a significant risk to peace and stability. The important shipping lanes and choke points of our region are vulnerable to disruption, piracy and in the worst case, closure —with serious implications on safety of trade and security of energy flows. And if that were not enough, our region is home to 70 per cent of the world's natural disasters. Can we find individual solutions to all these challenges that stare us in the face? Or does it make more sense to hold hands and find collective answers? I think the choice is clear.

Inter-operability is another word that is much bandied about these days. It too evokes strong mental images that pervade the shared consciousness of our contemporary society. 'Inter-operability' is sometimes maligned at the altar of ignorance, by associating the word solely with material or equipment-based issues. Inter-operability, of course, is much more than that. In a humanitarian assistance mission, it is what allows your ships and aircraft to talk to mine, through commonly-held Standard Operating Procedures (SOPs). It is what assures me that you are reacting in a given manner to a given stimulus for reasons that I am familiar with. It is what allows my boat to be lifted by the davits on your ship. It is what allows your medical or non-combatant evacuation procedures to be readily understood by me and mine by you. It is what allows me to be trained by you or you by me, so that we are able to recognise what is normal within the maritime domain, which we need to be able to do before we can discern what is abnormal. These are issues that are addressed through training. The sharing of such knowledge and training would enrich us all without diminishing any. These are the facets of inter-operability that we should focus on. Interoperability is about much more than commonality of equipment, and we would be unwise to restrict ourselves to unduly narrow mental constructs. Inter-operability is certainly one of the core aims of the IONS Initiative.

The fleshing out of these thoughts, the provision of tangible form to this intent—this is the task that my fellow Chiefs and I will take up in right earnest in the 'Conclave-of-Chiefs' tomorrow and the day after. Today, as always, we prepare for the morrow. This seminar, for whose conduct I must express my heartfelt thanks to Admiral KK Nayyar and his tireless staff at the National Maritime Foundation, will, I am certain, provide us with the overview that we need the backdrop against which the steadfast characteristics of all our plans and actions will be clearly shown to be cooperative, inclusive, consultative, consensual and progressive, in the pursuit of regional stability and security, so that we and our people may prosper, both individually and collectively.

With these words, I welcome you once again to the birth of the IONS Initiative. May we be united in our resolve and may this movement grow from strength to strength, sustained by the firm conviction that what we do, we do for the good of all. ■

Index

Ravi Vohra

Admiral **Ravi Vohra** had a distinguished career in the Indian Navy including Command of ships and a diplomatic assignment as the Naval Attache in Bonn, Germany. As a Flag Officer he held the appointments of Flag Officer Offshore Defence Advisory Group and Assistant Controller of Warship Production and Acquisition.

He is a keen student of International Relations and has written a paper on Confidence Building Measuresbetween India and Pakistan in the maritime scenario.

PK Ghosh

Captain **PK Ghosh** specializes in the fields of Maritime Security, Strategic Nuclear Triad, missile proliferation and Chinese Maritime Forces. He is one of the very few serious researchers in the region who has worked on the Ballistic Missile Defence Shield (BMDS). He has numerous papers and books to his credit.

D Chakraborty

Commander **D Chakraborty** is currently attached with National Maritime Foundation (NMF), New Delhi. His areas of interest are Marine Navigation and Operations, India's External Trade, International Trade Logistics, Maritime Transportation.